GRACE'S CARD

A NOTE ON THE AUTHOR

Charles Chenevix Trench is of a minor Ascendancy family, of Huguenot origin, which settled in Galway in about 1600. He has spent most of his working life abroad. After taking a degree at Oxford, he served for twelve years in the Indian Army (winning a Military Cross in Italy) and then as a District Commissioner in Kenya. He now lives in County Tipperary, running a small farm, reviewing and writing books. His books include biographies of O'Connell (*The Great Dan*), General Gordon and John Wilkes, and historical studies of the Royal Malady of George III, the Monmouth Rebellion, the Indian Army and horsemanship.

Grace's Card
Irish Catholic Landlords
1690–1800

Charles Chenevix Trench

Mercier Press

First published in 1997 by
Mercier Press
PO Box 5, 5 French Church Street, Cork
16 Hume Street Dublin 2
Trade enquiries to CMD Distribution
55A Spruce Avenue
Stillorgan Industrial Park
Blackrock County Dublin

ISBN 1 85635 163 7

10 9 8 7 6 5 4 3 2 1

A CIP record for this title is available
from the British Library

Cover design by Penhouse Design
Set by Richard Parfrey
Printed in Ireland by Colour Books,
Baldoyle Industrial Estate, Dublin 13

To Charlotte, Priscilla and Richard

GRACE'S CARD

In 1689 emissaries of William of Orange called on John Grace, Baron of Courtstown, with an invitation to join the army of the usurper. On a playing-card lying on the table beside him he scrawled a contemptuous refusal: 'Tell your master I despise his offer'; and proceeded to raise a regiment for James II. A hundred years later, in Kilkenny, the six of hearts was still known as 'Grace's Card'.

CONTENTS

INTRODUCTION

This is a political history of Irish Catholic landlords from 1690 to 1800. Many had lost part of their estates under Queen Elizabeth, and most lost all under Cromwell. Those who supported James II against William of Orange – and most did so – lost what they had recovered under the Restoration, except for about 1,200, who were allowed by the Articles of the Treaty of Limerick to keep their land. Some also who had behaved generously to Protestants during James II's reign were pardoned. The British and Irish governments, and the legal profession, respected Catholic rights in this matter.

The Irish Parliament (wholly Protestant) saw this, however, as scandalous lenity which they set out to rectify by the Penal Laws. The most important of these was the Act of 1704 'to prevent the further growth of Popery'.

But Catholics with good legal advice could find ways round many of its provisions. They were not, for instance, allowed to buy land from Protestants or to lease it for more than thirty-one years; so they got trusty Protestant friends to 'hold' land for them while swearing 'the print out of the Bible' that they were doing nothing of the kind. (The two Protestants who thus obliged Lord Fingall and Maurice O'Connell eventually had to break it to them that, being old and near their deaths, they could no longer perjure themselves, 'even for such old and valued friends'.)

In order to break up large Catholic estates, the practice of primogeniture was forbidden to Catholics: on the death of a landowner, the estate had to be divided equally between all his sons. But an Act of Parliament could not override existing entails, which saved many a Catholic estate. Sir Laurence

Esmonde of County Wexford, acting no doubt on a tip-off, entailed his land just before the 1704 Act came into effect. In many cases the younger sons had too much family loyalty to claim their legal rights, preferring to seek their fortunes in foreign military service, on West Indian plantations or in 'the mercantile career' at home or abroad. In some families there was a remarkable succession of only sons. Charles Chenevix Trench quotes the celebrated raconteur Eoin 'The Pope' O'Mahony on this delicate subject: 'It was all done by *continence*. They were *martyrs*.' So be it.

The salvation of the Catholic landed families came with the passing of the Catholic Relief Acts of 1778 and 1782 which gave them all normal rights in purchasing, leasing and bequeathing land. In 1792 they were permitted to take commissions up to the rank of lieutenant colonel in the British army and navy, and to become barristers and solicitors. In 1793 they were allowed to vote for Members of Parliament and to become Justices of the Peace. The great boon of Catholic Emancipation – the right to enter Parliament and to hold political office – was withheld until 1829.

The author examines the substantial minority of Catholic landowners who conformed to the Church of Ireland – either to make sure of their land, to enter politics or the legal profession, to take commissions in the British army and navy, or even out of religious conviction. Most remained Catholic in their sympathies, and the many Catholics who did not convert relied heavily on them for legal services and advice.

Chenevix Trench also examines the tendency of some very efficient tenant farmers to enlarge their holdings by leasing land and eventually buying it, blossoming at last into substantial landowners. Among these were the Scullys of Kilfeakle in County Tipperary. In the 1860s William Scully owned the second largest agricultural estate in the USA. Another Catholic family which rose in the eighteenth century from strong tenant farmer to landowner was that of Ryan, of Ballyvistea and Scarteen. They kept a pack of foxhounds, later famous as the Black and Tans, for which Daniel O'Connell sent some of his beloved Kerry Beagles as breeding stock.

Charles Chenevix Trench, who has an active historical mind, has already made a valuable contribution to Irish history with his biography of Daniel O'Connell; this book on Catholic landed families under the Penal Laws extends that contribution. He writes ably, objectively and with humour. Perhaps he finds it easy to sympathise with any people under persecution because his own family, Irish Protestant Ascendancy during the eighteenth century, first arrived in Ireland as Huguenot refugees from religious persecution in France. Where Irish Catholics were a majority surrounded by friends, Huguenots were a small minority surrounded by enemies.

Professor Maurice R. O'Connell

AUTHOR'S FOREWORD

In the great debate between tradition and revision in Irish history, the author sits firmly on the fence. It is indisputable that the eighteenth century Penal Laws were a dishonest and dishonourable attempt by the Irish Parliament (entirely Protestant) to renege on the Treaty of Limerick. Parliament's intention was to discourage, without actually banning, Catholicism; and, far more important, to deny to Catholics all political power, which then depended entirely on landownership. But the Penal Laws were far less effective than those who framed them intended. They were laxly enforced, and Catholics were able to hold, throughout the eighteenth century, many large estates. This they did with the connivance of trusty Protestant friends and relations, and by adroit use of the law; for there were ways round most of the Penal Laws if one could find them. How they contrived to do so, how their younger, landless sons fared and how the Penal Laws were eventually repealed is the theme of this book.

ACKNOWLEDGEMENTS

This book does not break virgin soil. It has been thoroughly cultivated by eminent academic historians including the late Maureen Wall, J. G. Simms, L. M. Cullen, Kevin Whelan, W. N. Osborough, Karen J. Harvey and others. I can only express my admiration for the vast quantity and high quality of their original research, and my gratitude for making it available to non-academics such as myself.

I have sought help and advice from many people more knowledgeable than myself. For advice on legal matters I am indebted to Mr Marcus Bourke, Mr Vincent Grogan SC of the Legal Draftsman's Office, Dublin; Professor W. N. Osborough of the Department of Law, Trinity College, Dublin; and Mr Peter Paul Ryan.

For general help I am particularly grateful to Dr John Andrews, Sir David Goodall, Mr A. P. W. Malcomson, Mr D. G. Marnane, Dr Harmon Murtagh, Mr Patrick Melvin, Professor Maurice R. O'Connell and the Reverend Mark Tierney.

Those who have made available to me family records and traditions include Mr R. R. Barnewall, the Hon'ble Bryan Bellew, Mrs Joyce Green and the late Mrs Rosamund Lombard (*née* Blake), Mr Sean N. Cloney, Mr Jim Condon, Mrs Olive Daly, Lord Dunboyne, the late Count Edmund and Mr Nigel De la Poer, the late Mr Owen Esmonde, Mr Richard H. A. J. Everard, Mr Adrian Fitzgerald, the Knight of Glin, Viscount Gormanston, Brigadier W. S. Hickie, Miss Melosina Lenox Conyngham, Madam MacDermot, Mr B. C. McDermot, Brigadier W. M. T. Magan, Mr Patrick Mansfield, Mr Pyers O'Conor Nash, Count Eoin O'Kelly, Mr Arthur Ryan, Mr Thady Ryan, Dr T. C. I. Ryan and Mr John Wilkinson.

I am most grateful to the staffs of the National Library, the County Libraries of Thurles and Nenagh, the Library of Trinity College, the Royal Irish Academy, the Public Records Office of Northern Ireland, the Freemasons' Hall in Dublin and the Registry of Deeds.

Miss Rachel Furmston in Belfast and Mr Sean Murphy in Dublin gave me invaluable help in research.

1

―

The War of the Two Kings

The war in Ireland of 1689–91 was about the ownership of Irish land. To the gentry who ran the country and officered the armies that was far more important than the question of whether the King of Ireland should be a Calvinist Dutchman or a Catholic half-French Englishman of Scottish descent. Political power, local and parliamentary, depended on landownership; and gentry status, even for younger sons who owned not an acre, depended on family ties with those who did.

The Normans, who first arrived in Ireland in 1170 under Richard de Clare – 'Strongbow' – and became known as the 'Old English', established a *modus vivendi* with the Irish, fighting with or against them, taking over and losing much of their country, intermarrying with them and in many cases adopting the Irish language and lifestyle. There were no religious barriers between them as all were Catholics. But the Reformation and Queen Elizabeth's war against Spain promoted the policy of 'planting' Protestants in areas of strategic importance. Some 22,000 'New English' Protestants were planted in Munster living on fairly relaxed terms with the Irish though a Catholic could not prosper in public life. The planting of Ulster by James I was denser and more rigid in the expulsion of 'Papists' or their reduction to small tenant farmers. It was mainly by Presbyterian Scots, radical in their politics and almost as hostile to the Anglican episcopacy as to Popery.

In 1641 the Irish in Ulster rose against the planters and killed some 4,000 of them. There were instant reprisals and folklore on both sides cherishes the atrocities: to this day Ulster Protestants exhort one another to 'remember the steel of Sir Phelim O'Neill who slaughtered our fathers with Catholic zeal'. Eight years later Cromwell, having disposed of the Cavaliers at Naseby and their king on the scaffold, brought his invincible New Model Army to Ireland primarily to avenge 1641, which he did bloodily at Drogheda and Wexford. Having a cash-flow problem, he paid his army with grants of Irish land.

To make room for them, most Catholic landowners east of the Shannon were expropriated and resettled in Connaught and County Clare. It was a fairly orderly process. A Catholic landowner from, say, Meath, reported to the Commissioner for Delinquency in Athlone and was allocated land in, say, Galway, which was supposed to be proportionate to the estates which he had lost and adequate for the livestock he brought with him. The Powers, for instance, whose Munster estates were forfeited, were given no less that 4,000 acres in Galway; and the Chevers protested vigorously because their new Galway estates were too small, and contained no suitable residence. But in general the new estate in the stony west was only about half the size of the estate which had been confiscated and of far lower productivity. Of course the existing proprietors in Galway, native Irish or 'tribal',* had to make room for the newcomers, which strained their Catholic sympathies.

The forfeiting proprietors in Leinster and Munster were replaced by Roundhead soldiers or 'adventurers' (investors) who

---

* The 'tribes' of Galway were fourteen families, mainly of Old English stock, who had made money in commerce in Galway city and were buying land and setting up as country gentry. They were the families of Athy, Blake, Browne, Bodkin, D'Arcy, Dene, Fote, Ffrench, Joyce, Kirwan, Lynch, Morris, Martin and Skerret.

had financed Cromwell's campaign with this in mind. Common soldiers, who were given smallholdings in lieu of their pay and had no wish to settle in a barbarous foreign land, sold their holdings to officers or adventurers so that the average Cromwellian settler ended up with about 700 productive acres. Many of the old proprietors did not bother actually to move. John Ryan of Inch, for instance, a substantial landowner in County Tipperary, rather than trek off to County Clare, spurned the miserable 239 acres he was allotted there in exchange for his 1,000 good acres, and stayed on at Inch as a tenant of his supplanter, not perhaps much worse off financially but with a lower status. The net result of the Cromwellian confiscations was that the 60 per cent of land owned by Catholics in 1641 was reduced to about 9 per cent by 1660.

The 'Interregnum' lasted only from 1650 to the Restoration of Charles II in 1660. Naturally all those whose estates had been stolen by the Lord Protector expected to have them restored by the king. But it was Stuart instinct to appease a foe at the cost of a friend, and Charles II was well aware that he had been restored to the throne not by Catholics and Cavaliers but by the New Model Army. He was far too prudent to offend the Roundhead grandees who now governed Ireland, who would be prepared to accept him as king provided he left them with their loot. At first the only Cromwellians to forfeit their estates were the 'regicides' who had signed Charles I's death warrant. But this did not begin to satisfy Catholic claims, so other Cromwellians were persuaded to give up a third of their estates on condition that they could keep the rest. Thus by the Acts of Settlement (1662) and Explanation (1665) Charles II restored to 'innocent Papists' who had not been prominent in the rebellions of the 1640s, and to those who had friends at court, enough of their estates to keep them quiet. Most of those who benefited from the Restoration settlement were Old English Catholics rather than Gaelic Catholics, and many were relatives and protégés of the newly created Duke of Ormond, head of the Butlers and Charles's Viceroy in Ireland, himself a Protestant but always sympathetic to Catholics and particularly to Catholic Butlers. Other Catholics were able to buy land. William Fogarty, for instance, a doctor from Tipperary practising in London, in 1662 bought back his family estates from the adventurer who had acquired them.[1] Martin Blake, of the prominent tribal family, in 1672 bought the Ballyglunin estate, well over 10,000 productive acres, from the Cromwellian adventurer Holcroft.[2] Sir Edward Tyrrell, described as 'of any or no religion, sometimes a Roman Catholic, sometimes a Protestant', accumulated large estates by purchase from soldiers and adventurers. Sir Patrick Trant bought the Cork and Kerry estates granted to Lord Arlington, and Sir Richard Talbot, later Lord Tyrconnell, bought estates in Leinster.

Some of the Cromwellian grandees were not easily dislodged but by 1680 1,300 Catholics owned 1,700,000 productive acres – excluding mountain and bog – or 22 per cent of the total.[3] Their land was mainly across the Shannon or in County Kerry, but included large estates, giving considerable local power, in Antrim, Louth, Meath, Kildare, Tipperary, Kilkenny and Cork. No one was satisfied by this compromise, but none was outraged to the point of rebelling against it.

In 1685 Charles died and was succeeded by his Catholic brother James II. He was a far less intelligent and flexible man, but did not tamper with the Restoration Settlement in Ireland, though under strong Catholic pressure to do so. What he did, however, raised every Protestant's hackles: he appointed first as Lord General of the army in Ireland, then as Viceroy with the title of Lord Deputy, the Catholic Earl of Tyrconnell, a domineering and deeply suspect character known to his non-admirers as 'Lying Dick Talbot'. Tyrconnell immediately set to work Catholicising the Irish army, and by 1688 three-quarters of the rank-and-file were Catholics, only a handful of Protestant officers remaining on sufferance.

Sooner or later the Irish Parliament, which had not met since 1666, would have to be summoned, if only to vote taxes to pay for the army.* A Catholic majority had to be ensured. Of 300 members of the House of Commons, sixty-four sat for the thirty-two counties, two for Trinity College and 234 for 117 two-member boroughs, many with few – if any – inhabitants and most with franchises restricted to very few voters – Freemen perhaps, or Mayor and Corporation. Sixty-two of these had been created by James I and Charles I, and provided with charters designed to produce a Protestant majority in a Parliament from which Catholics were not specifically excluded. This Tyrconnell had to rectify, resorting to the well-tried methods used in England by Cromwell and Charles II. Boroughs were issued with *quo warranto* notices, challenging the validity of their charters. To examine these, a commission was set up headed by the Attorney General, Sir Richard Nagle, and two extremely capable lawyers, Sir Toby Butler and Sir Stephen Rice, all Catholics. It was not hard for these ingenious men to find flaws in charters, or abuses of them, and it was very expensive for a small borough to defend itself against such heavy legal metal. Most, therefore, thought it prudent to surrender their charters and then apply for new ones. These invariably ensured a majority of Catholic voters. Catholics were appointed judges, Privy Councillors and Sheriffs, the last being key men since as Returning Officers they decided the winners of disputed elections

---

* As in England, only Parliament could impose taxes. It was their attempt to raise money by dubious methods without Parliament's consent that got the Stuart kings into trouble.

– and many elections were disputed. By 1688 Tyrconnell could guarantee the king a Catholic Parliament in Dublin.[4]

Whether James II's intention was merely to give Catholics a fair share of the loaves and fishes or to convert his three kingdoms to his faith, can still be argued. The point is that an overwhelming number of Protestants, even sons of Cavaliers who had fought for Charles I, even the second Duke of Ormond, believed that their Anglican church was in danger and in 1689 joined, reluctantly, William of Orange when he invaded England to usurp his father-in-law's throne.

Chased out of England and Scotland, James was effectively king only of Ireland. But for the fact that William was engaged in a desperate struggle with Louis XIV's France, the strongest military power in Europe, James might almost have been left there. But Ireland became an important sideshow in the main war. James and Tyrconnell, with meagre French help, expanded the Irish army to 35,000, raised and commanded by the wealthier Catholic magnates and officered by their relatives and friends, few of whom had any military experience. Although it contained a small number of Protestant Jacobites, it was essentially a Catholic army.

To pay for it, Parliament was summoned on 7 May 1689, soon after James's arrival in Ireland. Tyrconnell's management of the boroughs had been brilliantly successful, and he was helped by the departure to England of many Protestant MPs and landed magnates, while those who remained kept very quiet. For this parliament, there seems to have been only one contested election. The counties of Donegal, Derry and Fermanagh, and a number of boroughs, mainly in Ulster, returned no members. The final count was 230 members of the House of Commons – out of a possible total of 300 – of whom only six were Protestants. Of thirty members of the House of Lords, five were

Protestants. Two-thirds of the Lords and Commons were of Old English families, which James and Tyrconnell greatly preferred to the Gaelic Irish. They wanted an Ireland, albeit Catholic, still linked to and governed from England.

The Catholics were in a militant mood, far more so than their king, who still had hopes of English Tories and did not wish to upset them. The key issue was landownership, as established by the Act of Settlement, which Catholics thought monstrously unfair. Under parliament's threat that it would refuse otherwise to vote taxes, James II very reluctantly signed an act restoring the estates, without compensation to the present proprietors, to all who had lost them since 1641. Parliament also passed an Act of Attainder requiring about 2,000 anti-Jacobites to stand trial for treason.

William's parliament at Westminster was equally hard on those whom it deemed traitors: the fifty-seven most prominent Irish Jacobites were indicted in England for treason; and clearly, if the Williamites prevailed, thousands more would be indicted in Ireland. Those found guilty could be drawn, hanged and quartered – though none were executed in the forthcoming struggle – and would certainly lose their estates. So the stakes were on the table. Officers of the defeated army and the civilian functionaries who supported them might keep their lives and their religion, but would lose land, goods and chattels, political power, gentry status – all that made life worth living. The winners would take all.[5]

On 22 February 1689, nine days after he and his wife Mary – James II's daughter – were jointly crowned, William of Orange issued a declaration that all rebels who submitted before 10 April would be pardoned and left with their estates. It was too soon. The Jacobites were still bursting with confidence and only a few of the elderly, infirm and unwarlike accepted the offer. Among these was Theobald Butler, seventh Lord Cahir, who resigned his commission in King James's army and departed with relief to his wide estates in County Tipperary.

In May 1689 the war between the two kings broke out in Ulster. Neither side enjoyed a monopoly of military ineptitude but the Williamite defence of Derry (Londonderry) against the smaller force of besiegers ranks high in Protestant legend. When the siege was lifted both sides moved to the east coast south of Dundalk, where they spent a sodden autumn making faces at each other before retiring into winter quarters.

James expected his Irish recruits to run away at the first shot and William thought his English regulars would probably change sides, as they had already done once. Both kings wanted the fighting in Ireland to end as soon as possible, but it was in Louis XIV's interest to keep the pot there boiling. He therefore lent James six regular regiments of the French army in exchange for an equal number of Irish recruits who were regrouped into three regiments – Mountcashel's, Dillon's, Clare's. When they had been trained and equipped, these fought magnificently in Flanders and Italy and established the fame of the Irish Brigade in the French army. William sent over to Ireland 7,000 of his reliable Dutchmen and an equal number of Protestant mercenaries hired from the King of Denmark. /

The armies spent the winter training, reorganising and re-equipping.

The Jacobites' mercurial spirits were raised by news from the west: Patrick Sarsfield, half-Old English, half-Irish, with the reputation of a dashing cavalry commander on the continent and against the Monmouth rebels in England, had driven the Williamites out of Enniskillen into Sligo and there made them surrender. King James's men began to think they were doing rather well, and would do better when the campaigning season opened in 1690.

William regarded the Irish war as a distraction from his main business of fighting Louis XIV. In order to end it as soon as possible, he crossed over to Ireland in June to take personal command of his army. He was neither a military genius nor a particularly attractive character. But he was, in conspicuous contrast to the Stuarts, a man of his word.

On 1 July 1690 there was fought the battle of the Boyne, a river which provided the last position defending Dublin against an attack from the north. The Jacobites were outnumbered (24,000 to 36,000) and still outmatched in training, discipline and weapons. But the Irish Horse, led by Lord Dominick Sheldon and James's young bastard son, the Duke of Berwick, performed brilliantly, charging again and again; and the infantry fought as well as could reasonably be expected. With a bit of luck, if the cannonball which grazed William's shoulder had been aimed two inches to the left, the Irish might have won the battle. But at last the Jacobite infantry broke and fled towards Dublin, its retreat covered by Sheldon's devoted Horse.

On arrival in Dublin James remarked sourly to Lady Tyrconnell: 'Your countrymen, madam, can run well.'

'But I see,' she replied, 'that Your Majesty has won the race.'

The battle of the Boyne need not have been – indeed was not – decisive, but it was a severe blow to Irish morale; and King James himself, no coward but a man given to despondency, left his last kingdom, afflicted by a bad nosebleed, never to return.

While the Irish army withdrew in creditable order towards Limerick, William made a triumphal entry into Dublin, then largely a Protestant city, and on 7 July 1690 issued the Declaration of Finglas, which was an obvious attempt to separate the rank-and-file of the Irish army from the officers. It promised pardon 'to all poor labourers, common soldiers, country farmers, ploughmen and cottiers . . . as also citizens, tradesmen, towns-men and artificers' who laid down their arms before 1 August. 'But for the desperate leaders of the rebellion . . . we are resolved to leave them to the event of war unless by great and manifest demonstrations we shall be convinced that they deserve our mercy.'

The Declaration of Finglas failed in its intention. Landowners noted that it contained no promise to respect their estates, nor did it promise to anyone religious toleration. The common soldiers proved commendably loyal to their officers. But thinking Jacobites realised that outright victory and the recovery of all Catholic-owned estates lost since 1641 was now unlikely; the best they could look for was a peace settlement which would leave them with what they already had. This to a great extent they achieved. The few who gave up in response to the Declaration of Finglas and William's offer of 1689 were to regret doing so.

Once established in Dublin and the eastern half of the country, the Williamite authorities proceeded to indict for high treason within Ireland, and subsequently to outlaw, about 2,600 Irish Jacobites in addition to the fifty-seven already indicted in England. The figures are imprecise: many were indicted in several counties, and there were as yet no returns from counties which the Williamites did not control. Most were charged with holding civil or military office under King James since 10 April 1689, the deadline set by William in his declaration of 22 February. Most of those indicted were not themselves landowners – the total number of estates forfeited was 457 – but younger brothers and sons of landowners: they included also yeomen, tenant farmers, sailors, artisans, boatmen and priests.[6]

By no means were all the officers in the Jacobite army indicted. The names of many well-liked by Protestant neighbours or not particularly conspicuous in their 'treason' were left out.

Some brought to trial were acquitted by juries who were unhappy at classing as 'treason' adherence to one who could be regarded as the rightful king. Maurice FitzGerald, eldest son of the Knight of Kerry, was captured at the Boyne, aged only eighteen. He was brought to trial but put on such an act of youthful and irresponsible high spirits that the jury with a smile threw out the case.[7] Nicolas Taaffe, second Viscount Carlingford, a volunteer in the Jacobite army, was killed leading a charge at the Boyne. That his estate of 1,975 Irish acres* was not confiscated was due to the fact that his younger brother and heir, Francis, was a distinguished officer in the Austrian service, and William did not want to offend his ally, the Emperor.[8] The Mulloys were a Catholic family of divided loyalties, being hereditary bearers of the English standard in Ireland. Captain William Mulloy and several more were in the Jacobite army; but Theobald was a lieutenant in a regiment of Williamite dragoons and, when King William's horse was shot, gave the king his own. Among the prisoners taken by his regiment was his own seventeen-year-old son, who was pardoned.[9]

Indictment, attainder and outlawry were not arbitrary acts of the executive but legal processes in courts of law. The first step was for the county's Grand Jury to file a Bill of Indictment charging the accused with high treason. The county sheriff then issued a Writ of Capias, requiring him to appear for trial. If after two Writs of Capias he still did not appear, a Writ of Exigent was issued, directing the sheriff to have the accused named on five successive county court days, charging him to appear on pain of outlawry. Only if he still failed to appear was he declared an outlaw, which would mean the forfeiture of all landed property, of unexpired leases, of mortgage claims, and of goods and

---

* The old Irish acre was nearly twice the size of the English acre.

chattels even down to clothes and blankets. That was the prospect which faced the Irish army as it established itself in Limerick and prepared to stand a siege.[10]

Tyrconnell thought that all was lost and they had better throw in their hand. But the hard line of the Declaration of Finglas did not suggest that William's terms would be lenient. The Lord Deputy's pessimistic view was fiercely opposed by the bitter-enders led by Sarsfield, the 'darling of the army' and undoubtedly the bravest of the brave, though perhaps not the brightest of the bright.* They pointed out that they held all the country west of the Shannon including the port of Galway, as well as the ports of Kinsale and Cork; and that Britannia did not rule the waves. Athlone was putting up a stout resistance: its Governor, Colonel Richard Grace, a veteran who had fought against Cromwell, when summoned by the Williamite General Douglas to surrender on terms, fired a shot into the ground and replied: 'These are my terms, this only will I give or receive. When my provisions are consumed, I shall defend until I eat my boots.'

He then destroyed the bridge and held the Connaught side of the town while Sarsfield led 15,000 men to his relief. On 25 July 1690, Douglas, whose forces had nearly run out of food, withdrew lest his communications with Dublin be cut.[11]

Limerick was a strong city, its walls in good condition, built on an island in the Shannon. The Williamites held only the left bank: on the right bank opposite the city were Sarsfield's formidable Horse. The rest of County Clare could best be described as no man's land owing to the equivocal attitude of its most powerful family, the O'Briens.

---

* 'Un fort brave homme, mais qui n'avoit point de tête.' D'Avaux, Négotiations, 159.

That branch of the family which was headed by the Earl of Inchiquin was Protestant, though wavering in its allegiance to church and state and with a propensity for changing sides at the wrong time. The second earl, although apparently a Catholic in 1659, was attainted by the Jacobite Irish Parliament thirty years later. Another branch was staunchly Catholic and its head, Viscount Clare, had raised and commanded one of the regiments which went to France with Mountcashel. Conor O'Brien of Lemanagh Castle in mid-Clare was married to a formidable lady called Moira Rua (Red Mary) née MacMahon, who was tried but acquitted of murdering her first husband, a Colonel Neylon. In 1651 Conor was killed in a skirmish against the Cromwellians. With a firm grasp of priorities, his sorrowing widow drove at top speed to Limerick, demanded an interview with General Ireton and offered, if her son were allowed to keep the family estates, to marry any officer of the Limerick garrison. The hero volunteering, or detailed, for this duty was a Cornet Cooper.

According to family tradition, the marriage was a happy one and the children were devoted to their stepfather. Mrs Cooper, as she incongruously became, and her Neylon sons remained Catholic but her O'Brien sons were brought up as Protestants. The eldest, Donogh, took up residence in more fertile country at Dromoland. He was created a baronet in 1685 and in 1689, as sheriff of the county, was commissioned by King James to raise a regiment of dragoons for the cause. He procrastinated and excused himself from joining the Irish army until begged by his neighbours to do something about the raparees* who were plaguing the county. He then raised a troop which he used only for internal security, and hanged thirteen of Sarsfield's men for

---

* Raparees were Jacobite irregulars, or *banditti*, according to one's point of view.

looting. Sarsfield was furious and thought he was not doing his bit but nothing would shift him from his seat on the fence.[12]

William could not really begin operations until his heavy artillery arrived. On 11 August Sarsfield learned that the siege-train was approaching, and set out on 'Sarsfield's Ride', his most celebrated exploit. With 500 horse and sixty dragoons he rode through the Clare hills to Killaloe, forded the Shannon, circled round and intercepted William's siege-train ten miles south-east of Limerick. After a brief fight, the guns and ammunition were piled together and blown up in a tremendous explosion which was heard even in Limerick.

Without siege artillery and with an army hungry, cold and miserable in the waterlogged trenches, William made a futile attempt to storm the city through an inadequate breach in the wall. The Irish fought with desperate valour, with grenades, musketry and cannon flanking the breach. Even the women took part, hurling stones and broken bottles at the storming parties. Eventually these withdrew, and on 29 August William's army marched away. He himself returned to England and the French to France, accompanied by Tyrconnell to report to his royal master. It was a famous victory, outweighing in its moral effect the far more important loss of Cork and Kinsale in the autumn, by which the Jacobites lost their direct communications with France. Instead of relieving these, Berwick and Sarsfield wasted time on an irrelevant and unsuccessful siege of Birr Castle.

William handed his army over to the Dutch Baron Ginkel, a good soldier and a very decent man.

Jacobites and Williamites were not always at daggers drawn. Colonel George Hamilton wrote to his Jacobite foe, Colonel Daniel O'Donovan:

There being one John Jackson, sergeant, lately
taken by some raparees, if you will send him to
Dunmanway, I will send you Sergeant Deady in
exchange . . . John Roche is at Dunmanway, though
a very notorious robber, yet if you own him as your
soldier, he is at your service . . . I am very sensible
of your kindness in treating my soldiers so kindly,
and if ever it be my good fortune to have any of
your soldiers prisoners, you may assure yourself
that they will have no worse usage. I shall be glad
if time allows us to drink a bottle.

A week later, time did allow.

If you please, I could meet you at your daughter's
or privately or publicly at Skibbereen . . . If you
will allow me that honour, I will drink a bottle with
you very heartily . . . My service to your lady,
daughter and other friends, and we drink your
health at present with a cup of punch.

In the spring Hamilton offered his opposite number freedom
from all prosecution if he would change sides.

Believe me, it will not be in my power to procure
such conditions for the future or yet for you to
expect larger terms than now offered . . . On
Saturday between 8 and 9, if it please God, I will
meet you at Clough Castle with my daughter Nell
and an officer or two, and from thence to do myself
the honour to wait upon you and your lady at your
quarters.[13]

But on that day, not before time, Colonel O'Donovan was ordered to march his regiment to Limerick.

The Duke of Würtemburg wrote to the King of Denmark in September 1690:

> If an amnesty could be given to the leading people, the war would soon come to an end. But the amnesty is limited to the poor common soldiers, as the English are very eager for the confiscation of the Catholics' estates. For the Irish say openly, 'We are fighting not for King James or the Popish religion, but for our estates.'[14]

That being so, it is remarkable that the 'poor common soldiers' who had no estates should continue to fight so well.

With so much at stake, many gentlemen hedged their bets. The Dalys were a Catholic family transplanted to Galway, where they invested in West Indian plantations, prospered and bought land. Denis Daly of Carnakelly was a judge and Privy Councillor of King James, a man much respected by both Catholics and Protestants. In Galway city he canvassed the opinions of many who saw no hope of victory, and sent a message to Ginkel that the city was ripe for surrender.[15] Another of King James's judges, Baron Riverston of the Nugent family, which had also been transplanted to Galway, had urged James after the Boyne to get out of Ireland quickly. On Sarsfield's insistence, Berwick imprisoned them both but Tyrconnell returned in January and released them.[16] In May there arrived a very experienced French general, St Ruth, who brought with him more French officers, cannon, 16,000 muskets, shiploads of miscellaneous stores, and an excellent opinion of Irish soldiers, whom he had commanded in Italy.

In June Ginkel moved on Athlone. The valiant Colonel Grace had been killed and on 30 June, after a heavy bombardment, Williamite storm-troops waded shoulder-deep across the Shannon and drove the Irish from their defences. It was a shattering blow, and some Jacobites responded to another declaration on 7 July, which promised pardon to all who submitted in three weeks.

However, ten days later they stood to fight in a strong position behind stone walls and a bog at Aughrim, nineteen miles south-west of Athlone. For once the Jacobite horse was ineffective but the infantry fought well and St Ruth exclaimed exultantly, *'Le jour est à nous, mes enfants!'* A few minutes later a cannonball took off his head* and the Jacobites broke.

It later transpired that Colonel Henry Luttrell, whose regiment had not distinguished itself, had been in communication with Ginkel over peace terms. D'Usson, St Ruth's successor, would have had him court-martialled and shot had not Ginkel threatened to hang every Irish officer in his hands.

Aughrim was decisive. After it, the Jacobites had no chance of victory and knew it. If they did not, it was pointed out to them by John Bellew of Barmeath Castle in County Louth, a member of an impeccably Catholic family, who had been since May arguing the case for a negotiated surrender. He was 'outlawed by his own consent to prevent the enemies having any suspicion of the services he was doing their majesties in the enemies' quarters'; but was of course pardoned.[17]

Galway, the city of the tribes, was Ginkel's next objective, and did not detain him long. Perhaps the tribes' background of commerce, with West Indian, French and Spanish connections,

---

* The cannon aimed at him could not be sufficiently depressed until the author's ancestor, the Reverend John Trench, of a Huguenot family settled in Galway, hacked off the heel of his boot and thrust it under the gun's breech. A century later Protestants in that area still swore by 'the heel of the Dean of Rafoe'.

made them more pliable, readier to make the best of what could not be mended, than the Os and Macs and Old English dynasties of the Pale. Most of the tribal family of Ffrench fought for King James, but Colonel John French – the spelling was interchangeable – for King William. Lieutenant Marcus Ffrench of Rahasane fought with conspicuous gallantry at Aughrim, was promoted captain, and then defected to Ginkel with full details of the Galway garrison.[18] Arthur French of Tyrone, Mayor of Galway, was imprisoned by Sarsfield for communicating with Ginkel.[19] Richard Martin – another tribesman – of Dangan, one of King James's judges and a captain in Luttrell's Horse, after Aughrim took half his troop and seven 'serviceable horses' over to Ginkel, thereby earning the sobriquet of 'Nimble Dick'.[20] Of the non-tribal families, Francis Forster, son of the High Sheriff of Galway, also defected to Ginkel with half his troop.[21]

As soon as Ginkel arrived before Galway a deputation led by Sir John Kirwan, a former mayor, waited on him, assured him that the city would not stand a siege, and obtained from him terms which Protestants thought scandalously lenient. Those who wanted to continue the struggle could march off to Limerick with all their weapons, drums beating and colours flying; those who did not could keep their estates, their religion, their right to bear arms and, if they were lawyers, the right to practise their profession.[22] Most of the garrison marched away, but Colonel Walter Blake of Menlo, who had been wounded at Aughrim, became the first Catholic to raise a regiment for King William. They did not fight against their former comrades, but were engaged in internal security duties and 'behaved themselves with great care and fidelity'.[23]

In Limerick, roles were now reversed. Sarsfield was for peace in Ireland and continuing the war abroad. Tyrconnell, who had been promised large French reinforcements, was for fighting on.

But on 14 September Tyrconnell died of a stroke. At the end of the month Ginkel's army arrived and the second siege of Limerick began, with the Irish in far worse shape than they had been a year earlier; only the cavalry, concentrated in south Clare, being in any condition to continue fighting. On 22 September the Williamites seized the Thomond bridge over the Shannon, by which means alone the garrison had contact with the cavalry. There being no news of the French relief force, on the next day the Jacobites 'beat a parley' and there was a three days' ceasefire.

Peace terms were argued long and hard but with surprising cordiality. 'Change kings,' Sarsfield assured the Williamite officers, 'and we'll fight you again.' The principal negotiators on the Irish side were Sarsfield himself, the Catholic lawyer Sir Theobald (Toby) Butler, and the cavalry commanders Lords Galmoy and Trimleston.

The Limerick garrison and the Irish forces still in arms in Counties Clare, Cork, Kerry and Mayo were offered the choice of:

1 Going to France, there to join the French army and continue to fight for King James.
2 Joining King William's army.
3 Resuming possession of their estates, having 'submitted to their Majesties obedience' and sworn the oath of allegiance.

The first was Sarsfield's strong preference. The French of course favoured it, as did Ginkel, for it would remove from Ireland a lot of volatile material.

Since soldiering was generally regarded not as a crusade but as the only profession, apart from the law, open to a gentleman, about a thousand chose the second option. About 12,000 sailed with Sarsfield to France.

The Wild Geese took to France not only their swords and their fidelity but the tenets of Freemasonry, which for the next half-century was strongly implanted in Jacobite circles. Pope Clement XII's Bull of 1738 denouncing Freemasonry was not promulgated in Ireland, where Masonry was neither anti-Christian nor republican, until 1797; and until then many Catholic laymen and even priests were Masons. According to a French history of Freemasonry, *L'Etat du Grand Orient*, written in 1777, the first lodge in France, established in 1688 (sic), was the regimental lodge of the corps which later became Dorington's, then Walsh's. From this sprang innumerable lodges in France, largely Irish Jacobite in composition. At least two Grand Masters of the Grand Lodge of Ireland – the fourth Lord Kingston and Thomas Nugent – had served in the Irish Brigade. Another Catholic Grand Master was Viscount Barnewall of Kingsland. Loyalty to the king was a principle of Irish, English and Scottish Freemasonry, but to which king?

> God bless the King! God bless the Faith's Defender!
> God bless (no harm in blessing) the Pretender!
> But who Pretender is, and who is King,
> God bless us all! That's quite another thing.

Gradually Freemasonry with a Jacobite tinge was replaced by military and civilian lodges loyal to the Hanoverians; and at the end of the century in Belfast, as on the Continent, by lodges with republican leanings. But despite political differences, Masons were all brothers, and in times of trouble could count as individuals on a brother's help. A sort of handbook of Belfast Freemasonry was entitled *Ahimon Rezon or Help to a Brother*, the very essence of the Craft.[24]

Generally the Wild Geese were the landless younger sons,

though to this generalisation there were exceptions such as Lords Galmoy, Clare and Trimleston. Those who formed the largest category in the Jacobite army, known as the 'Articlemen', took advantage of the Articles of Limerick and Galway to stay at home on their estates – if they had any – and enjoy such freedom of worship 'as was consistent with the laws of Ireland or as they did enjoy in the reign of Charles II'. The grander ones rode off, like Lieutenant Colonel Mathias Everard, with pistols, sword and gun, family, servants, tenants, horses, cattle and Ginkel's safe conduct.[25] The humbler articlemen walked or jogged home on their farm nags.

On Sarsfield's insistence that he would fight on and 'lay his bones in these old walls rather than not take care of those who stuck by us all along', the terms offered to the Irish army were extended to 'all such as are under its protection in Counties Limerick, Cork, Kerry, Clare and Mayo'. This was included in the negotiated draft but, apparently by mistake, omitted from the signed fair copy. Ginkel assured the Irish that the 'missing clause' would be re-inserted. It was not. But although, to appease the more militant Protestants, it was omitted from the treaty presented to the Irish Parliament for ratification, it seems in fact to have been honoured, in that Jacobites in those counties who wanted to stay were treated as Articlemen.[26]

In Tyrone's rebellion of 1594–1603, in the Great Rebellion of 1641 and in Cromwell's war in Ireland, the leaders of the vanquished expected to be hanged; during the English Civil War, Irishmen caught fighting for the king were invariably butchered, with their women and children, by the Cromwellians; as late as 1685 the Duke of Monmouth had been beheaded for his rebellion, scores of his Anabaptist followers drawn, hanged and quartered, and hundreds exported to work and die as slaves in the West Indies. Nothing of the kind happened during this civil war in Ireland, which was fought with chivalry and restraint. One cannot imagine the Williamites charging with the war-cry 'Jesus and no quarter!', or Marlborough treating Cork as Cromwell had treated Drogheda; the Jacobites never dreamed of slaughtering 'with Catholic zeal' hundreds of Protestant men, women and children. By 1689 the age of religious enthusiasm was fading out, the Age of Reason was setting in and would last for exactly a hundred years. The Jacobites obtained far better terms than losers might expect, certainly better than they would have obtained after the Boyne.

Exasperated Irish Protestants thought they had won the war but lost the peace:

> Hard fate that still attends our Irish war,
> The conquerors lose, the conquered gainers are;
> The pen's the symbol of the sword's defeat,
> We fight like heroes but like fools we treat.[27]

It was a situation which their Parliament was resolved to rectify.

---

1 Fogarty family papers in County Library, Thurles; Melvin, *Irish Genealogist*, 90.

2 *Blake Family Records*, 214; *Tuam Herald*, 3 October 1991.

3 J. G. Simms, *Williamite Confiscations*, 17.

4 *Ibid.*, 22; J. H. Plumb, *The Growth of Political Stability in England 1675-1725*, 52-6; Angus MacIntyre, *The Liberator: Daniel O'Connell and the Irish Party 1830-1847*, 232; Robert Shepherd, *Ireland's Fate*, 12, 55-6.

5 *Ibid.*, 56; Simms, *op. cit.*, 32.

6 *Ibid.*, 33-40, 176.

7 *Ibid.*, 38 and FitzGerald family tradition.

8 *Ibid.*, 79-80; Dalton, *King James's Irish Army List*, II, 51-2; TCD MSS. N1, 3.

9 Dalton, *op. cit.*, II, 537.

10 Simms, *op. cit.*, 30.

11 Dalton, *op. cit.*, II, 567.

12 Donough O'Brien, *History of the O'Briens*, 203; Inchiquin MSS nos. 20-22, 54, 55, 57.
13 Dalton, *op. cit.*, II, 716-8.
14 Quoted by Robert Shepherd, *op. cit.*, 140.
15 Hardiman, *A History of Galway*, II, 157.
16 Dalton, *op. cit.*, II, 474.
17 Simms, *Irish Jacobites*, 131.
18 Dalton, *op. cit.*, II, 674; J. Fahey, *History and Antiquities of the Diocese of Kilmacduagh*, 316.
19 *Ibid.*
20 Simms, *Williamite Confiscations*, 77-8, and *Irish Jacobites*, 132.
21 *Ibid.*, 133.
22 Hardiman, *op. cit.*, 161, 219.
23 *Ibid.*, 162-3; Dalton, *op. cit.*, II, 271.
24 *New Catholic Encyclopaedia*, 135; Michael Baigent and Richard Lee, *The Temple and the Lodge*, 184; R. E. Parkinson, *History of the Grand Lodge of Ireland*, II, 215.
25 R. H. A. J. Everard, 'The Family of Everard', IV, 32 in Melvin, *op. cit.*, VII.
26 Simms, *Williamite Confiscations*, 55-62, 65; Simms, *The Treaty of Limerick*, 12-14.
27 *Ibid.*, 12.

2

The Post-War Settlement

To about 2,600 indictments for high treason in Ireland were now added 1,261 for foreign treason, about one in fourteen of those who had gone to France with Mountcashel and Sarsfield. (None of these figures are quite accurate owing to duplications and incomplete returns.) Few of those charged with foreign treason returned home to stand trial and of those charged with high treason in Ireland, most could plead the Articles of Galway or Limerick. Adjudications were made from 1691 to 1694 by the Privy Council, and from 1697 to 1699 by a panel of nine judges. All one needed was three witnesses (including one Protestant) to swear that one was in the Galway garrison or covered by the Limerick Articles. 1,263 claims were made under the Articles, seventy-eight for Galway and the remainder for Limerick, of which all but sixteen were granted. The usual ground for refusal was that the applicant had 'taken protection' after the battle of the Boyne, but had then taken up arms again.[1]

Thady Quinn of Askeaton in County Limerick was adjudged not to be protected by the Articles on these grounds. Attempts were made to indict him for high treason in three counties. In two, grand juries returned findings of *ignoramus*. In the third, County Limerick, he was released on bail pending his trial, whereupon the High Sheriff, grand jury and numerous Protestant gentry and clergy petitioned the Chief Justice that he had not plundered or oppressed Protestants but had protected them during the Jacobite regime. The case against him was withdrawn.[2]

Those who chose to stand trial had a good chance of acquittal. In Galway it was notoriously impossible to pick a jury free of Jacobite sympathies. There is an apocryphal story that at one assizes forty men were charged with domestic treason in that they had fought for King James. So had most members of the jury, but they were articlemen. They had no difficulty in acquitting thirty-nine; but the case of the fortieth, Kirwan, was more difficult, since the foreman of the jury had been his commanding officer. From this embarrassing situation the twelve good men and true could extricate themselves only by drawing lots for one who would fall suddenly sick. Without a full jury, the case against Kirwan had to be dropped.[3]

Outside Galway too, Protestant freeholders, 'contracting new friendships with the Irish', as jurymen were inclined to view fighting for King James as misguided but not treasonable. They were angry at seeing 60 per cent of the forfeited estates divided among seven of King William's Dutch and Huguenot favourites and his mistress. Many were distressed by the anomalies of forfeiture and non-forfeiture, it being remarked that many Jacobites kept their estates under the Articles while others, 'who had submitted after the Boyne and had since remained quiet, lost all. This is such a wondrous inequality.' So prosecution virtually stopped when the fighting finished and many who were attainted and were known to be in Ireland, were never brought to trial.[4]

Much depended on sheer luck. The great Catholic family of Esmonde was strongly Jacobite in sympathy, but Laurence the second baronet died in 1688 and Laurence the third baronet was aged only thirteen at the time of the battle of the Boyne, so the family escaped forfeiture.[5] Luke Plunkett, the third Earl of Fingall, was included in the list of outlawries though he had died in 1685; his eldest son Peter was born in 1678 and was not in

Ireland during the war, so they too escaped forfeiture.[6]

Eleven Jacobite peers recovered their forfeited lands thanks to the Articles. None had more enemies than Alastair MacDonnell, Earl of Antrim, who owned vast estates in a fiercely anti-Papist province. These were lost to Cromwell, restored by Charles II, lost in 1690, restored in 1692. Many were waiting to grab them the instant they were forfeited, and William Connolly (who despite his name was a Protestant, Speaker of the House of Commons, and had made a fortune from forfeited estates) wrote wistfully, 'I fear he will be restored, for we have no evidence against him' – no evidence, that is, which might invalidate his plea under the Articles.[7]

Jenico, seventh Viscount Gormanston, head of the Old English family of Preston, raised a regiment of infantry for King James, was attainted in 1691 and died without issue soon afterwards. His heir was another Jenico, his nephew, who under the Articles of Limerick should have been able to recover the estates (9,009 Irish acres in county Meath and 972 in King's County): they had, however, been acquired by a former Cromwellian, latterly Williamite, Colonel Richard Coote, who refused to disgorge, obstructed and beat up the bailiffs and generally behaved in a most reprehensible manner. By paying out money like water (including £12/6/11 on dinners for two juries), Jenico obtained a court order ejecting Coote. Coote refused to be ejected and petitioned Parliament to pass a special act in his favour. The petition was rejected; but in 1697, while Coote was still in possession in defiance of the court, Jenico died and was succeeded as ninth Viscount by his younger brother, Anthony. Coote then appealed to the English House of Lords as the ultimate court of appeal. This power of appeal was of very long standing but had been abolished by King James's Irish Parliament in 1689. In 1695 the Acts of this Parliament were annulled, so the English House of Lords retained its appellate powers. They were formally confirmed, and the appellate powers of the Irish House of Lords removed, by the Declaratory Act of 1720. In the case of Coote's appeal, their lordships upheld the decision of the Irish court in favour of a Catholic Jacobite against a Protestant Williamite.

That was the end of Coote's pretensions, but Anthony was not yet out of the wood. The Trustees for Forfeited Estates held that although he and his elder brother had been adjudged within the Articles of Limerick, their uncle, the seventh Viscount, from whom they inherited, had been attainted, was not covered by the Articles, but had nevertheless held the estates for several months in 1689-91. The estates were therefore forfeited to the Trustees. However, they were good to Anthony and his wife, granting the estates in trust to him for 500 years provided he paid her £3,000 a year (probably by a former marriage settlement). The remainder went to him in tail. So in effect Anthony got all the estates, but the fact that they were entailed was to be of vital importance.[8]

The Barnewalls were descended from a Norman knight who had arrived in Ireland even before Strongbow, and acquired wide estates in Counties Meath, Louth and Dublin. In 1689 there were three main branches of the family, headed respectively by Nicholas, third Viscount Barnewall of Kingsland, Mathias, tenth Baron Trimleston, and Sir Patrick Barnewall, Bart. Fifteen Barnewalls were outlawed for high treason in Ireland, of whom only five, including the viscount and the baronet, were adjudged under the Articles and retained their estates, in both these cases entailed.

Mathias Barnewall, Lord Trimleston, a captain in Galmoy's Horse, had been one of those who negotiated the Treaty of Limerick. He could have pleaded the Articles, but elected to go to France and was killed the next year fighting in Germany.

Although the estate was entailed, the prospect of his younger brother, John, recovering it must have seemed remote, especially as he had been educated in France from the age of twelve. He was accordingly indicted, despite his tender years, of foreign treason. One of the judges considering claims under the Articles wrote:

> I shall be sorry if poor Lord Trimleston loses his
> property . . . Supposing he was an ensign in King
> James's Guards, I do not think his guilt is so great
> that he should lose his property on that account;
> for he was a mere child, for whom his relatives had
> secured his commission to give him the wherewithal
> to live at the college.

The Lords Justice gave orders to prosecute but nothing was ever done about it, and in the end the Trustees allowed young Lord Trimleston to retain the family estates in tail.[9]

An even harder case was that of Jane Lavallin, outlawed for foreign treason because she had been taken to France at the age of three. It took a private Act of Parliament to get her estate restored.[10]

Nicolas Cusack was an MP in 1689, rose to colonel in the Jacobite army and negotiated the civil Articles of Limerick. He had been attainted in 1691 but was of course covered by the Articles. He owned various freehold properties in Counties Dublin and Kildare which had come to him as part of his wife's dowry. His son, Robert, was not an articleman but was allowed a remainder in tail of these properties, inheriting them on his father's death.[11]

No family was more Jacobite than the Dillons. They raised two infantry regiments, one of which went to France with

Mountcashel and one with Sarsfield. Twenty-two Dillons were outlawed for high treason in Ireland, seventeen for foreign treason. Only five pleaded the Articles of Limerick. Theobald, seventh Viscount Dillon, had 4,723 statute acres in Counties Roscommon and Mayo, which had been entailed in 1680. Although he remained in France, he was given a royal pardon in 1694 for the sake of his son, Henry, the eighth viscount, who was covered by the Articles of Limerick and inherited the estates.[12]

The Brownes of Kerry were unusual in being an English family who had settled in Ireland in the sixteenth century but remained Catholic, intermarrying with O'Sullivans and McCarthys. Sir Valentine Browne was one of James II's Privy Councillors and was created Viscount Kenmare. He raised Lord Kenmare's Infantry, and his son raised Colonel Nicholas Browne's Infantry. Kenmare died in 1694 and Colonel Nicholas, his estates forfeited, went abroad and died in Ghent in 1720. The recovery of the vast Kenmare estates must have seemed a forlorn hope, but the Trustees of Forfeited Estates ordered that Nicholas's life interest in them be sold to the Trustees, who would hold them in trust for Valentine, the third viscount, who was a child during the war and on whom the property had been settled in infancy.[13]

Naturally the Butlers, kin of the Duke of Ormond, did all right. Besides Lord Cahir, there were four Catholic Butler peers. Nothing could be done for Lord Galmoy but wish him luck in the French army, in which he rose to be Lieutenant General. But Lords Dunboyne, Ikerrin and Mountgarret all recovered their estates under the Articles of Limerick. Mountgarret was extremely lucky to do so: he had been captured in 1689 leading the forlorn hope against the walls of Derry; but he was, doubtless with Ormond's help, exchanged, and was therefore at Limerick and able to plead the Articles.[14]

Those who were captured or surrendered at Derry, the Boyne or Cork were unlucky; those covered by the Articles of Galway or Limerick, or whom the courts acquitted or never got round to prosecuting, were in luck.

One who was conspicuously unlucky was John Grace, Baron of Courtstown. His grandfather, the first baron, who owned 32,870 statute acres in County Kilkenny, had been High Sheriff in 1686 and MP in 1689. An approach had been made to him by an emissary of Schomberg to side with William and Mary. Picking up a playing card (the six of hearts, known in Kilkenny a century later as 'Grace's Card') he wrote on it his contemptuous reply and told Schomberg's men, 'Go, tell your master I despise his offer.' He raised a regiment of foot and a troop of horse for King James; but he died in 1690 before they went into action, without, it seems, being attainted. His heir was his eldest son, Robert, who died at the end of 1691 from wounds received at Aughrim, but who was covered by the Articles of Limerick. The property then passed to Robert's eldest son, Oliver, who had been attainted for the modest help he had given King James but was a 'sad invalid' in the south of France. He survived his father by only nine days, and never knew he had inherited.

The second son, John, who had been Sarsfield's *aide-de-camp*, then inherited the title and, as an articleman, took over the estate. He was a model landlord, popular with tenants and neighbours, Protestant and Catholic, for ten years. There was a flaw in his title, in that the estate had been owned for nine days by his brother Oliver; but he must have thought that nine days were neither here nor there. No one but he knew about them, so the less said the better. Unfortunately an aunt knew, and intimated that unless he made it worth her while to keep silent, she would disclose all. John refused to be blackmailed, so disclose all she did, and the Trustees of Forfeited Estates declared his estate to be forfeited by Oliver. John appealed for help to his kinsman, the Duke of Buckingham, to whose large estates he was the heir presumptive. The duke promised to use all his influence to get the matter satisfactorily settled by an Act of the English Parliament; so John, leaving his wife in Ireland, went over to England to see the business through. Unfortunately there was in the ducal household, living *en famille*, the duke's nubile illegitimate daughter, whom John Grace fancied, and she him. Within a few months the fruit of their mutual regard became embarrassingly apparent; the duke cut Grace out of his will and refused to do anything to help him. So for his pleasure John Grace paid dearly, losing his Irish estates and his English expectations. No doubt his wife had something to say about it, too.[15]

A Catholic family could keep out of trouble by keeping its head down, if that is possible while sitting on the fence. The Magans of County Westmeath are a Celtic sept of very ancient lineage, kin to MacDermot and O'Conor Don. In the early seventeenth century Humphrey Magan while at home lived, dressed, spoke and behaved like a Celtic chieftain, while in Dublin like a French or English gentleman. By what was apparently his deliberate decision Richard, his elder son, remained a Catholic, while Morgan, his younger son, became a Protestant. When Cromwell ruled Ireland, Morgan gave Richard such protection as was needed; when James ruled, Richard protected Morgan. They weathered the Cromwellian storm and even retained their estates, prospered modestly after the Restoration, and avoided plunging on either side in 1689-91. Neither the Protestant Magans under James II, nor the Catholic Magans under William and Mary, were attainted.

In this way they were more fortunate than their cousin 'Young D'Alton', who joined King James's army but at Athlone deserted to join the Williamites. He was unwise enough to take advantage of a truce to visit his cronies in Westmeath to drink and reminisce. They received him with open arms, threw a party for him, kept him at the bottle until the truce expired and then made him prisoner. They asked his father what they should do with him. 'Haven't you hanged the rascal?' he replied. So they did.

The Catholic Magans seem to have suffered no disabilities whatever during the eighteenth century. They retained their estates intact, and with their Protestant cousins High Sheriff and grand jurymen, no one harassed them. Even when Richard, a Catholic, illegally inherited an estate from a Protestant cousin, he got away with it.[16]

In 1696 there was a plot to assassinate King William. It was reported to the authorities by Thomas Prendergast, a Catholic of an Old English family who had been a captain of Horse in the Jacobite army. He was himself implicated in the plot, perhaps the man who was to shoot the king with a 'musketoon that carried six or eight bullets'. At the last moment, however, his conscience or his sense of self-preservation baulked at regicide. He was rewarded a 7,082 acre estate at Gort in County Galway, forfeited by Sir Roger O'Shaughnessy and his son William, who had gone to France with Clare's regiment in 1690 and had brilliant careers in the Irish Brigade. Prendergast became a Brigadier General in the British army and was mortally wounded at Malplaquet.[17]

Sixty-five royal pardons were granted between 1690 and 1698. Those pardoned included John Bellew, for unspecified 'services to their Majesties in the enemies' quarters'; John Kerdiff who had 'always behaved with great affection towards the Protestants'; John Browne and John Malone who had 'behaved with great tenderness towards the Protestants'; Captain Richard

Martin 'by His Majesty's favour'; Denis Daly 'by a promise made under the hand of General Ginkel at His Majesty's camp near Galway he was to enjoy his estate to him and his heirs free from all forfeitures as the Protestants of Ireland enjoyed theirs'; Francis Forster for 'bringing in part of his troop'; Thomas Nugent, Baron Riverston, for reasons which were not stated but one can guess; Patrick French 'by his being instrumental in the surrender of Galway'; Charles Whyte 'by the king's favour . . . by the interposition of His Imperial Majesty'; Martin Blake of Moyne who had been imprisoned by the Jacobites for corresponding with Ginkel; Robert Longfield 'by the king's favour without any merit appearing'; and twenty-seven more simply by 'His Majesty's' or 'Their Majesties' favour', no other reason being given.[18]

Tyrconnell's widow had been outlawed and thus debarred from claiming her jointure of his forfeited estates. The Irish Lord Justices refused to reconsider her case, telling Queen Mary that she had acted not only in duty to her husband but 'in malice to Protestants'. However, she was sister to the Duchess of Marlborough, so when after Queen Anne's succession the Marlboroughs were in the ascendant, a private bill was pushed through Parliament on her behalf. Wrote a disgusted bishop: 'Thus it is to be the sister of a favourite.'[19]

The English Parliament had been outraged by the grant of so many forfeited estates to the king's foreign favourites instead of their sale to worthy English and Irish Protestants, thereby relieving the taxpayer of the cost of the war. In 1700 it passed an Act of Resumption, mortifying to the king, which declared null and void all previous grants and vested all forfeited estates in thirteen Trustees for re-allocation.

This greatly inconvenienced Captain Mark Baggot of Grace's Infantry. He was covered by the Articles of Limerick but his father, also attainted, was not, and the family estate of more than 3,000 acres in County Carlow was accordingly granted to Lord Albemarle, the king's Dutch favourite. On his father's death Mark produced proof that the property was settled on him. Albemarle agreed out of court, and sold him his own estate for the modest sum of £300. But with the Act of Resumption the whole issue was reopened; the Trustees of Forfeited Estates took over the property and Mark had to lodge his claim before them. His Protestant neighbours now weighed in with the petition to Ormond from the High Sheriff, Grand Jury *et al.* The duke was urged to:

> obstruct and discountenance Mark Baggot, a violent Papist, from having his abode among us; the said Mark having been titular High Sheriff in 1689 and acted as such with that insufferable pride, rigour and insolence towards the Protestants as will never be forgotten.

But if Mark Baggot had Protestant enemies in County Carlow, he had in Dublin a very useful Protestant friend, Bishop King of Derry, shortly to be Archbishop of Dublin, with whom he shared an improbable interest in mathematics and portable barometers. With episcopal support, Baggot was able to convince the Trustees that the property was part of a marriage contract which was revocable only with the consent of his wife's trustees. So, in the face of strong local opposition, a not very likeable Catholic recovered his family estates.[20]

James Nugent died in 1690 and was outlawed after his death, when his property was already in the possession of his son Edward, who was covered by the Articles of Limerick. But in 1700 the Trustees of Forfeited Estates took the property over.

Edward argued that but for the Act of Resumption he would have a good title to the estate by virtue of the Articles, and that the Trustees' interpretation of the Act was in breach of the Articles. His arguments did not prevail with the Trustees, but he had enough influence and friends in Parliament to get a private bill passed restoring the estates to him with the proviso that, although he need not conform to the established church, his heir (as yet unborn) must do so. His heir duly conformed thirty-four years later.[21]

On the whole Catholics benefited from the Act of Resumption. Working for two years flat out, the Trustees heard 3,140 claims and allowed in whole or in part 1,861, nearly half by Catholics. Forty freehold estates, totalling 70,000 acres, were restored to former Catholic proprietors. In the case of fifteen others a life interest for the lifetime of the forfeiting proprietor was sold, but his heir would inherit after his death. They also settled innumerable claims on forfeited estates by mortgage-holders, lessors and lessees, widows claiming jointures and daughters claiming marriage portions. Most of the estates which stayed forfeit were sold to deserving individuals or to institutions, notably Trinity College, Dublin and the Hollow Blades Sword Company, which sank without trace in the South Sea Bubble in 1721, when the South Sea Company went bust, setting off a general collapse in the London and Dublin stock exchanges which ruined thousands of people.

That concluded the Williamite confiscations. According to a manuscript list made at the time, 1,699,343 profitable statute acres were confiscated and 985,786 were restored, about 30 per cent by royal favour, the rest under the Articles of Galway and Limerick. Various historians give various estimates of the proportions of land left in Catholic hands. J. G. Simms, in the most authoritative calculation, estimates that the Catholic-owned share of profitable land declined from 22 per cent in 1688 to 14 per cent in 1703.

> Almost half the area ... was held by persons adjudged within the Articles of Limerick and Galway ... Pardons and successful claims accounted for a further fifth. The balance was held by persons whose trials were dropped, or ended in acquittal, or against whom no proceedings were taken.[22]

1   Simms, *Williamite Confiscations*, 33-42, 46, 47.
2   *Ibid.*, 40, 52-3.
3   Mary Anne Hickson, *Old Kerry Records*, I, 205-6.
4   Simms, *op. cit.*, 39.
5   Esmonde family papers.
6   Simms, *op. cit.*, 75.
7   *Ibid.*, 46, 50, 53; W. A. Maguire, *Kings in Conflict*, 147.
8   Simms, *op. cit.*, 137-8; Dalton, *King James's Irish Army List*, II, 238.
9   Simms, *op. cit.*, 138-9.
10 *Ibid.*, 41.
11 Dalton, *op. cit.*, I, 91.
12 *Ibid.*, 247-249; Simms, *op. cit.*, 77; and Simms, *Irish Jacobites*, 135.
13 Dalton, *op. cit.*, II, 638; MacLysaght, *Kenmare Papers*, XI.
14 Simms, *Williamite Confiscations*, 114-5; Lodge, *Peerage of Ireland*, II, 316; IV, 71.
15 Sheffield Grace, *Memoirs of the Family of Grace*, 42-5.
16 William Magan, *Umma More*, 128-30, 135.
17 Simms, *Williamite Confiscations*, 90-1; J. Fahey, *History and Antiquities of the Diocese of Kilmacduagh*, 330-2.
18 Simms, *Irish Jacobites*, 130–5.
19 Simms, *Williamite Confiscations*, 131–2.
20 *Ibid.*, 141-3.
21 *Ibid.*, 128-9.
22 *Ibid.*, 159-62; TCD MSS N1, 3ff; 77-100.

3

—

THE PENAL LAWS

Protestants on both sides of the Irish Sea were appalled by the Treaty of Limerick and pointed out that there was now in France a formidable Irish army dedicated to the invasion of England. In 1691 the English Parliament passed an Act applying to Ireland the Test Act of 1678 which had previously applied only to England. This excluded from public office and from Parliament not only those who would not take the oath of allegiance (which was fair enough) but also those who would not take the oath of supremacy which denied the Pope's temporal *and spiritual* authority in the kingdom, and who would not make a declaration denouncing the Catholic doctrine of transubstantiation, the sacrifice of the Mass, and the 'idolatry' of the invocation of the Virgin Mary and saints. Clearly this broke the promise in the Treaty of Limerick that Catholics would enjoy the same degree of religious freedom that they had enjoyed in the reign of Charles II, for no Catholic could take the oath of supremacy or make so impious a declaration. The Irish Parliament, elected and meeting in 1702 for the first time since the war, was thus totally purged of Papists. Richard Butler, the fifth Viscount Mountgarrett, immediately tested the law. He claimed his seat in the House of Lords and swore the oath of allegiance, but refused to swear the oath of supremacy, and was not allowed to take his seat. But as an articleman he retained his estates.[1]

This Protestant Parliament lost no time in annulling all acts

of the Jacobite Parliament of 1689, thereby restoring the English
Parliament's right to legislate for Ireland and the English House
of Lord's appellate powers over decisions in Irish courts. There
were very soon protests against this subordination of Ireland to
England, starting with *The Cast of Ireland Stated*, published in
1698 by William Molyneux, MP for Trinity College, Dublin.
In 1707 Jonathan (later Dean) Swift wrote *The Story of the
Injured Lady*, on the same theme. But these were Protestant
protests: politics, even political protests, were not for Catholics.

Although the Irish Parliament met again in 1695 (William
needed money), it was not until its 1697 session that it turned
its attention to the Treaty of Limerick, treating it with the
contempt that the honourable members thought it deserved. The
'missing clause'[2] (included in the draft treaty as negotiated and
agreed, but omitted, apparently in error, from the official version
of the treaty) remained missing. The clause granting Catholics
the religious freedoms they had enjoyed during the reign of
Charles II was omitted, leaving them only such freedom of
worship 'as was consistent with the laws of Ireland'.* Also
omitted was Article 9, which required of Catholics *only* the Oath
of Allegiance: now, if they wanted office, they must swear also
the Oath of Supremacy which denied the spiritual authority of
the Pope, and make a declaration denouncing their faith. So only
when the Treaty of Limerick had been rendered innocuous did
the Irish Parliament ratify it.[3]

Metaphorically rubbing its hands, Parliament then set about
Papists in earnest. Under the Act of 1697 for the Better Securing
of Government by Disarming Papists, Catholics (unless specifically licensed to do so) were forbidden to carry arms, in an age

---

* This was not at all the same thing, for Charles II, himself a crypto-
Catholic, had turned a blind eye to sundry breaches of religious law
by Catholics. Nor was the Test Act applied to them during his reign.

when highwaymen and ex-raparees infested the roads and when a rapier and a readiness to use it were the perquisites of a gentleman. Only about 130 Catholics were so licensed, but this does not seem to have inhibited duelling with sword and pistol. With painful memories of the efficacy of the Irish cavalry, Parliament – as every schoolboy knows – laid down that if any Papist was seen riding a horse worth more that £5, any Protestant could buy it from him for £5. What every schoolboy does not know is that in 1709 Parliament exempted from this law stud mares, stud stallions and their progeny up to five-year-olds.[3] So a horsey Catholic with a helpful vet, fiddling the foaling dates and perhaps 'bishoping' the teeth to make a horse look younger, could ride rings round the law. I do not think this law was strictly enforced. Horses specifically bequeathed in Catholic wills, such as the 'young grey mare' left by Robert Keating to Lord Cahir's eldest son 'in token of my love to him', were by implication valuable animals. Hare- and fox-hunting were to be the passion of country gentlemen, Catholic and Protestant, all through the eighteenth century, and one could hardly ride to hounds on a £4 horse.

One of the few documented cases of anyone taking advantage of the £5 horse law concerns Father John Barnewall, the registered parish priest of Rathboyne in County Meath. He was a relative of Lord Trimleston, and one of the family had given him an exceptionally fine horse which he used to ride round on his parish duties. One day a low scoundrel of a priest-hunter accosted him and claimed the horse for £5.

> For a time there was an inward struggle between
> nature and grace. The blood of the old princely
> house of Barnewall boiled within him as he thought
> of the base minion who ventured to rob and insult

him. He thought too of the spiritual privations to which the flock would be exposed if anything happened to the pastor.

Grace prevailed. He pocketed the £5 and meekly dismounted. The priest-hunter mounted his prize and was about to depart. 'Not so fast,' said Father Barnewall, 'give me my saddle and bridle. The law gives you my horse but nothing else.' The priest-hunter laughed him to scorn. So Father Barnewall, a tall powerful man, seized the bridle, knocked the fellow to the ground and rode off saying, 'Take that, you scoundrel. You'll get no horse from me.' The fracas landed him in court, but the magistrate decided that he was perfectly entitled to use force in resisting the attempted robbery of his property. History does not record whether or not he returned the £5.[4]

Other Acts of Parliament during the next five years forbade marriage between Catholics and Protestants and expelled from the kingdom Papist bishops, deans, monks, friars and 'regular' priests (i.e. priests of regular orders such as the Benedictines or Dominicans). Any of these returning to the kingdom after being expelled could be deemed guilty of high treason and executed. Many returned, but none were executed. Lay (i.e. parish) priests had to register, and to remain in the county in which they were registered; but were then free to perform all their priestly duties. There was no ban on Catholicism as in Cromwellian times.[5]

In 1702 King William's horse stumbled in a mole-hole, fell and rolled on him, causing injuries from which he died. Jacobites drank to 'the chestnut horse' and the 'little gentleman in black velvet'. His successor was his sister-in-law, Anne. The 'Church of England's Glory' was far more anti-Catholic than the Calvinist Dutchman, and in the early part of her reign the Whigs were in the ascendant. Tories were always a trifle ambivalent about the 'Glorious Revolution' in which, basing their political creed on church and king, to save their church they had connived at the expulsion of their king. But the Whigs had no such doubts, professing always the firmest adherence to the 'Principles of the Revolution', the most important of which was that Whigs should enjoy a monopoly of power and perks. Whigs were more anti-Catholic, anti-Irish and anti-Jacobite than Tories, and at a time when England was locked in a death-grapple with France, saw Irish Catholics as allies of France. Most Irish Protestants shared these views. Besides, as Sir Richard Cox, Chief Justice of the Irish Queen's Bench said in 1714:

> Too many of them [the Catholics] think we are
> incorrigible rebels and have no title to our land and
> not much to our goods; and consequently if they
> had the opportunity, would deprive us of both.[6]

So in 1704 the Irish Parliament passed an Act for the Prevention of the Further Growth of Popery.[7] Its object, and that of other Penal Laws, was to make Popery not illegal, but expensive, inconvenient and socially unrewarding; and, above all, to destroy the Catholic landed interest, the ownership of land being the source of all political power. No doubt some Protestants, particularly the clergy, had concern for Catholics' salvation, and rejoiced in every brand plucked from the burning. But in this not all were agreed: Protestants were privileged people, and it would never do to dilute their privileges by sharing them with too many converts. In the House of Lords the Earl of Drogheda, when urged to support a very stringent anti-Catholic bill, would be:

very glad to see the Protestant religion strengthened,
but what shall we do for hewers of wood and
drawers of water? For labouring men to plough our
fields and thresh our corn?

He did not want the country flooded with Protestants:

for there is not one of them but wears a sword and
thinks himself as good a gentleman as I am; and
possibly would offer to fight me, should I find fault
with him.[8]

The Protestant gentry, particularly the more public-spirited who
would seek election to Parliament, were far more interested in
eliminating Catholics' power than in saving Papists' souls; and
many gentry, while subscribing to both these desirable objects,
did so with reservations: 'Of course I'm all for keeping Papists down
– but not neighbour Dominick, we've been friends for thirty years.'

According to this act of 1704 Catholics were forbidden to
'pervert' Protestants to the Popish religion; to send their children
abroad to be educated; to buy houses in corporate towns; or to
come and live in Limerick and Galway; and those already there
must give surety for good behaviour.

Marriages between Catholics and Protestants were forbidden;
as were pilgrimages or gatherings at holy wells and such places
of 'pretended sanctity'; all 'such meetings and assemblies shall
be judged unlawful assemblies'. There was a sweetener of £20
a year for any priest who conformed to the Church of Ireland.

Such laws were largely ineffective. A more serious one barred
Catholics from all but the most lowly offices, civil and military,
under the Crown. More serious still was the ban on Catholics
becoming guardians of minors, a shrewd blow at the Catholic

community. The MacDonnells, of whom the head was the Earl of Antrim, were staunch Catholics and Jacobites until the fifth Earl, who succeeded as a minor, was provided willy-nilly with a Protestant guardian and brought up a Protestant, as were all his successors.

But there were ways round this. The Dowager Countess of Fingall wrote to her uncle soon after the death of her husband, the fifth earl, in 1717:

> I have desired the Earl of Arran [younger brother of the second Duke of Ormond] to let me make use of his name to screen me from the law and to secure him [young son of the fifth earl] from being bred a Protestant, and am persuaded I could not make a better choice, being the next Protestant relation which is agreeable to the law and that I am well satisfied he will not give any trouble about his religion.

Selected with equal care was the Protestant guardian of the seventh earl who inherited in 1734 at the age of seven. He was George Howard, a substantial tenant on the Fingall estate, holding his land on a ninety-nine-year lease, and a friend of the family. The boy was *not* brought up as a Protestant.[9]

The most important provisions of the Act concerned land ownership. Any Catholic who received from a Protestant landed property by bequest, gift or inheritance must conform within six months, or the property went to his nearest Protestant relative. A Catholic could not buy land or lease it for more than thirty-one years or at a rent less than two-thirds of is assessed annual value. If the eldest son of a Catholic landowner conformed, he forthwith obtained the reversion of the estate and his father became only tenant for life. (But the reversion was burdened by the estate's previous debts and by the obligation to provide for his brothers and sisters, Catholic and Protestant, which somewhat lessened its attraction.)

Most damaging to the Catholic landed interest was Clause X of the Act:

> hereafter all lands . . . whereof any Papist now is
> or shall be seized in fee simple or fee tail*. . . shall
> be of the nature of gavelkind . . . and be inherited
> by all and every the sons of such Papist . . . to share
> and share alike . . . and not to descend to the eldest
> of such sons only. [And, in want of sons, to
> daughters.]

Only if the eldest son conformed to the Church of Ireland could he inherit the whole estate. This was intended to break up the great Catholic estates by ending the normal practice (at least in Old English families) of primogeniture. With a handful of named exceptions, it applied to *all* Catholics, even to the few who had sided with King William. It was a crafty, and could have been a devastating, blow.

There being no Catholic members of Parliament, two Catholic lawyers, Sir Toby Butler and Sir Stephen Rice, were permitted to put the Catholic case from the Bar of the House. Butler argued that the bill was an infamous breach of the Treaty of Limerick by which the Jacobites had been induced to surrender when they might still have fought on; and that the gavelling clause introduced to Ireland a practice hitherto known only in a remote corner of Kent. Rice compared it unfavourably with

---

* 'Fee simple' meant outright ownership. 'Fee tail' meant entailed.

Louis XIV's revocation of the Edict of Nantes.* But they pleaded in vain: Parliament was not open to argument, least of all argument by Catholic lawyers who had secured a Catholic majority in the Parliament of 1689.

Two general factors blunted the Penal Laws. The eighteenth century was the age of reason, not of bigotry. It was also the age of legality, when men set much store on the letter of the law. James II thought nothing of breaking or ignoring the law for what he saw as a good cause. His successors would never do so. So although the Penal Laws were grossly unfair to Catholics, their interpretation by the courts was strict but impartial. The remark of John Bowes, Chief Baron of the Exchequer, that the law did not presume a Catholic to exist except for the purpose of punishment, which has been quoted *ad nauseam*, was nonsense. Lord Earlsfort, Chief Justice of the King's Bench, was much nearer the mark when he said that the Penal Laws (with Catholics trying to circumvent them and Protestants to enforce them) were 'the principal topic and source of emolument to the legal profession.'[10] So in the front line of Catholic resistance to the Penal Laws were lawyers, generally Protestants or crypto-Catholic converts from Catholic families.

There were two kinds of juries. Grand Juries, consisting of twenty-three gentlemen of property selected by the sheriff of each country, did not try cases, but decided whether there was a sufficiently strong case against the accused for him to be

---

* In the sixteenth century French Protestants (Huguenots) had been a powerful state within the state, iron men, a formidable challenge to the government. In 1598 Henri IV had negotiated with them a treaty formalised by the Edict of Nantes which allowed them religious freedom and the possession of several towns and fortresses. It was this that Louis XIV revoked in the 1670s, causing some two hundred thousand Huguenots to risk the galleys by emigrating to enrich with their skills and strengthen with their military expertise the enemies of France.

required to stand trial. They also had local governmental function, including responsibility for roads, bridges and prisons within the county. Under 6 Anne, Ch. 6, V, Catholics could not be Grand Jurymen unless there were not enough Protestants suitable for nomination – as there always were. There was no general rule against Catholics serving in petty (or, as we would say, trial) juries. But the inclusion of one in a panel from which the jury would be drawn to hear a case which might threaten the Protestant interest would be immediately challenged. Only in cases arising from bills of discovery under the anti-Popery acts of 1703 and 1708 was it enacted that juries must consist only of Protestants.

The actual duties of juries in those days has been described as one of the unsolved mysteries of the English, and hence of the Irish, legal systems. It seems that issues of fact would be submitted to a jury chosen from men who should know the facts, e.g. from local knowledge. They collected and gave evidence of such facts, but were not required to assess the reliability of witnesses, or to give anything in the nature of a unanimous verdict.[11]

In cases concerning land ownership, bills of discovery were presented to one of the two equity (or, as we would say, civil) courts, the Chancery or the Exchequer. The judge might then decide them on his own; or he might refer one or more points at issue to judge and jury in a common law court, at the assizes. In the latter case the opinion of the jury would be reported back to the equity court which would proceed accordingly.

Obviously the criteria which guided equity court judges in referring or not referring cases to the jury of a common law court were of great importance to Catholic landowners, but this is another unsolved legal mystery. Much must have depended on individual judges, and on the political and religious climate at the time. One would expect a judge, albeit Protestant, to be less biased in discovery cases then a Protestant jury.*

Before Catholics were banned from the legal profession in 1727[12] there were three very able Catholic lawyers in practice. Counsellor Terence MacDonagh was also a distinguished soldier. In 1660 he had been a lieutenant in Charles II's army overseas, and returned to Ireland to study law and be called to the Bar. In 1689 he became MP for Sligo and a captain in Dillon's. Promoted lieutenant colonel, he commanded the Sligo garrison in 1691, and after a stout defence negotiated an honourable surrender which allowed him to take his men to Limerick. Before he reached there, Limerick capitulated, but he could still plead the Articles. He resumed his Bar practice until his death in 1713 and was one of the Catholics licensed to carry arms.[13]

Sir Theobald (Toby) Butler was a member of the Dunboyne branch of the family. His mother had the good fortune to be first cousin to the first Duke of Ormond, which helped him in his career; and his grandfather the bad fortune to be drawn, hanged and quartered during the Interregnum, when Toby was seven. He read for the Bar in England and was called to the Irish Bar in 1676. He prospered and was a rich man in his mid-thirties. In 1688 he was a member of a commission appointed to adjust the charters of Irish boroughs so that the Catholic interest would prevail in the forthcoming elections. He was knighted in 1689, sat in the House of Commons and was appointed Solicitor General. A plump, jovial *bon viveur*, addicted to the bottle, he was a less martial figure than MacDonagh, but was the chief negotiator on the Irish side of the civil Articles of Limerick. Just before the passing of the anti-Popery Act of 1704, he took the

---

* For this information on eighteenth century juries I am indebted to Professor W. N. Osborough of the Department of Law, Trinity College, Dublin, and to Mr Vincent Grogan, SC, of the Legal Draftman's Office, Dublin.

prudent step of conveying all his property to a Protestant friend, Richard Tisdale. This was among the first of the collusive Catholic-to-Protestant land conveyances by which, advised by lawyers such as Toby Butler, Catholics frustrated the intention of the Penal Laws. The trust was honourably kept, the land being handed back in due course to Toby's heirs. He, too, was licensed to carry arms. He was quarrelsome in his cups, and after spending a whole night imbibing Canary at the London Tavern in Waterford, got involved in a brawl with a fellow barrister who alleged that Toby had belaboured him with a 'great unwieldy cane' so that he was obliged to defend himself with a 'small little pocket-knife'. In Galway he was in disrepute for felling, while a case about the ownership was still pending, many hundreds of fine trees until the market was so glutted that they fetched only sixpence each. He had his shortcomings, but moral cowardice was not among them.[14]

Sir Stephen Rice was appointed Privy Councillor on James's accession, the first Catholic to hold this position since the Reformation. Four years later, as a Baron of the Exchequer, he laboured with Sir Toby Butler to secure a Catholic majority in the Parliament of 1689. He was attainted in 1691, but adjudged under the Articles of Limerick. He would have had to gavel his own estates had not his eldest son Edward conformed, obviously a conversion of convenience rather than conviction.[15]

One of the Protestant lawyers with many Catholic clients was Counsellor Robert French, from whom Dr Thomas Fogarty asked for an opinion on the matter of gavelling. The Fogarty estates had been entailed since 1698. On the death of Cornelius Fogarty, Timothy, his eldest son, had inherited the entire estate by primogeniture. He died without issue and the estate passed intact to his brother, Dr Thomas: it was not gavelled with the two younger brothers. Everyone concerned was a Catholic. Dr Thomas asked

Counsellor French if he was the lawful owner of the entire estate, or whether it should be gavelled. French replied that he was the lawful owner subject to the entail, and that the gavelling clauses of the anti-Popery Acts were *not* retrospective. Unfortunately French's original opinion does not survive: all that is in the Fogarty papers is a modern language paraphrase of the original.[16]

The wording of the Act is that an estate 'whereof any Papist now is or hereafter shall be seized in fee simple [outright ownership] or fee tail [entailed]' shall be gavelled. This sounds retrospective; but perhaps Counsel for a Catholic who had not gavelled could argue, 'Eager as my client is to comply with the wishes of the Legislature, in this matter he cannot do so. He is not the outright owner of the estate. He holds it in trust for his eldest son, and that son's eldest son, and he cannot break the entail without that son's consent.'* Evidently there was a 'grey area' in the law on this matter. According to a modern legal historian: 'the better view prevailed that pre-1704 family settlements were generally left unaffected by the new Act.' Such family settlements included not only entails but leases with covenants for renewal, a hole in the law limiting Catholics to thirty-one-year leases. One whose legal advisers took this view was Sir Laurence Esmonde, the third baronet. In July 1703 he entailed all the Esmonde land, two months before the first reading of the anti-Popery Bill. One can surmise that he had a tip-off. The Esmonde estates remained ungavelled.[17]

By 1708 it was evident that the 1704 Act to Prevent the Further Growth of Popery was not working. This was due partly to the weakness of the machinery for enforcing the law – constable, sheriffs, magistrates, Grand Juries – and partly to

---

* I have consulted two eminent lawers, Mr Marcus Bourke and Mr Peter Paul Ryan, on this. Each said that, if it were his case, he would argue on these lines with considerable confidence.

Irish lack of enthusiasm for law enforcement. In 1709 there was passed an Act for 'explaining and amending' the 1704 Act – in short, to plug the holes in it.[18]

One gaping hole was in the gavelling clauses of the 1703 Bill, which had become the 1704 Act. It was now laid down that no entail made in order to evade the intention of the law could prevent gavelling. 21 September 1703 (by which time the intention of the Bill must have been known), was set as the date after which new entails in this context would be invalid. This implies the validity of earlier entails.

To frustrate conformity by the eldest son in alternate generations, the Act laid down that Catholics could neither inherit land from nor bequeath it to Protestants. To remedy the scandal of convert lawyers acting always in the Catholic interest while their families remained Catholic, it was enacted that the children of convert lawyers must be brought up as Protestants.

The definition of convert was tightened up. The 1704 Act had stipulated that he must make publicly, in church, a formal denunciation of the Popish doctrine of transubstantiation, the invocation of the Virgin Mary and saints and the sacrifice of the Mass as idolatrous and superstitious; and take an oath declaring fidelity to Queen Anne and abjuring Stuart pretensions. Having done so, he must obtain a bishop's certificate to that effect. The 1709 Act added that he must within six months of his declaration take the sacrament according to the usages of the Church of Ireland, and obtain another certificate from a bishop.

To 'animate the Popery laws', provision was made for Protestant 'discoverers' of unlawful purchase of property, leases for more than thirty-one years or for less than the stipulated minimum rent and other such malpractices, to be rewarded by taking over the land or lease concerned. This vicious clause, encouraging all sorts of sneaks, *agents provocateurs* and 'horrid pests of society', was to be the subject of innumerable court cases.

Finally two Catholic landowners were specifically exempted from all disabilities laid on their fellow Catholics: Oliver Martin of Tulira in County Galway for his 'kindness to Protestants in distress, many of whom he supported in his family and by his charity and goodness saved their lives'; and Colonel Henry Luttrell for his tergiversation in 1691.

Fortunately for Catholic landowners, the Protestant 'discoverers' had no *locus standi* in relation to gavelling; so unless the younger sons claimed their rights, the estate remained in possession of the eldest son by primogeniture. Most younger sons had too much family loyalty to make trouble in this way.

The simplest way of evading the gavelling law was by having, or acknowledging, only one legitimate son. For instance, Sir Valentine Browne, first Viscount Kenmare, had six sons, but five died without issue, leaving only Nicholas to inherit. Nicholas had two sons, but one died without issue, leaving only Valentine to inherit. Valentine also had only two sons, of whom one died without issue, leaving only Thomas to inherit. So for three successive generations the estate could not be gavelled.[19]

Christopher Bellew of Mount Bellew in County Galway had only one son, Michael, in the crucial generation after the 1704 Act, who inherited the whole estate. Michael's three sons must have agreed not to gavel, for it was inherited intact by the eldest, Christopher. He, when making his will in 1769, simply ignored the law, bequeathing all the real estate to his eldest son, Michael, while buying off the younger sons with £1,800 each: 'I direct that if any of my younger sons shall set up a right to gavel my real estate, the said sum shall be raised out of my real estate.' In the event they accepted these payments rather than face heavy legal costs and family discord. Instead of hanging about Mount Bellew as younger sons, they set up as merchants in Dublin.[20]

Let the last word on the only sons of Catholic landowning families be with the Dublin wit, Eoin ('The Pope') O'Mahony: 'It was all done by *continence*. They were *martyrs*.' So be it.

With three ways of avoiding gavelling, by the mid-eighteenth century it was generally recognised that this law could not be enforced. But it remained on the statute books until 1778.

Between 1716 and 1779, 903 discoveries were filed outside Dublin,[21] an average of about fifteen a year, of which a considerable number were 'collusive' discoveries. One would have expected the number to be larger but as it was, the Protestant discoverer on the prowl, snooping and prodding and ferreting round for any transaction which could be turned to his advantage, was the nightmare of every Catholic landowner.

The thirty-one-year limit on a Catholic leasing land was very damaging: it was hardly worth investing money in draining and improving land for tillage unless one could be sure of holding it for much longer. So Catholics holding leased land favoured livestock farming, which required less labour and fewer sub-tenants than tillage, and was therefore resented in the countryside. It would obviously be helpful if one could, before the expiry of a thirty-one-year lease, arrange for its renewal. But was that a 'discoverable interest' in that in effect it made a lease longer than thirty-one years? In 1719 and 1729 two cases held that it *was* discoverable, and there the matter rested until 1772, when this was challenged in the case of Windis *v.* Power.

Power, a Catholic, made arrangements for a thirty-one-year lease to be renewed two months before its expiry, so that in effect his new lease was for thirty-one years and two months. Windis, a Protestant, 'discovered' this. The Chancellor held that Power had by his arrangement frustrated the intent of the anti-Popery Act. Two months were neither here nor there, but 'one day has the effect of ever so many'. Where could a line be drawn? A

Catholic might renew a lease seven years before the expiry of the old lease. He found for the discoverer. But on appeal the English House of Lords reversed his judgement and thereby overturned, to Catholic advantage, a ruling which had prevailed for fifty years.[22]

During the 1720s Sir Gerald Aylmer, a Protestant, granted a lease for more than thirty-one years to Patrick Plunkett, his Catholic tenant. A discoverer, Gardner, then filed a bill of discovery and got his decree. But Aylmer filed a cross-bill against both of them, alleging collusion to end a high-rent lease, with Gardner, the discoverer, agreeing to surrender the land to Plunkett when he had obtained it for nothing. In the end there was a compromise, but such cases made lawyers' fortunes.[23]

The easiest way round the Penal Laws relating to land was for a Catholic secretly to convey his land to a trusty Protestant friend who would hold it for him while swearing that he was doing nothing of the kind. There were innumerable examples of this device, which was of course easier between kith and kin. The Plunketts, a family of Danish origin in County Meath, were divided into a Catholic branch, headed by the Earl of Fingall, and a branch which conformed during the eighteenth century, headed by Baron Dunsany. Almost as a matter of course the Dunsanys acted as 'holders' for the Fingalls, until the twelfth Baron Dunsany wrote:

> My dear Fingall, I am now an old man and will soon have to meet my Maker. I do not want to go to him with a lie on my soul. Could you not get someone else to swear that the land and property are theirs?[24]

A similar service was performed for the O'Connells of County

Kerry by a Protestant cousin, Hugh Falvey, who 'held' land for them. Himself challenged by a potential discoverer, Falvey retorted, 'Swear away and be hanged to you! I'm ready to swear the print out of the Bible that I bought the land for myself.' But he too in old age suffered from qualms of conscience, writing to Maurice O'Connell of Derrynane, the Liberator's uncle:

> My dear Maurice, Were I a few years younger, I should be as willing to oblige a friend as ever. I regret that I am now too near my end to perjure myself any more, even for so old and valued a friend as yourself.[25]

The Catholic Butlers of Bunnahow in County Clare had land held for them by Protestant Butlers.

It was rare for the 'trusty' Protestant friend to prove otherwise but it did occasionally happen. The Protestant who held Sir Francis O'Neill's estates in County Meath and leased them back to him was a neighbour named Brabazon. But 'in confidence of friendship' Sir Francis surrendered them to Brabazon for a new lease on better terms. Brabazon then had him evicted to a small farm, and he ended up in a four-room cabin-shop and dairy, while his sons carted meal for hire. The youngest son enlisted as a private in the Connaught Rangers and fought at Fuentes d'Onoro, Busaco, Cuidad Rodrigo, Badajoz and Salamanca, rising to be a company sergeant-major and retiring in Dublin on a pension of 2s/2d a day.[26]

A more sophisticated ploy was the 'collusive discovery', getting a Protestant friend, if one's land or lease seemed to be in danger of discovery, to file a discovery himself, take it over and then hold it in secret trust to oneself. The Fithmore estate in County Tipperary, bought by Dr William Fogarty from a

Cromwellian 'adventurer' had been divided. By 1730 part was owned by Dr Thomas Fogarty and part by his distant cousin and brother-in-law, Thady Fogarty. Having cleared with Counsellor French his own legal position, Dr Thomas turned his attention to that of Thady, which was precarious. Thady was a Catholic, but the estate came down to him, through his wife, from Philip Fogarty who had conformed, and a Catholic could not inherit from a Protestant. So Dr Thomas, to safeguard Thady, induced another brother-in-law, William Meyler, a Protestant, to file a bill of discovery and hold the land in trust for the Fogartys. No sooner was this done when Thady died, leaving one son, Denis, a minor. Perhaps William Meyler's Protestantism was in question: he had married a Catholic; so Dr Thomas got Denis's guardians, necessarily Protestants, to file a bill of discovery against him and Meyler; and then got another Protestant named Collier to file a bill against the guardians, Meyler and Denis. Finally he got a Dublin gunsmith, Weatherall, to file bills of discovery against Collier, the guardians, Meyler and Denis. But he had been too clever by half. A genuine Protestant discoverer appeared on the scene, filed bills against all of them and acquired the estate, leaving poor Denis penniless.[27]

Complicated arrangements could go very wrong and the courts showed no particular favour to converts. Sir Walter Blake was a Catholic and a frequent litigant, not least because his family was divided between Catholics and Protestants. In the 1720s he bought land in the names of two Protestant friends, Bingham and Lynch. Twelve years later he conformed and openly conveyed the lands to himself. Promptly a discovery was filed by a Protestant Blake, on the grounds that the original purchase had been unlawful: for twelve years Sir Walter had enjoyed the lands and taken the profit from them without the least interference from the nominal owners, Bingham and

Lynch. So the lands were decreed discoverable 'for that they, being purchased in trust for a Papist, no subsequent conveyance to him could avoid a discovery against him.' Sir Walter, also, had been too clever.[28]

A controversial issue was whether a discovery could be proved by 'parole' or verbal evidence, or whether written proof was required. Written proof, in the shape of wills, conveyances, mortgages, leases, all signed and witnessed, was naturally a great deal more difficult, often impossible, to produce. The issue was finally settled in Low v. Espinasse in 1762. The Dean and Chapter of Christ Church, Dublin, leased land to William Espinasse, a Protestant, which had formerly been leased to Raymond FitzSimon, a Catholic. Espinasse claimed that he had fairly purchased FitzSimon's interest; but a discoverer, Low, alleged collusion between them, Espinasse holding it in secret trust for FitzSimon, whose 'parole' evidence seemed to confirm this. Low contended that this was enough: to insist on written proof would be 'a certain means of furnishing an evasion of the Act'. The Irish Court of the Exchequer decreed for Low, the discoverer; but the English House of Lords reversed the decision. Thereafter written proof from documents was always required and seldom obtainable.[29]

In Brogden v. Murray in 1726, 'JS', a Catholic, took a lease for more than thirty-one years. A Protestant, Murray, then filed a bill of discovery. But it was alleged that there was collusion between the two, with 'JS' protecting his interest by getting Murray to take over the lease and hold it in trust for him. This suspicion seemed to be confirmed when Murray married a Catholic. Brogden then filed a bill of discovery against Murray and 'JS' on the grounds that Murray was a Papist. Murray insisted that he was holding the lease for his own benefit, not for 'JS'. As to his religion, he had been a Protestant since infancy;

and he refused to answer questions about his marriage since to admit it would expose him to prosecution. The Lord Chancellor ruled that: 'Although a man who married a Papist shall be deemed a Papist . . . yet in reality he [Murray] is not a Papist, nor shall he be obliged to answer such things as may subject him to penalties.' He found against Brogden, thereby allowing Murray's discovery, perhaps collusive, to take effect.[30]

What was a Catholic and what was a Protestant? That was the essence of many a case. In 1752 Edward Cusack of Athboy near Dublin, supposedly a Protestant, died, having bequeathed land to Dr Steven's Hospital, a Protestant charity. A discoverer, Swan, then alleged that Cusack was a Catholic and that the bequest was therefore illegal. Cusack's witnesses swore he had been an 'ostentatious' Protestant all his life, and had hobbled to the Protestant church when 'troubled with gout and scarce able to stand'; Swan's witnesses insisted that Cusack had been seen several times at Mass, watching it sometimes through a window; that he consorted with priests, had given land for a 'Mass house' and allowed Mass to be celebrated in his stables; and that the priest, Father Plunkett, had been to his house the night of his death. ('To play cards,' said Cusack's witnesses.) The case finally went to the British House of Lords, where the Chancellor ruled against Swan who 'might style himself a Protestant discoverer, but was in reality only a common informer.'[31]

Such are the imperfections of human nature that discoverers were not infrequently their victims' kin, individuals who had conformed for the basest of motives, cupidity outweighing family feeling. No family was held in higher esteem than that of O'Conor Don in County Roscommon, whose forebears had been High Kings of Ireland. J. Dalton, compiler of *King James's Irish Army List*, lamented that a family as distinguished and patriotic did nothing very much for King James. None were commissioned in his army, none served him in a civil capacity so conspicuously as to be recorded in history; Charles (or Cathal) O'Conor of Belanagare, County Roscommon, first cousin once removed to O'Conor Don, was too old to fight in 1689, and his son Denis (Donogh Lia, Denis of the Grey Hair) was too young.

In 1699 Charles of Belanagare died, and Denis mortgaged part of his estate to John French. In 1701 there was a complicated legal settlement between the O'Conors, the Frenches and the Trustees of Forfeited Estates. How the Trustees were involved is not clear;* but the outcome was an agreement that because of Charles's outlawry (*sic*) a quarter of his estate should be forfeited and sold, and the remainder divided between his three sons, Denis, Phelim and Daniel. Phelim and Daniel died without issue leaving their shares to Denis subject to the French mortgage. Denis and his heirs, it was agreed, should enjoy and work their portion of the estate in perpetuity, paying to John French and his heirs an annual rent of £79 – not much for 448 profitable and 422 unprofitable acres. This arrangement was probably worked out by John French himself and Terence McDonagh, Denis's uncle, who signed it. Both were lawyers, both retired colonels of the Williamite and Jacobite armies respectively. It was, as will be seen, a very crafty, watertight arrangement. Denis held the Belanagare land in 'base fee', which was something between a lease and fee simple (outright ownership). It admitted of a rent being paid to French, but nonetheless Denis and his

---

* A Charles Connor of Carrowbane in County Roscommon was outlawed, but for *foreign* treason, so he cannot be Charles O'Conor of Belanagare who never went abroad. A Charles O'Conor, described only as being 'of Roscommon' forfeited 175 acres, but there is no record of his being outlawed or convicted of treason. However, the records are incomplete: this may be Charles of Belanagare, let off lightly because his services to King James were modest.

heirs, not French, *owned* the land, and could do so in perpetuity provided they did not default on the rent.[32]

It was certainly a collusive arrangement. When Denis entered into possession of Belanagare, which for some unexplained and inexplicable reason was not until 1720, French wrote to him:

> I shall be very glad to see you at all times, and you
> may depend upon it I shall ever be punctually just
> to whatever I have promised you and will perform
> it as far as in me lies. When you and my son
> [Robert, also a lawyer] have to both your likings
> prepared what is fit for me to sign, I will do it.

Such a letter could not have been written had they been at variance. The O'Conors remained on excellent terms with the Frenches, who had the reputation of being liberal and helpful to Catholics; and in 1837 Daniel O'Connell and O'Conor Don exerted themselves in Parliament to obtain a peerage for Arthur, the then head of the French family.[33]

It was nearly eighty years before the legal subtlety of this arrangement was tested. Denis died in 1750 and was succeeded by his eldest son, Charles, who became famous as an Irish linguist, historian and antiquarian. In 1777 his younger brother, Hugh, conformed and tried to get hold of the estate. Charles was outraged by this attempt by 'an apostate and perjurer' to 'wrest from me the poor plank that brought my father to shore after the great wreck of the family fortunes':

> To qualify my youngest brother [Hugh] to marry
> I handed over to him a property exceeding £800
> in value. But having wasted that and his wife's
> portion he, by conforming to the established church,

[73]

sought to repair his broken fortune either by the
Gavel Act of by a bill of discovery . . .

My father held his estate by what they call a
'base tenure"* and therefore not open to the Gavel
Act as my lawyers assure me. My brother, however,
has filed a bill against me suing for a gavel; but lest
that should not succeed, he has armed himself with
another bill against me suing for the whole property
of Belanagare as a Protestant discoverer, pretending
that my father's agreement with Mr French was in
the nature of a perpetual lease whereas a Papist can
have no perpetuity nor a tenure beyond thirty-one
years. If lawyers do not give me flattering hopes
for my money, the agreement of my father with Mr
French has no intercommunity with the lease law,
and in either case my adversary will be defeated.[34]

He had confidence 'in the present lenient interpretation of the
Penal Laws', and his confidence was not misplaced. In short, and
in plain language, Hugh claimed first that the estate be gavelled.
'No,' replied Charles's lawyers, 'the gavelling clause of the anti-
Popery Act of 1704 applied only to land held in fee simple or
fee tail. This is held in base fee.' 'Then,' claimed Hugh, 'the land
is held by a perpetual lease, which is unlawful for a Papist.' 'No,'
replied Charles's lawyers, 'it is not a lease. Your brother *owns* the
land.' In the event Charles O'Conor prevailed, but the case ran
on for seven years to the satisfaction of the lawyers on both sides.

---

* The antiquarian got it wrong. Holding land by base 'tenure' was a
medieval concept of holding it by a tenure less honourable than by
military service, e.g. by so many days' ploughing a year. He obviously
meant 'base fee'. For this information, vital to the understanding of a
case which has been so much misunderstood, I am indebted to Mr
Marcus Bourke.

The delay was due partly to the antiquarian's tendency to play for time in the hope that the repeal of the Penal Laws and the Statute of Limitations, which restricted a civil suit to fifty years after its original cause, would come to his aid. When the relevant Catholic Relief Act was passed, it was not retrospective; and the Statue of Limitations also proved a broken reed. It is gratifying to record that Hugh eventually returned to the faith of his fathers and was kindly received at Belanagare.[35]

Hugh's misconduct was nothing to that of the Abbé FitzMaurice, a priest in France, who in 1768 conformed and filed a discovery on a kinsman's Kerry estates. Captain Daniel Charles O'Connell of Derrynane, in the French army, was 'sorry to hear of the low sentiments of my former friend, the Abbé FitzMaurice. I should never have thought him capable of a step of that nature.'[36]

By far the most common way of evading the Penal Laws was by conforming to the Church of Ireland. In the Age of Reason, to many it seemed that holding estates which had been in the family for generations was infinitely more important that whether one went to Mass or Holy Communion. The matter was put in a nutshell by the gentleman who, asked by the bishop signing his certificate of conversion what were his grounds for embracing the tenets of the Church of Ireland, replied cheerfully, 'I can tell you easily, my Lord. 2,500 acres of the finest grounds in the county of Roscommon.'

About 4,000 men conformed between 1703 and 1789, their wives generally following suit. At least 1,700 were identifiable as being of landowning gentry families. Certainly many more were so, though they are not listed in the *Convert Rolls* as 'Mr' or 'Esquire'. There was hardly any pretence that gentlemen conformed for any reason other than to safeguard their estates, to be called to the Bar, or occasionally to obtain a commission in the British army. In 1727 the Irish Privy Council wrote more in sorrow than in anger to the English Privy Council:

> Temporal considerations make many men pretend to be converts who are not really and sincerely such ... Many such converts continue to breed their children or some of them Papists, suffer Mass to be often said in their houses and upon all occasions give great countenance to the popish interest, which under the mask of being Protestants they have better opportunity of promoting; they themselves all the while seldom or never appearing at any public Protestant worship.[37]

The Starkies of Rosscarbery, County Cork, perfected this system. No Starkie married a Protestant, but in every generation the eldest son was brought up as a Protestant, the others all as Catholics.[38]

Landed gentry who conformed to keep their estates do not seem to have been resented by laymen whose Church they left: it is Catholic clergy and Victorian writers who denounce their apostasy, though no doubt many a Catholic must have thought, 'There, but for the grace of God, go I.' Nearly all remained pro-Catholic in political and social attitudes. They served a very useful purpose as 'holders' of land, collusive trusts and leases, as voters and borough mongers in elections, as MPs pressing for the relaxation of the Penal Laws, as sheriffs, Grand Jurymen and magistrates who performed the functions of local government; and above all as lawyers in the Catholic interest. Only four men are described in *The Convert Rolls* as lawyers, but many described as 'Mr', 'Gent.' or 'Esquire' had converted to become lawyers after an Act in 1727 laid down that barristers, solicitors, attorneys and court officials had to be Protestants for two years before applying for call or admission. It has been calculated that of 331 barristers and 680 solicitors and attorneys practising in 1765, thirty-one and seventy-five respectively were converts; many more were born Protestants, sons and grandsons of converts. Members of Parliament from convert families formed a significant proportion of the Irish House of Commons: out of 300 members, they varied in number between forty and fifty-two during the years 1727–83. About a quarter were themselves converts, others from convert families.

There are fifteen army officers in *The Convert Rolls*, but a number of those described as 'Mr', 'Gent.' or 'Esquire' converted in order to apply for commissions, such as Charles McCarthy Mór, who was a captain in the First Footguards in 1770. Sixty-two priests conformed between 1703 and 1789, most of them presumably for reasons of conscience or because of quarrels with their superiors. The £20 bribe cannot have seduced many, for priests were from affluent families since education in French or Spanish seminaries was expensive. About sixty merchants conformed, since as Catholics they could not be full members of Guilds, which handicapped them in business. A disproportionate number of converts (2,176) were described as 'of Dublin'. Many country gentlemen, whatever their motives and however shallow their religious convictions, must have thought it would be embarrassing publicly to denounce, as impious and idolatrous, in their own villages, the faith of their fathers which they themselves had been practising a few days before: better get it over in a city a hundred miles away where one was not known. Perhaps, too, they reflected that it would be easier to continue in Catholic practices if one had conformed in Dublin rather than at home.[39]

From 1703 to 1720 there were only 252 conversions, mainly

by 'persons of large estates in real landed property'. Thereafter the number of conversions varied between forty-one and ninety-three a year with no very clear pattern. But from 1761 to 1776 numbers were much higher, ninety to 210 a year. This seems to have been due mainly to agricultural prosperity making land ownership and long leases more desirable. The Whiteboy troubles in the 1760s may also have put numbers up; as many Protestants attributed them (with no truth whatsoever) to French propaganda and Jacobitism, the harassment of Papists increased and, with it, conversions.[40]

The overriding reason for gentlemen conforming was land. The estimated fall in Catholic land ownership from 14 per cent in 1700 to 5 per cent in 1780 was due not to Catholics losing their land to Protestants, but to Catholics retaining their land by becoming Protestants.[41]

Of the 'licitness' of Catholic gentlemen giving their daughters in marriage to Catholics who 'pretend heresy for worldly reasons', the hierarchy seem to have been in two minds.[42]

Conversions in families other than landed gentry seem to have been more widely resented. It was felt that they had no valid reason for changing their faith; neither could they do much to help Catholics.

The Penal Laws relating to religion were to some extent enforced during the wars against the France of Louis XIV because the Catholic Church was suspected of aiding the enemy. This was not entirely without reason: in the archives of the Diocese of Meath there is an undated memorandum summarising the resolution of an unidentified body, presumably of Catholic clergy, to encourage ' in a prudent quiet way' recruitment to the Irish Brigade in the French army. Thus Catholic bishops, if found in the country, were expelled; so were friars and 'regular' priests, i.e. those of regular orders such as Benedictines and

Dominicans. 'Lay' clergy, that is parish or diocesan priests, had to register, but could then perform all their priestly duties.

But after peace was made with France in 1713 and the abortive Jacobite rebellion two years later, the pressure on Popery was eased. 'Priest-hunters' looking for unregistered or 'regular' priests were in general disrepute, even with magistrates. John Wilkinson, for instance, a magistrate in County Meath, was asked by a priest on the run for shelter. He took the fugitive into a barn and put him in a large barrel of which the bung had been removed for air. When soldiers arrived and began to search the outhouses, he perched himself on the barrel and directed their efforts.

An official report[43] to the House of Lords in 1732 found that priests were even getting above themselves, 'terrifying some poor Protestants on their sick-beds so that they sometimes suffer themselves to be anointed and to have Mass said over them, and they say that though it may be safe and convenient to live in the Protestant Church, yet it is dangerous and damnable to die in it.'

There were in the kingdom at least 892 Catholic churches, 'Mass houses', some of them 'large and pompous buildings' served by 1,445 registered diocesan priests, and many private chapels. Catholic bishops exercised their functions quite openly, though their presence was legally unrecognised.

As for Catholic schools, totally illegal, there were seventy-four in the Dublin diocese alone, including three convent girls' schools and the 'nunnery in Channel Row which commonly goes under the name of boarding-school'.

---

1   English Parliament, 3 W & M, Ch. 2; Lodge, *Peerage of Ireland*, IV, 71.

2   Simms, *Treaty of Limerick*, 12-16.

3   7 W, Ch. 5, III ; 8 Anne, Ch. 3, XXXIV.

4   A. Cogan, *Diocese of Meath*, II, 267.

5   9 W, Ch. 1, III; 2 Anne, Ch. 3.

6   W. N. Osborough in Power and Whelan (eds.), *Endurance and Emergence*, 21.

7   2 Anne, Ch. 6.

8   Maureen Wall, *Catholic Ireland in the Eighteenth Century*, 6.

9   Mary Rose Carty, *History of Killeen Castle*, 21; NLI MSS 8024 (3).

10   Patrick J. Corish, *The Catholic Community in the Seventeenth and Eighteenth Centuries*, 73; W. N. Osborough in Power and Whelan (eds.), *op. cit.*, 27.

11   6 Anne, Ch. 6, V; 8 Anne, Ch. 3, XXX; E. Jenks, *A Short History of the English Law*, (London, 1912), 163.

12   1 G, Ch. 20, II.

13   J. G. MacDonagh, 'Counsellor Terence MacDonagh', in *Studies*, XXXVI, no. 143, Sept 1947, 307-318.

14   Toby Butler, 'Sir Toby Butler', in *Butler Society Journal*, 1975-6, Vol. I, no. 6, 364ff.

15   Dalton, *King James's Irish Army List*, I, 110, 202; Robert Shepherd, *Ireland's Fate*, 181-2; Howard, *Several Special Cases in the Laws Against the Further Growth of Popery*, 71.

16   Fogarty family papers in County Library, Thurles.

17   Esmonde family papers; W. N. Osborough in Power and Whelan (eds.), *op. cit.*, 35

18   8 Anne, Ch. 3.

19   Burke, *Peerage, Baronetage and Knightage*, 1024.

20   Karen J. Harvey in Power and Whelan (eds.), *op. cit.*,175, 177-9.

21   Maureen Wall, *op. cit.*,189, fn 2.

22   Howard, *Several Special Cases in the Laws Against the Further Growth of Popery*, 217, 196, 357; Annesley papers in PRONI.

23   Howard, *op. cit.*, 61.

24   Countess of Fingall, *Seventy Years Young*, 104.

25   Mrs M. J. O'Connell, *The Last Colonel of the Irish Brigade*, I, 56-7.

26   Bernard Burke, *Vicissitudes of Families*, (London, 1889), 130-1.

27   Fogarty family papers in County Library, Thurles.

28   Annesley papers in PRONI.

29   Howard, *op. cit.*, 140.

30   *Ibid.*, 20-4.

31   *Ibid.*, 136.

32   Dalton, *op. cit.*, I, 143-4; Simms, *Irish Jacobites*, 181; G. W. Dunleavy and J. E. Dunleavy (eds.), *O'Conor Papers*, 8.X SH.0006, 7.4.EH.0008, 8.1.HE.018, 8.1.ES.022, 8.1.HE.023; Lord Halsbury, *Laws of England*, (London, 1975), 262.

33   Dunleavy, *op. cit.*, 8.1.SE.019; M. R. O'Connell, *O'Connell Correspondence*, 2430, 2913.

34 C. C. and R. E. Ward (eds.), *Letters of Charles O'Connell of Belanagare*, Preface, XI; B. C. MacDermot, *Letters*, 281, 288, 368.

35 *Ibid.*, 368; Dunleavy, *op. cit.*, 8.4.EH.222.

36 M. J. O'Connell, *op. cit.*, I. 122, 123.

37 Eileen O'Byrne, *The Convert Rolls*, Preface, X-XVI; T. P. Power in Power and Whelan (eds.), *op. cit.*, 101-7; Lecky, *Ireland in the Eighteenth Century*, I, 282-3.

38 Enid Starkie, *A Lady's Child*, (London, 1941), 55.

39 T. P. Power in Power and Whelan (eds.), *op. cit.*, 101-7.

40 *Ibid.*, 202.

41 *Ibid.*, 110; Simms, *Williamite Confiscations*, 160.

42 A. Cogan, *Diocese of Meath*, III, 59, 671.

43 *Report by His Grace the Lord Primate for the Lords Committee Appointed to Enquire into the Present State of Popery in the Kingdom*, (Dublin, 1732).

4

—

SOME CATHOLIC FAMILIES IN CONNAUGHT

The Catholic landed interest was strongest in Galway. The gentry there and in the adjoining counties of Mayo, Sligo and Roscommon were a hotchpotch of races, traditions and loyalties. The O'Conors, MacDermots, O'Haras, O'Malleys, O'Flahertys, Dalys and Donnellans had always been there. The Burkes (de Burgo, Bourke) led the Norman influx in the fourteenth century. The 'tribal' families, nearly all of Old English or Welsh origin, were well dug into the commerce of Galway city by the fifteenth century and thereafter spread out as rich *parvenus* landowners. The Brownes, Sussex gentry, emigrated in 1580 to Mayo in much the same spirit as thirty years later they might have migrated to Virginia, and bought a great deal of land from the natives. Next to arrive, in the late sixteenth century, were the Trenches who, as Huguenots, could pride themselves that they had not become Protestant in order to better their material circumstances. They proved very apt at advantageous marriages and land acquisition. The Lamberts, Eyres and Blakeneys were Cromwellian grandees. Many Catholic families from Leinster – Nugent, Bellew, Aylward and others – were transplanted to Galway by Cromwell, and Catholic families already there had to move over and make room for them. In 1689 all except the Huguenots, the Cromwellians and, strangely enough, some Dalys and Donnellans were Catholics. During the eighteenth century more Catholic gentry in Galway conformed (395) than in any other county outside Dublin.

The mix of cultures, the modifying of Jacobite zeal by self-interest made for a greater sectarian tolerance than elsewhere in Ireland, coexisting with a propensity for duelling and violence that was notorious. 'The man for Galway' at election time was said to be he who would fight a duel in the morning, hunt all day, get drunk at night and fight another duel the next morning. Whiskey-punch, indifferent claret and excellent port stimulated their exertions.

Jonah Barrington, who had Galway connections, identified three categories of Galway gentry:

1 'Half-mounted gentlemen', squireens with un-polished boots, hunting on good horses which jumped well but were never groomed, owning and farming about 200 acres.
2 'Gentlemen every inch of them', but a bit short of cash, public-spirited and influential at elections.
3 'Gentlemen to the backbone', the oldest families, rather too grand for many but deeply respected by their tenantry, from whom they could at any time raise a formidable private army.

All three categories included Catholics and Protestants. Nearly all lived on their estates or, if occasionally absentee, no further away than Dublin. They were very close to their tenants, even leading them in faction fights on such occasions as Ballinasloe Fair. During the early part of the eighteenth century their relations with tenants and servants were governed by the standards of the Middle Ages rather than the Age of Reason. As Barrington recalled:

My grandfather, Mr French of county Galway, was a remarkably small, nice little man, but of an extremely irritable temperament. He was an excellent swordsman and, as was often the case in that county, proud to excess . . . He had conceived a contempt for, and antipathy to, a sturdy half-mounted gentleman, one Mr Denis Bodkin, who, having an independent mind, entertained an equal aversion to the arrogance of my grandfather, and took every possible opportunity of irritating and opposing him.

My grandmother, an O'Brien, was high and proud . . . disposed to be rather violent at time in her contempts and animosities, and entirely agreed with her husband in his detestation of Mr Denis Bodkin.

On some occasion or other Mr Denis Bodkin had outdone his usual outdoings, and chagrined the squire and his lady most outrageously. A large company dined at my grandfather's and my grandmother launched out in her abuse of Denis, concluding her exordium, 'I wish the fellow's ears were cut off. That might quieten him.'

[A while later] when everyone was in full glee, the old butler, Ned Regan (who had drunk enough) came in; joy was in his eye; and whispering something to his mistress, he put a large snuff-box into her hand. She opened the box and shook out the contents; when, lo and behold, a considerable portion of a pair of bloody ears dropped onto the table . . . at which old Ned exclaimed, 'Sure, my lady you wished Denis Bodkin's ears were cut off,

> so I told old Gahagan [the gamekeeper] and he took a few boys with him and brought back Denis Bodkin's ears – and there they are, and I hope you're pleased, my lady.'

Denis Bodkin sought satisfaction at Galway Assizes, but lost his case because all the dinner guests testified that their hostess had not really meant what she said.[1]

The most powerful family in Galway were the Bourkes, of whom the head was the Earl of Clanrickard. Once they had held sway from the Shannon to the Atlantic but by the seventeenth century they were somewhat reduced. Lord Bophin, second son of the eighth earl, had raised a regiment of infantry which was wholly Galway in its officers and other ranks. He had been wounded and captured at Aughrim and taken to England. Being there, he could not take advantage of the Articles of Galway which required that officers of the Jacobite army not actually in the city's garrison must submit within three weeks. On Ginkel's intervention, he was released, took the Oath of Allegiance to William and Mary and remained in possession of his estates until 1697, when the judges held that he was not covered by the Articles. Again Ginkel spoke up for him, and the king wrote to the judges that he was 'particularly intended to be within the Articles.' Nevertheless the Irish Solicitor General insisted that the royal intention could not override the law. Bophin then dropped his claim under the Articles and asked for pardon. Unfortunately his estates had been granted to the Earl of Albemarle,* one of William's Dutch favourites. Finally the English Parliament, overriding the Irish Parliament, by a special act reversed his outlawry and put the estate under trustees for

---

* Not to be confused with the seventeenth century Dukes of Albemarle, the English family of Monck.

his children, provided he pay £25,000 as a sweetener to Albemarle, and his children be brought up as Protestants. So Lord Bophin, later the ninth Earl of Clanrickard, remained a Catholic but subsequent earls were all Protestants, generally acting on the Catholic interest. Throughout the eighteenth century Bourkes and Burkes conformed in shoals – twenty-eight Bourkes and 107 Burkes, not all from Galway as the name was common also in Leinster and Munster. While Protestant Bourkes protected Catholic families, the Bourkes of Ower, Catholics, had collusive arrangements with the Brownes of the Neale, and the Burkes of Marble Hill with the Masons.[2]

These Brownes were much later arrivals than the Browne family which was one of the tribes and had lately provided a Mayor of Galway. They had settled in the sixteenth century in Mayo, buying much land from the O'Malleys, and remaining Catholic. Sir John Browne of the Neale was a barrister in peacetime and raised a regiment of foot for King James in 1689. In September he was ordered to join the king's army at Dundalk. Addressing his letter to 'Colonel John Browne wherever to be found,' a staff officer wrote, 'If they have no firearms let them get at least a half-pike and a skean [long dagger] and what other accoutrements they can'. It seems to have occurred to someone that, rather than lead a bunch of untrained, unarmed peasants, Sir John would be better employed making arms for them in his foundries and workshops in Mayo. He was appointed commander of all the troops there, and a stream of letters from King James himself, from Tyrconnell, Berwick, Sarsfield and Sir Richard Nagle placed orders on him for firelocks, bayonets, swords, hand-grenades, shovels, pickaxes, cannonballs, horseshoes, uniforms, forage, oatmeal, bullocks and sheep. He was even required to recover from the piratical O'Malleys of Achill an enemy ship which they had hijacked, and convert it into a privateer. He was in Galway when it fell, and then marched with the rest of the army to Limerick.

Having helped to negotiate the Articles, he did not suffer the forfeiture of his estates but was nevertheless ruined. For all the arms and equipment he had provided for the Jacobite army, King James couldn't pay and no one else would. Browne was clapped into a debtors' prison, and his estates were sequestered to satisfy his numerous creditors. Altogether 114,323 Irish acres in Mayo and 41,127 in Galway[3] were sold for £47,769. From time to time he was allowed to travel to Dublin to untangle his affairs; and in 1704 he simply disappeared and a special Act of Parliament declared him dead. In fact he lived on until 1711 or 1712, but found it more convenient to be legally deceased.

He was succeeded by his eldest son, Peter, born in 1670. Peter's part in the war had not been so conspicuous that he was outlawed: he did not hold a commission in the Jacobite army but was perhaps a volunteer. In 1707 he married the daughter of Denis Daly of Carnakelly, a Protestant. His daughters were Catholic, as was he, but his only son was brought up as a Protestant and the family have been Protestants ever since. It was Peter's son, John, who restored the family fortunes and enlarged the family seat, Westport House.

The Brownes were uncomfortable neighbours of the O'Malleys and the O'Flahertys. An inscription on the west gate of Galway city used to read 'From the ferocious O'Flahertys, good Lord deliver us.' Pushed or bought out off their estates by the tribal Martins, the O'Flahertys had turned to smuggling and stock theft. Everyone had it in for the O'Flahertys, and they for everyone else.

The O'Malleys of Achill looked back with pride to Granuaile O'Malley, a sort of pirate queen in the sixteenth century. The tale, doubtless apocryphal, is told that she paid a visit to Queen

Elizabeth, who received her at the Tower of London. Granuaile was accompanied by a bodyguard of rough Mayo diamonds from whose vicinity the scented and bejewelled courtiers withdrew pointedly to windward, which did not escape her notice. To end the audience, Queen Elizabeth presented her with a beautiful lace handkerchief. She accepted it with becoming thanks, wiped her nose delicately and dropped it over the parapet into the Thames:

> 'Madam,' one of the courtiers reproached her, 'you have thrown away a most precious gift which Her Grace bestowed on you.'
>
> 'I never use them things twice,' she replied.

The largest and most prestigious of the tribes were the Blakes. Blow-ins from Wales, they had originally been named Cadwallader, meaning 'black'. From this, transition over the centuries to Blake and Cadell (a name common in Ireland) was easy. They had built up their fortunes in Galway by trade with France and Spain, and had become gentry by the possession of over thirty landed estates in Galway, including at least six of over 2,000 acres. At the end of the nineteenth century they still owned a dozen estates of over 1,000 acres. In 1689 they were all Catholic, but not all Jacobites.

Richard Blake of Ardfry was so conspicuously neutral that the Jacobites burnt down his house and ravaged his estates. Ginkel promised him relief, which he eventually obtained after ejecting with some difficulty those who had moved on to his land.

Martin Blake of Moyne was imprisoned by the Jacobites for corresponding with the enemy. Having been outlawed for treason, he obtained a royal pardon.

The leading Blake in 1689 was Sir Walter of Menlo, the sixth baronet. His seat was a fortified Elizabethan house on a creek some three miles west of Galway city. His father had lost it during the Interregnum but recovered it under the Restoration Settlement, and Sir Walter had entailed it in 1688. As second-in-command of Colonel Henry Dillon's regiment of foot he had, of course, been outlawed, but under the Articles of Galway he recovered his estate, which was never gavelled because of the entail. No doubt the fact that he had raised a Catholic regiment for William and Mary in 1691 helped to safeguard his position; and he was kept further beyond reach of want by sugar plantations in Barbados and Monserrat, and a family wine business in Bordeaux. He died in 1746 and was succeeded by his son, Thomas, who was also a Catholic. But Thomas's son, Ulick, conformed in 1738 in order to be admitted to Middle Temple to read for the Bar; and the ninth baronet, Thomas, from Bordeaux, conformed in 1766.

A branch of the family which remained Catholic were the Blakes of Ballyglunin. Martin Blake bought Ballyglunin from a Cromwellian, Charles Holcroft, in 1671. His heir, Peter, was about forty-six at the start of the Williamite war, took no part in it, and died in 1691. Peter's heir, Martin, born in 1670, presumably fought in the war though he was not outlawed and was pardoned in 1698 'by His Majesty's favour'. Martin had two sons, Edmund, the elder, and Martin, and the estate might have been gavelled between them had not Martin emigrated to Antigua, so for that generation it was spared. Edmund had four sons: one died young and two were priests, so again the estate escaped gavelling. So the Blakes of Ballyglunin, on their 10,000 acres, remained Catholic, prosperous and obscure, but so influential that in the nineteenth century they used their influence to have the railway diverted to Ballyglunin and to have a post office there.

The Blakes of Muckiness in County Clare also remained Catholic. John Blake was killed at Aughrim and his estates forfeited. But because they had been entailed in 1678, the Trustees of Forfeited Estates restored them to his infant son, Isidore. Having been entailed, they could not be gavelled.

Fifty-eight Blakes conformed in the eighteenth century, but many remained Catholic.[4]

Another important tribal family were the Martins (or Martyns) who acquired in the seventeenth century much O'Flaherty land and, with it, the enmity of the O'Flahertys. Oliver Martyn of Tulira, who had been MP for Galway in 1689, was of course outlawed, but was adjudged under the Articles of Limerick and Galway, and so retained his estates. Indeed with Ginkel putting in a word for him and because of his conspicuous kindness to Protestants, he was allowed, by a special clause of the anti-Popery Act of 1708, to hold them as if he had been a Protestant, passing them on by primogeniture and free of all restrictions imposed on Papists.[5]

Richard Martin of Dangan, 'Nimble Dick', owned the largest estate in the British Isles, 192,000 acres, mainly mountain and bog, along eighty miles of indented coastline, largely bought from the O'Flahertys. As a captain in Luttrell's Horse he had been outlawed, and his confiscated estate had been bought by John French who had fought for King William. By his timely surrender he had hoped to rectify this; but as he was neither a member of the garrison nor a freeman of the city of Galway, he was not covered by the Articles, and was obliged to go to London with 'a hatful of guineas' and 'plausible discourses' to negotiate his pardon and the restoration of his mountains and bog, in which he succeeded. His huge estates were governed from three seats, Bursthall on the shore of Lough Corrib, Dangan just across the creek from Sir Walter Blake's house at

Menlo, and Claremont. In 1695, 'sensible of His Majesty's grace and favour', he petitioned that Claremont be designated a manor with its own manorial court, competent to try all kinds of civil cases and to hold fairs and markets. This was granted in 1698 and promptly the Irish House of Commons, 'sensible of the great inconvenience of the grant of manors and royalties to Papists' and of the danger of them communicating with enemy warships, prayed that no more favours be extended to Catholics or to those holding land in trust for them. But King William had given his word and kept it.

In 1707 Richard Martin, on behalf of himself and others, petitioned for troops, which he would house, as protection against outlaws and malefactors. They came, and arrested three O'Flahertys. It was probably no coincidence that soon after this the horse of Martin's eldest son came galloping home riderless: the son had been murdered. The second son, Anthony, succeeded to the property.

Anthony Martin, a quiet, steady man, arranged for his second son, Robert, born in 1714, to be educated (albeit illegally) at Louvain. Robert returned home a fanatical Jacobite and a swashbuckling swordsman. He killed in a duel an army officer who had insulted him; and followed to London the Governor of Galway, Stratford Eyre, fought him in St James's Street and gave him 'the most unmerciful drubbing that ever was heard of.' In 1745 he set off for England, disguised as a farm labourer, to join Prince Charles Edward. Unfortunately he gave himself away by ordering fricassee of chicken at a common alehouse, and was arrested. Released because he had committed no crime, he returned to Dangan (which he leased from his elder brother, Richard, for a peppercorn rent) and was rumoured to be fitting out a privateer for the Pretender. The Governor described him as 'the most dangerous, murdering Jacobite' who could 'bring in

[91]

twenty-four hours to the gate of Galway 800 villains as desperate and as absolutely at his devotion as the Camerons to Lochiel.'

In October 1745, Robert Martin conformed. Why he did so is not clear: perhaps there was a Protestant discoverer in the offing, and the lease of Dangan at a peppercorn rent was certainly discoverable. He may also have felt that it guarded him against charges of Jacobitism. A few months later the Jacobite cause went down in irretrievable ruin at Culloden.[6]

As though to lend spice to a life which had become weary, stale, flat and unprofitable, he took to 'free trading' (a euphemism for smuggling) on a large scale. The west coast of Ireland with its long, deep inlets and a population congenitally averse to law-enforcement, was a smugglers' paradise, and the English Navigation Acts invited evasion. Ireland had three main exports, wool, hides and butter (to say nothing of 'Wild Geese') for which there was a strong demand in France and Spain. Returning ships brought wine, brandy, tea and silk. Everyone was in it – Martins, Blakes, Lynches, Brownes, and of course O'Malleys and O'Flahertys. In County Clare on the south shore of Galway Bay which was alive with smugglers, resided Daniel MacNamara and his son, Teigue, on an estate so barren that its only conceivable asset was a view across and access to Kinvara Bay and a half-dozen rock-bound lagoons where at high tide the skipper of a shallow-draught vessel could land a cargo on a dark night. From there it would be taken on ponies along secret paths through the Burren where no revenue officer dared follow. Even the O'Briens, pillars of the English Ascendancy, were not above a little free trade. Edward O'Brien, grandson of Sir Donough of Lemanagh, wrote to a kinsman, 'A small two-masted vessel will come to anchor or run aground *by chance* near Nick McInnerhinny's carrying choice burgundy, champagne and claret, very cheap. But this is *entre nous.*[7]

In 1753 Robert Martin married a daughter of Lord Trimleston, a Catholic, who died ten years later having born him one son, Dick. Robert's elder brother also died, unmarried, so Robert became the owner of the whole huge estate.

When Dick, born in 1754, was twelve, and was sailing one rough day with his father on Lough Corrib, Robert told the boy of the plans for him: he would be brought up as a Protestant, be called to the Bar, enter Parliament, and must always work in the Catholic interest. This was exactly what he did. He became famous as 'Humanity Dick' because of his lifelong campaign against cruelty to domestic animals (foxes didn't count); he got through Parliament as a private bill the first legislation on that subject. He was the terror of London and Dublin coachmen, carters and donkey-drivers. He was also known, for reasons which need no explanation, as 'Hairtrigger Dick'. When someone commented on his different attitudes towards animals and humans, he replied simply, 'Bullocks can't point a pistol.' And when the Prince of Wales asked him who was likely to win a Galway election, he replied, 'The survivor, Sir.'

His wife was wanton. Her first lover was the children's tutor and private secretary at Dangan, a young man named Theobald Wolfe Tone. Had Hairtrigger Dick known of this, the history of Ireland might have been different. Her last lover was found by the butler entwined with her on the sofa, one arm round her neck, the other hand 'employed between her legs'. Uncharacteristically, Martin sued him for criminal conversation, and was awarded £10,000 damages. Rather than profit from his wife's dishonour, he scattered it all through his coach windows in villages between Dublin and Dangan, and had his horses shod with silver shoes.

Dick inherited an estate encumbered by enormous debts and left it still encumbered. He was an indulgent landlord, evicting nobody and taking no rent from widows; but he kept a private prison on an island on Ballinahinch Lake in which were interned malefactors sentenced in his court. He was, in his way, a great man, and certainly 'the man for Galway'.[8]

A family which owned little land but was nevertheless socially accepted was that of Mahon. They were originally O'Briens from Clare, who changed their name; but having lost their Clare estates, they moved into Galway under the protection of Clanrickard and made a good recovery. It was Bryan Mahon's athletic prowess that got him the job of Clanrickard's family tutor, in which capacity he saved the earl from an attempt by the countess to murder him. For this he was promoted agent for the Clanrickard estates, and in 1689 given a captain's commission in the regiment of Clanrickard's son. When the war was lost and his patron was attainted, Mahon raised several thousand pounds from the estates, which he passed into the Treasury to expedite the reversal of the earl's attainder. In 1700 he bought the Castlegar estate, previously leased by Clanrickard to O'Shaughnessys and O'Flahertys. He was a capable, not to say sharp, operator. In 1708 he conformed, traditionally after inviting Catholic and Protestant clergymen to debate their differences in his presence, and deciding that the Protestants had the better case.

The Mahons of County Roscommon stemmed from Captain Nicholas Mahon, a Catholic who had fought for Charles I and been despatched by Cromwell to 'Hell or Connaught'. The Commissioner for Delinquency allocated to him an estate at Strokestown, on which he elected to stay after the Restoration. He conformed but his wife remained a Catholic. He died in 1780, having arranged for his sons to be brought up as Protestants and his daughters as Catholics. Thus insured against all contingencies, the family kept a low profile during the Williamite war, and afterwards slid effortlessly into the upper echelons of the Protestant Ascendancy.

One of this family, Gilly Mahon, surfaced in London, where he was known to William Hickey as 'an Irish adventurer who lived by his wits.' He took under protection a Ms Russell, 'a smart dashing girl of good family', and they set up in Paris. 'Her five brothers swore vengeance against their sister's seducer; nor would Mahon, who was as brave as a lion, have hesitated to meet them all in turn had he been called upon, which he was not, for prudence prevailed and they decided to leave the inconsiderate girl to her fate.' After a few months the lovebirds parted on good terms and Ms Russell returned to London, where she embarked on splendid prostitution, being known to the *ton* as 'The Bird of Paradise'. There was a Mrs Mahon in the background, and when she died Ms Russell wrote to her former protector that she would now like to bear his name and perhaps sometimes make him liable for a milliner's bill, so they were joined in Holy Matrimony. They lived apart, but were on the most cordial terms whenever they happened to meet. Somehow there seems to be about the eighteenth-century Mahon males the faint flavour of a chancer.[9]

The Kirwans, although addicted to duelling, seem to have been of a more intellectual bent than other tribal families. Before 1689 they owned about 7,000 acres. Sir John Kirwan, Mayor of Galway in 1686 and MP in 1689, was best known for introducing modern glass windows instead of lead lattices. He was never attainted. Nor was his son, Richard, though a captain in Lord Bophin's infantry. He had three sons, Martin, the eldest; George killed in a duel in France; and Richard ('Nineteen Duel Dick') who did well in the Irish Brigade, fought at Fontenoy and was a protégé of Marshal Saxe. Because his brothers were in France, Martin inherited the estate ungavelled. So did his eldest son, Patrick, and to facilitate this, it was decided that the next son, Richard, should be a priest. He entered the Jesuit novitiate, and his Latin was so good that the Jesuits appointed him Professor of Humanities. But when Patrick was killed in a duel, Richard decided to return to Ireland and run the estates.

He was described walking:

> of a Sunday to the Mass House, in a rich suit of embroidered clothes; his *chapeau bras* under his arm, and picking his steps along the dirty road, with brilliant stone buckles in his shoes. He was a tall, elegant, comely young man, and spoke good Irish, though sometimes too fond of interlarding his discourse with foreign words.

He married Anne Blake of Menlo who had 'every amiable qualification' including a fortune of £4,000. For some years they lived at Menlo, where he built up a good library and spent too much time in it, to the detriment of his married life: his mother-in-law protested that she 'never intended her daughter to be the wife of a monk.' He then decided on a legal career, which necessitated conforming in 1764. But his real bent was for science, and after his wife's death he concentrated entirely on it, becoming President of the Royal Irish Academy and a prolific writer on chemistry and geology.

Walter Blake Kirwan, also educated by the Jesuits, became a priest in 1778 and conformed seven years later. His brother, also a priest, nearly died of grief and broke the news to his uncle, an archbishop, that Walter was changing his religion. His Grace took the matter quite calmly, 'Tut, man, he has no religion to change.' So much for a Jesuit education.[10]

The O'Kellys (or Kellys) were thoroughly Jacobite. Twenty-two, including ten from Galway and Roscommon, were indicted for treason, but they largely survived the Williamite confiscations since the holders of their principal estates were protected by the Articles of Galway. Among these was Captain William O'Kelly, who thereby retained his estates at Tycooly near Portumna. His eldest son having died young, the estate passed to the second son, Festus. He had two sons, Connor and Dillon. That the estate was not gavelled, but passed intact to Connor, was probably due to Dillon making his career in the service of the Austrian Emperor, first as a soldier, later as ambassador and Grand Chamberlain. He was created a count of the Holy Roman Empire, and when he died without issue, the title passed through his father to his elder brother Connor, who already had the Tycooly estates.

Connor was much in London and William Hickey knew him as a man about town, owner of the famous racehorse, Eclipse, and protector of the equally famous courtesan, Emily Warren, much in demand among the *ton*. From him the title and property passed to his son Festus, whose descendants are still Catholics, still counts of the Holy Roman Empire and still proprietors of Tycooly, now known as Gurtray.[11]

The Kellys were cushioned against adversity by West Indian money. This enabled Denis Kelly of Lisduff, known as 'Jamaica Kelly' and lately Chief Justice of that island, to buy from Denis Daly the estate of Ramore, 1,482 Irish acres for under £4,000.

'Jamaica Kelly' was presumably a Protestant. His Catholic kinsmen lived at Turrock in County Roscommon, with estates straddling the Roscommon-Galway border. For some reason not now clear, Daniel Kelly of Turrock felt threatened by discovery. He could not escape merely by conforming, for a discovery could be retrospective; so he arranged for a Protestant friend, Anthony Lyster, to file a discovery himself, and having gained possession of the Turrock estate, to hold it in trust for its true owner. As a Catholic, Kelly could not receive the estate from a Protestant, so in 1719 he conformed; and in due course, Lyster conveyed the estate back to him. There was nothing hole-in-corner about this collusion: its essential details are set out in a deed duly signed, witnessed and deposited in the Registry of Deeds: it was a lawful transaction. But of course it depended entirely on the gentlemens' agreement that Lyster, having become the lawful owner of 1,071 acres, would return it to Kelly. This he did, for £10.

Ninety-nine Kellys conformed during the eighteenth century, mostly from Connaught or giving Dublin addresses which may mean anything. Many, it seems, did so in order to obtain commissions in the British army; for the Kellys over many generations combined military service to the Crown with fervent Irish nationalism. From this generalisation must be excluded Denis Kelly of Castle Kelly, near Ballygar, who was an Irish scholar and antiquarian and an Orangeman, surely a unique combination.[12]

Of all the Galway gentry, Catholic and Protestant, the joker in the pack was Lucas Dillon of Clonbrook, whose daughter became the wife of Captain William O'Kelly of Tycooly. He was described by Clanrickard as the leader of 'that party who care neither for King, Pope nor Parliament, but only for the salvation of their own estates.' John Trench, the heel of whose boot had won the battle of Aughrim, tried to get hold of those estates on the grounds that Dillon had fought there on the wrong side; but Dillon was able to prove that he hadn't, or not very hard, and was able to plead the Articles of Limerick. He remained at least nominally Catholic and died in 1717, leaving five sons. The eldest, mindful perhaps of the possibility of his brothers claiming to gavel, conformed three years later, and became MP for Dungarvan. Altogether forty-four Dillons conformed; but many remained staunchly Catholic and Jacobite.[13]

Many Catholic landed families went under in the aftermath of the Williamite war but those who managed to keep their heads above water were not materially much worse off. They suffered from a moral malaise. They had lost a just war which they had expected to win. Now they were treated (to use an anachronism) as second-class citizens in their own country. They had, unless they conformed, no future in public life: they could not even become magistrates or Grand Jurymen. Their estates were always at risk of discovery, and their safety lay in never drawing attention to themselves. So while their Protestant neighbours built Palladian mansions, or at least substantial square Georgian houses, it might be prudent for them merely to do up the old tower-house.

They even had to pay tithes, based on their acreage of tillage (but not of grazing) to the local Protestant parson. Oddly enough, their only public function was as vestrymen in the Protestant parish. The vestry was an assembly of all solvent resident householders, including Catholics. It had modest responsibilities, including poor relief and the upkeep of the church, for which a cess could be levied. Catholics sometimes packed a vestry meeting to block some project of which they disapproved. Ironically, they were sometimes elected church-wardens, an unwelcome distinction as they would then be responsible for collecting the cess.

The final straw is generally thought to have been the Electoral Reform Act of 1727 which deprived Catholics of the vote.[14] This, in fact, was not such a heavy blow as it sounds. The vast majority of Catholic (and Protestant) voters were not landowners but were 'forty-shilling freeholders', which meant that they leased land for two or more lives worth forty shillings a year after payment of rent; which ruled out from the start tenants on a thirty-one-year lease. It was assumed that these freeholders' votes would be entirely at their immediate landlord's disposal; he would tell them how to vote and they would obey him. So Catholics when they lost the vote lost very little. As for the Catholic landlords, they still expected their Protestant tenants to vote as they directed, even though they themselves could not vote. So, if they had Protestant tenants – which many preferred because they were more regular with the rent – they could take a very active part in elections. Sir Patrick Bellew of Mount Bellew, a Catholic, before an election wrote to his cousin Michael:

> I hope Mr Daly will carry the election. I was obliged to promise our neighbours here that I would do all I could for Billy Trench, so I beg you'll speak to Grace [a Protestant voter] if he means to pay me any compliment for his freehold to vote for him and Denis Daly. . . . I am determined to make a score of [Protestant] freeholders at Newtown Bellew which I shall certainly give for the future to Daly.[15]

There were complaints during an election for County Roscommon in 1713 that 'Papist gentlemen well mounted, well armed [in despite of the law] and in red coats with their emissaries seduced and managed freeholders.' Fifty years later there were numerous complaints of Catholics intimidating voters in an election for County Tipperary, and Francis Mathew, who won a seat for Tipperary borough, was said to have 'come in by the Papist influence'.

The Catholic landowner's greatest difficulty was in finding suitable employment for his younger sons. The last thing he wanted was to have them hanging about at home with nothing to do but fight, hunt, seduce the tenants' daughters and perhaps discuss speculatively among themselves the gavelling clauses of the anti-Popery Acts. Protestant younger sons could go up to Trinity, be called to the Bar, obtain commissions in the British army and navy, or perhaps (if they could afford it) purchase a seat in Parliament. But all these outlets were closed to Catholics.

A Catholic younger son might obtain a commission in the French, Spanish or Austrian armies. This was not seriously opposed by the government, which had no wish to see Ireland swarming with idle swordsmen. He might become a priest, a doctor or a surgeon. He might obtain a commission or a collectorship in the service of the Honourable East India Company. Some Galway families had sugar plantations in the West Indies where there were openings for likely lads. Protestant gentry affected to look down on commerce, but Catholics could not afford to do so. Many younger sons, therefore, sought 'mercantile careers' in London, Dublin, Cork, France or Spain. There was no social stigma in this, especially for Galway families who had for centuries thrived on commerce.*

Many dispossessed Catholic landowners retained enough capital to rent and stock large farms for themselves or their sons. Landowners preferred them as intermediate tenants, provided they were not absentees and most were not, save for brief visits to Dublin. For the younger sons without the education or the inclination for a life off the land, this was the most promising role. The first half of the eighteenth century was a period of agricultural depression. Rents were low and difficult to extract. It saved the big landlords, especially recent arrivals in the country, a great deal of trouble and odium to have someone between them and the tillers of the soil, who would pay them

---

* These opportunities for younger sons are examined in more detail in Chapter 8.

a modest but regular rent, and themselves live off the rents of a couple of dozen small farms, covering several hundred acres.[16] These were the 'middlemen' denounced by Arthur Young, from whom all historians have until recently taken their tune:

> This is the class of little country gentlemen; tenants who drink their claret by means of profit rents; jobbing in farms; bucks; your fellow with round hats edged with gold who hunt in the day, get drunk in the evening and fight next morning. I shall not dwell upon a subject so perfectly disagreeable, but remark that these are the men whom drinking, wrangling, quarrelling, fighting and ravishing are found as in their native soil . . . The oppressive conduct of little country gentlemen, the vermin of the country . . . He yields obedience to no law but his will. A landlord can scarce invent an order which a servant, labourer or cottier dare refuse to execute. Disrespect or sauciness he may punish with his cane or his horsewhip. Knocking down is spoken of in a manner which makes an Englishman stare.

Young wrote in the 1780s, a time of agricultural prosperity with rising rents and profits, an economic miracle. He took his opinions from the big landlords in fee who by then had no use for intermediate tenants, preferring to collect their rents without difficulty direct from the actual farmers. But in the first half of the century, middlemen played a vital role in the countryside, collecting low rents from wide tracts of country, paying low rents to the landlords whose kinsmen they often were, in close touch with those above and those below them, acceptable to both.

Many, in some counties most, were the younger sons of Catholic gentry, themselves treasuring their gentry status.[17]

The abduction of unmarried women was somewhat prevalent in Ireland. Generally the abductor seems to have been attracted more by his victim's purse than her person. She would be carried off to a priest, probably unregistered, and offered the choice of marriage or a fate worse than death. Generally she chose the former option, in which case her husband was endowed with all her worldly goods. Abduction was a capital offence but abductors were very seldom executed. Sir Henry Hayes was let off with transportation to Botany Bay because 'he attempted to ravish but did not succeed, as the cock would not fight'. In Sydney he acquired a couple of hundred acres, built a mansion which is still a showpiece, and led a life very different from those who had been transported for picking pockets or shoplifting.

Comparative affluence, together with robust health and high spirits, resulted in a predatory hunt for peasant girls to seduce, a phenomenon not unknown in other countries and at other times. Many a landed family, Protestant and Catholic, has legends of dubious provenance of a neighbourhood peopled largely by its relations on the wrong side of the blanket. I have been told by an elderly Blake lady that when she was a girl it was well known that one of the maids was her second cousin. But there is no evidence whatsoever of any recognised *droit de seigneur* or *jus primae noctis* in eighteenth-century Ireland.*

With their drinking, gambling, wenching, smuggling and generally anarchic lifestyle, minor Catholic gentry were remarkably like their contemporaries in the English shires, only more so, particularly in the practice of duelling. Almost the first

---

* In France, but not I think in England or Ireland, a landlord had the right to deflower any woman on his estate before she married. The custom probably ceased after the Middle Ages.

question asked in Galway by a young lady's father about her suitor was, 'Has he blazed?' (duelled with pistols) – and a black mark against him if he hadn't.

Arthur Young certainly exaggerated the tyranny of the small gentry and middlemen towards tenants and servants. There is no evidence to confirm his allegations. Had they been, in general, anywhere near as bad as he made out, they would not have survived, in any sense. Perhaps, as occasionally happens in Ireland even today, his informants gave way to the temptation to cod an English visitor.[18]

It was almost unknown in eighteenth-century Ireland for country ladies to rear their male children at home. They were handed over to foster parents on the estate to toughen them up, give them some immunity to disease, and, no doubt, save mothers of large families a great deal of trouble. In these circumstances, particularly in the west, gentry children, even Protestants, spoke Irish before they spoke English. (Daniel O'Connell's wife was to comment unfavourably on this aspect of fosterage.) Of course they went on speaking it for communication with tenants and servants, and some from inclination. FitzJohn Trench, on his way out to India to join the Madras Light Cavalry, was delighted to find aboard a fellow Galway man, Lieutenant Donnellan: 'We converse daily in our native language.' A Dublin girl marrying into the Trench family was expected to learn Irish. There is still extant her notebook full of such useful phrases as: 'Come hither girl. How much are you asking for those eggs? . . . That is far too much. I will give you half.'[19]

Thomas Campbell, a visitor from England, was travelling in a coach from Galway to Dublin. His fellow passengers were a very pretty girl dressed *très comme il faut* for travelling in a feathered hat and plain riding habit; and a young fresh-faced squire, very 'Hibernian' in visage and manner. They were complete strangers but the young squire started to chat the girl up to discover who she was and whence she came. 'Madam, do you know So-and-So? . . . Or So-and-So?' Eventually they struck on a mutual acquaintance and he was well away, turning on his charm and breaking into Irish which 'betrayed her into all the Chesterfieldian indecorum of laughter.' He then sang to her in Irish 'with great softness.' He was 'perfectly good-humoured with a high flow of animal spirits.' His suit deserved success.[20]

We read much of bad landowners, but what made a good one? He was concerned not merely with collecting rent but with improving the land, encouraging or bullying his tenants to spread lime, dung, seaweed or marl (the fertility was thereby increased, and rents could be raised when present leases expired). He might make a lease conditional on the tenant draining the land, or fencing it properly, or building a slate-roofed house. He knew when to be firm over rents and when to be merciful. He knew his people, who was a good tenant and would improve the land, who was a troublemaker, who was always ready with excuses.

Many introduced cottage industries. In Meath, Arthur Young noted:

> Every farm has a little flax from a rood to an acre,
> and all the cottages a spot . . . [where] . . . they go
> through the whole process themselves, spin and
> weave it.[21]

This was done in most counties.

Whether landowners, middlemen or strong farmers, hare-and fox-hunting was the delight of the gentry. In Galway it was the fox. Early in the eighteenth century most of the land that was not mountain or bog consisted of open fields; but increasingly these were enclosed by banks, fences and drystone walls. Galway was noted for its walls: indeed the best way of clearing the stony land was to make walls round each field. It provided, and still provides, one of the most exhilarating countries in the world to ride over, jumping wall after wall after wall. The first master of the Galway Blazers was Denis Daly. It was not much like the Pythcley or the Quorn hunts in England:

> The rough horseman that hunted in the valley
> Till you turned them homewards and brought
>   them to your hall . . .
> Slender powerful horses and stable-boys to care
>   for them.[22]

When the ground was frozen too hard for hunting they relaxed in Homeric feasts described by Barrington:

> The old huntsman was the only male attendant and his ancient spouse was the cook, while the drudgery fell to the lot of the whipper-in. A prologue of cherry-bounce [brandy] preceded the entertainment. A large turf-fire seemed to court the gridiron; the pot bubbled up as if proud of its contents, while plump white chickens floated upon its surface. The claret was tapped. The pipers plied their chants. Collops from the hanging cow, sliced from the tenderest joints, grilled over the clear embers . . . Numerous toasts gave zest to the repast, every man shouting forth his fair favourite. The pipers jerked from their bags appropriate planxies [Irish melodies], the jokers cracked their usual

jests and ribaldry. Claret flowed, bumpers were multiplied. . .

My reason began to lighten me of its burden and kindly suggested the straw-chamber as my asylum.[23]

It was not a very edifying scene at a time when the country gentlemen were becoming more civilised. They were building houses to live in, not just to defend; box-like, with glass windows and slated roof, cheap, efficient and functional.

Near-illiteracy, common among the gentry at the beginning of the eighteenth century, was rare sixty years later. Books and newspapers were more easily obtainable. There were more consumer goods to buy. Better roads were being made; and transport contractors were setting up in business, including Burkes of Marble Hill in Galway.

After hunting, they were mad about dancing. Thomas Campbell attended an assembly in a country town:

Some nobility and all the gentry from near and far were gathered together. We had no less than two sets of dancers and three or four card tables. The ladies were not only well but elegantly dressed, in the *ton* of a winter to two since in London. (All . showed great vivacity.) The women vied with the men in the display of animal powers . . . We frog-blooded English dance as though the practice were not congenial to us; but here they move as if dancing had been the business of their lives . . . these people have quick and violent spirits betraying them sometimes into sudden starts of indecorum which the severity of punctilio would not fail to

censure, while candour would only consider them
as venial flashes of mirth and good humour.

Campbell was introduced by a Dr Carroll (a Catholic) to an
officer on leave from the Imperial Austrian army, and to partners
whose 'conversations were as spirited as their dancing. One of
them had a person that would be gazed at in St James's.'

Farmers and labourers were as keen on dancing as the gentry,
and itinerant dancing teachers made a good living from instructing
them in the latest steps.[24]

The improvements in living standards affected mainly the
gentry and better-off farmers, but the relatively poor were well
fed before the population explosion. (The population is believed
to have doubled during the eighteenth century, with the fastest
growth at the end of it.) In the seventeenth century the diet of
the poor had been mainly milk and milk products and oats. After
about 1750 bread and oatcakes were added; potatoes were more
prevalent, but not until the end of the century were they the
main diet of the poor. Compared to other Europeans, Irish
peasants ate a lot of meat – only the really destitute ate none.
Pork was the meat of the poor, beef and mutton of the more
affluent. A middling farmer ate meat three times a week.
According to Arthur Young (writing in the 1780s) even a farmer
of thirty acres would keep half a side of beef for the winter.
Freshwater and sea fish were widely eaten. Young made the point
that the children of the poor in Ireland were fed better than in
England, though they might go barefoot and in ragged clothes.
In England, they were clad better, but fed on tea and bread.
There were famines in 1728–29 and 1740–1; thereafter, increasing
prosperity for all classes. Even in years of shortage the cash
earned by cottage spinning and weaving staved off real hunger.[25]

Disputes about land were not always Catholic against

Protestant. The Dillons of Kinclare in County Galway remained Catholic. Henry Dillon had no son, but two daughters, Sibby married to Andrew French of Rahoon (a Catholic) and Jane, married to Michael Bellew of Mount Bellew (also a Catholic). According to the anti-Popery Act of 1704, there being no son, the estate should be divided between the daughters, but Henry Dillon had strong views about this: rather than see the family estates divided, and between women at that, he wanted to leave it intact to his cousin Garrett (or Gerald) Dillon of Dublin. In a draft will of 1763, which he seems to have discussed with his sons-in-law, he left only personal property, £1,300 each, to the daughters, and gave them the impression that the real estate would go to his cousin with only 'encumbrances' to the girls. The sons-in-law, while as Catholic landowners sympathetic to his wish not to gavel, naturally hoped that their wives would share the estate. However, encumbrances were better than nothing so they kept their thoughts to themselves.

But there was another matter to be thought of. Was Garrett Dillon Catholic or Protestant? If he were a Catholic, he might be vulnerable to a gavelling claim by Sibby and Jane. Henry, the testator, seems to have thought he was a Protestant, but the sons-in-law, Andrew French and Michael Bellew, doubted this. Perhaps with a view to putting pressure on him to forego the estate they started proceedings to show he was a Catholic. Finally Garrett yielded the estate to their wives on payment to him of £1,000 on Henry Dillon's death. But as Sibby French died before her father Henry Dillon, he changed his will in 1778 to leave the lot to Jane Bellew. Andrew French thought his brother-in-law had been guilty of sharp practice.[26]

The Bellews remained Catholic and prospered. They acquired land craftily, chose their tenants well, dealt in sheep and cattle on advantageous terms, encouraged linen manufacture and drained bogs. By the end of the century they had bought the Galway estates of their Barmeath cousins, 2,400 acres for £23,000 and owned over 40,000 acres in all. Their younger sons served in the Imperial Austrian army or became priests; set up as coffee and sugar planters in the West Indies; or followed the 'mercantile career' in Dublin, France and Spain. They complained a lot about the Penal Laws but contrived to circumvent them.[27]

To the north of Galway, Sligo and Roscommon were comparatively poor counties, containing much bog. In Sligo the main Catholic and Jacobite family was O'Hara. But in the mid-eighteenth century the estates were inherited by Kean O'Hara, a minor, who was provided perforce with a Protestant guardian and brought up as a Protestant. Nor were the O'Haras, like most converts, pro-Catholic in sympathy: they identified completely with the Protestant Ascendancy until the end of the century.[28]

The two main Catholic families in County Roscommon, of great antiquity and prestige, were O'Conor Don, descendants of the High Kings, and MacDermot, whose head was styled Prince of Coolavin. Both had suffered grievously from the Cromwellian confiscations, less so from the Williamite ones, and kept their heads just above water.

In the Restoration Settlement the MacDermots got back only about a third of their land, the rest remaining in the hands of the Ormsbys and the Kings, Elizabethan planters who had sided with Cromwell. But in 1669 Cathal Roe MacDermot leased back from William Ormsby Coolavin house and demesne, 383 acres. (The lease was renewed every thirty-one years until 1801 when Dr Hugh MacDermot bought back the land.) For reasons which are not clear, but with the consent of those concerned, in 1690 he made over the property not to his eldest son, Bryan, but to the second son, Hugh, in tail. After the fall of Limerick, Bryan departed to Spain and did not return. The peculiar arrangement turned out fortunately for the family, for at the beginning of the Williamite war Hugh commanded the Jacobite garrison of Sligo where many Protestants were interned. He was taken prisoner at Aughrim but released 'on the interest and by the influence of Sir Robert King' [commanding the Williamite forces in north Connaught] 'for the humanity and kindness evinced by him towards Protestant clergy and laity.' He was therefore not attainted and did not lose the remains of the family property, for what it was worth. Hugh's son, Charles, was not in the war, probably too young, and inherited in 1707.

The family tradition is that the MacDermots were penniless princes who sat by the shores of Lough Gara reading the Latin classics. This is broadly true. Of all their former estates there remained to them the 'Old Coolavin' lands, partly leased and part-entailed, and a third of the Moylurg lands, entailed – about 1,600 acres in all and pretty poor acres at that, largely bog and mountain. Charles MacDermot lived until 1758, a bitter and twisted old man. He bricked up those windows of his house which overlooked the land his family had once owned; and was so haughty that he would not bow to visitors but remained seated when they came in, and would not permit his wife and daughters to eat with him. So goes the legend about him, popularised and lampooned in a novel to the author of which his grandson, Dr Hugh MacDermot, wrote indignantly:

> Old Mr MacDermot, Madam, was neither a savage
> nor a lunatic. He was a worthy man who wanted
> neither talents nor virtue.

As for the canard that he would not permit his wife and daughters to eat with him:

Could you have believed such an absurdity? When the old man was confined to his room by the infirmity of age, it was natural that she should dine with her family [in the dining-room].[29]

Of MacDermot's four sons, Terence, the second, was a doctor; Roger, the third, joined the Spanish army; Hugh, the fourth, served in the army of the Honourable East India Company from 1769 to 1787 but he failed to give the pagoda tree a really good shake and died in his thirties, like so many Europeans in India.

The eldest son, Myles, lived in France from 1739 to 1754, when he returned to take over Coolavin from his aged father, who died in 1758. He was stubborn, ill-tempered and selfish, and his wife, a daughter of Charles O'Conor of Belanagare, had a lot to put up with. At one time she contemplated leaving him. Her father wrote:

> Poor Biddy, she accepted rather than made a choice. But . . . let her behave as reason notes and religion dictates.

His visitors, too, had a lot to put up with. Arthur Young relates (for what it is worth) a story that:

> MacDermot, who calls himself Prince of Coolavin, although he has not £100 a year,* will not admit his children to sit down in his presence. Lord Kingsborough, Mr Ponsonby, Mr O'Hara and Mr Sandford came to see him and his address was

---

* His son and heir, Dr Hugh MacDermot, received £300–£400 in rents.

curious. 'O'Hara, you are welcome. Sandford, I am glad to see your mother's son. (His mother was an O'Brien.) As for the rest of ye, come in as ye can.'

After his wife died, he sired three or four illegitimate children by a woman known as Kitty Bhán. She was probably an O'Conor, possibly an illegitimate daughter of Charles O'Conor of Belanagare, in which case she would be half-sister to Myles MacDermot's deceased wife, which might account for his not marrying her. The children seem to have been brought up at Belanagare but neither the MacDermot nor the O'Conor family records throw much light on this.

Being entailed, the MacDermot estates were not gavelled. Such of the younger sons who did not go soldiering in France, Spain or India went to seek their fortunes in the West Indies, or as wine merchants in Bordeaux and Dublin.[30]

The Cromwellian officer, John King, who was granted the MacDermot property of Moylurg and retained two-thirds of it at the Restoration Settlement, was elevated to the peerage as Lord Kingston for his zeal in promoting the Restoration. The MacDermots leased part of Moylurg back from him as they did Coolavin from the Ormsbys, and found him a good and resident landlord though somewhat bigoted in his anti-Popery. It was his eldest son, Sir Robert, a Williamite commander, who had interceded for Hugh MacDermot and stopped his attainder. But the younger son, John, married at the age of eighteen one of his mother's maidservants, Peg O'Cahan, turned Catholic himself and served in the Jacobite army. In 1692 he sought pardon, but it was objected that both his sons were Papists and in the French army; he would be pardoned only if they came home and all three conformed:

> Otherwise it may prove of ill-consequence to the
> public and be strengthening the Papist influence
> which by this means will have a man of quality to
> lead them, and if he recovers his brother's estate
> he will be very formidable in Connaught.

He did recover his brother's estate, and title, when Robert died
without issue; but he and both his sons conformed, albeit with
patent insincerity. Twenty years later his namesake, Archbishop
King, protested to him:

> I ought not to conceal from your lordship that it
> is much observed that your family is altogether
> Papist, and that you live in as much the old Irish
> style as the merest Irishman in the kingdom.

He and his sons remained Jacobite at heart. The eldest son,
James, fourth Lord Kingston, was a zealous Freemason, Grand
Master of the Grand Lodge of Ireland in 1731, 1735, 1745 and
1746.[31]

The *aisling** poets portrayed in Daniel Corkery's *Hidden
Ireland*, forever keening for a lost cause and a vanishing Gaelic
world, were men of Munster; but Corkery's 'Hidden Ireland' was
more real in MacDermot and O'Conor Don country than in the
south-west.

It has been related that the MacDermots' kinsman, Denis ('of
the Grey Hair') O'Conor, established a right to three-quarters
of the O'Conor estate at Belanagare, subject to an annual rent
of £79 to the Frenchs. Denis was at the time on a small farm,
presumably leased, at Knockmore, County Sligo. According to

---

* *Aisling*: an Irish word meaning 'vision'.

the family tradition he used to tell his sons, 'Boys, you must never be insolent to the poor. I am the son of a gentleman, but you are the sons of a ploughman.' This seems no more than a family joke. The settlement of the Belanagare estate was made in 1701. Denis must have known all about it from the lawyer, Terence McDonagh, who signed the agreement and probably negotiated it, whose niece Denis married and who did not die until 1713. Yet Denis did not take possession of Belanagare until 1720. If he were really poor, why did he not move earlier? Belanagare, with 448 profitable and 422 unprofitable acres, was not a great estate, but living and farming on it he would have been infinitely better off than as a ploughman at a shilling a day at Knockmore. A ploughman would not have made his house a 'general rendezvous for a number of unfortunate ladies and gentlemen who had lived in splendour' and were now very badly off. A ploughman would not have sent his seventeen-year-old son to a boarding-school in Dublin, nor employed a dancing master, a fencing master and an Irish master for his children. The family historian, Father Charles O'Conor Don, SJ, described Denis as 'poor, but not so poor as his neighbours.' Moreover, after he had made the move to Belanagare in 1720, he returned several times to Knockmore until 1724 when 'our houses [sic] at Knockmore were burnt.' The family legend that he walked barefoot to Dublin to settle the case in 1720 is most improbable: it had been settled in 1701.

His eldest son, Charles, had been educated in Sligo by local priests in local schools, perhaps even 'hedge schools' though they are not so described in Charles's diaries. He learned Latin and Irish – classical, properly accented, grammatical Irish: he must as a small boy have spoken it as a *patois*. In 1727 he was sent to Father Skelton's academy in Dublin to learn English, Greek, mathematics and physics. He was the pupil of Turlough Carolan, the blind harpist, equally apt at church music, Irish lays and drinking songs, who found that 'spirituous liquors lent strength to the flights of his genius.' Denis did not stint the whiskey-punch, for Carolan one night said to another harpist, 'I think when I am with the O'Conors the harp has the old sound in it.' 'No,' replied McCabe, 'but your soul has the old madness in it.' His harp is still with the O'Conor family.

Denis was a hospitable soul, and a frequent visitor was his brother-in-law, Thady O'Rourke, Bishop of Killala, in the guise of 'Mr Fitzgerald'. He wore the ring and pectoral cross given him by Prince Eugene of Savoy, whose chaplain he had been; and his chalice was divided into three parts for easier concealment.

In 1735 Denis set up a stone memorial inscribed in Latin:

> For his ancestors and his father and grandfather
>   here buried
> Who were to Faith and virtue most addicted
> And to religion and fatherland most constant
> But who were for the defence of both
> Reduced, despoiled, dispersed,
> This monument was erected by
> Denis O'Conor of Belanagare in 1735.[32]

When Charles's schooling was finished, he came home, hunted a little and ran a small farm which his father leased for him a mile or two from Belanagare. He drew in the hay and corn, went to fairs to buy sheep and cattle and filled his lungs with good country air after the smog of Dublin. It was mainly a stock farm, for with only a thirty-one-year lease, it was not worthwhile spending the capital needed for tillage. He wrote:

The Penal Laws now in force having thrown the principal Roman Catholics into the wasteful occupation of grazing, on account of the discoverable interest and the shortness of tenure, the poorer sort are thereby deprived of employment.

He had four brothers. Two became priests; one, Daniel, went off to the Irish Brigade in France; and Hugh, 'apostate and perjurer', conformed and tried to wrest from Charles the family estates. In 1731 Charles married. In the ten years before his wife died, he had a daughter, who married the disagreeable Myles MacDermot of Coolavin, and two sons. The elder, Denis, was all that a son should be, his father's best friend and confidant. The younger, Charles, wasn't.

Denis of the Grey Hair died in 1750 and Charles, a widower, moved into the house at Belanagare. He was incredibly busy, his finger in a dozen pies, and very, very, learned. He farmed; he collected ancient Irish documents; he assembled Irish genealogies; he became a member of the Royal Irish Academy. He was equally at ease in Irish, English, Latin, Greek, and competent in French. His first literary labour was ghost-writing a collection of Irish fables for an author who had no Irish. He next wrote a *Dissertation on the Ancient History of Ireland,* and made the mistake of sending it to a friend to read and criticise, which was the end of a friendship. In letter-writing he suffered from prolixity, his short letters being of eighteen or twenty pages. Edmund Burke, Dr Johnson and the Duke of Norfolk were among his long-suffering correspondents. He was involved, with General Vallancey, Engineer-in-Chief and an Irish scholar, in the Shannon Navigation Scheme.

He still found time to socialise with his bucolic neighbours, noting that he dined with Colonel French, 'a worthy man, an amiable person'; 'I sat with my host and three fox-hunters.' What did they talk about? *The Annals of the Four Masters* or last week's nine-mile point? But the sort of social occasion he really enjoyed was when Vallancey introduced him to:

> a most amiable gentleman, Colonel Burton, a Privy Councillor and Teller of the Exchequer. In a society of learned antiquarians I have dined at his fine house in Harcourt Place near Merrion Square. I could not have had a happier day and our conversation ran chiefly on Irish antiquities.

His younger son, Charles, was a problem. He wrote to Charles's brother, Denis:

> Your brother arrived here on Tuesday last in a threadbare coat, and yet (what I did not expect) he brought me the twenty guineas I paid for him here. He is endeavouring to obtain employment in the Shannon Navigation. He is fond of schemes, and none has ever succeeded for him. One who is always throwing the die must be happy if he is never [*sic*] favoured with a single lucky cast. . . . Your unhappy brother had the modesty lately to request I should advance him the sum of £60, after my late advance of £27 for him. I returned an answer with a severity unusual in me, and last post he put me to the expense of fourpence for an awkward apology for his conduct. Were he a man of industry or skill he would now have an opportunity of [leasing land] in a country open to improvement and profitable occupations. But I despair of him.

In 1751 he advised Denis:

> If you have any sagacity, strive to adapt it to the
> rank you are to fill hereafter: that of a Roman
> Catholic in a Protestant country, that of one in a
> low way, obnoxious to the laws.

It cannot be said that either the antiquarian or his son followed
this advice. From the mid-1750s onwards Charles Senior gave
more and more time to agitating (on paper) for the repeal of the
Penal Laws. In 1755 he ran off an eighty-page pamphlet on *The
Case of the Roman Catholics in Ireland*. Leading Catholics began
meeting together, informally, by invitation, to plan how to
proceed. At one of these meetings he met Dr John Curry, who
was to become his closest friend. In 1760 he, Curry and Thomas
Wyse of Waterford formed the Catholic Committee as a
pressure group for legislation to ease Catholic grievances. But
none of the family were anglophobes: as his grandson, Charles,
a priest, wrote: 'The English really think that Popery is
horrible . . . It is a pity that such good fellows could be so
misled by Methodists and mountebanks.'

Meanwhile, O'Conor Don lived at Clonalis, some ten miles
away, on a few hundred acres of the former family estates. His
family had suffered from Cromwellian rather than Williamite
confiscations, and their great possessions were reduced to a rent-
roll of £300 or £400 a year. Arthur Young noted: 'The common
people pay him the greatest respect and send him presents of
cattle etc. They consider him as the prince of a people involved
in one common ruin.' As a result of a series of early deaths and
childless marriages, Denis O'Conor's son Owen became O'Conor
Don in the nineteenth century.[33]

1 H. P. Staples (ed.), *The Ireland of Jonah Barrington*, 31-2.

2 Simms, *Williamite Confiscations*, 70-1; Melvin, *Irish Genealogist*, 85, 86, 88, 93; O'Byrne, *Convert Rolls*, 18-19, 27-33.

3 Marquess of Sligo, *Westport House and the Brownes*, (Moorland, 1981), 13-18.

4 Hardiman, *A History of Galway*,162-3; Martin Blake, *Blake Family Records*, 125, 136, 163, 179; Dalton, *King James's Irish Army List*, II, 270-1; Melvin, *op. cit.*, 90; Simms, *Irish Jacobites*, 133; Simms, *Williamite Confiscations*, 81; *Convert Rolls*.

5 8 Anne, Ch. 3, XXXIX.

6 Simms, *Williamite Confiscations*, 77-8; Shevawn Lynam, *Humanity Dick Martin*, XV-XVI, 46-7, 77.

7 Inchiquin MSS, 536.

8 Shevawn Lynam, *Humanity Dick Martin*, 82-5.

9 Melvin, *op. cit.*, 86; NLI MSS 17830 (9), (10); information from Mahon family papers supplied by Mr Luke Dodd of Strokestown; Hickey, *Memoirs*, I, 318-9.

10 R. Hayes, *A Biographical Dictionary of Irishmen in France*, 145; D Ó Cearbhaill, *Galway Town and Gown*, 111-12; Hardiman, *op. cit.*, 318.

11 Burke, *Landed Gentry of Ireland*, 535; Hickey, *op. cit.*, IV, 488 fn.

12 Registry of Deeds, 438-73, Book 45, f 526; *Convert Rolls*, 75-7.

13 Melvin, *op. cit.*, 85; Burke, *Peerage, Baronetage and Knightage, under Clonbrook*, 233; *Convert Rolls*, 75-7.

14 1 George, Ch. 9, II.

15 Karen J. Harvey in Power and Whelan (eds.), *Endurance and Emergence*, 188; E. and A. Porritt, *The Unreformed House of Commons*, II, 223.

16 L. M. Cullen, *The Emergence of Modern Ireland*, 17, 41, 47, 99.

17 Arthur Young, *A Tour in Ireland*, 189-90, 205; L.M. Cullen, *Life in Ireland*, 102.

18 *Ibid.*, 109.

19 Documents in possession of Mr. C. E. F. Trench.

20 T. Campbell, *A Philosophical Survey of the South of Ireland*, 289-90.

21 Arthur Young, *op. cit.*,10.

22 Eibhlín Dubh Ní Chonaill, *The Lament for Art O'Leary*, trans. E. Dillon.

23 H. P. Staples, *op. cit.*, 42-3.

24 Campbell, *op. cit.*, 202; Young, *op. cit.*, 202.

25 Cullen, *The Emergence of Modern Ireland*, 93, 144-7, 153, 163; Young, *op. cit.*, 183.

26 Harvey in Power and Whelan (eds.), *op. cit.*, 180-1.

27 *Ibid.*, 182-3, 192.

28 L. M. Cullen, *Catholics under the Penal Laws in Eighteenth Century Ireland*, I, 30.

29 Hugh MacDermot, *Letters*, no. 12.

30 Sir Dermot MacDermot, *The MacDermots of Moylurg and Coolavin*, 248-9, 254-6; Hugh MacDermot, *op. cit.*, nos. 1 fn, 47, 48; Young, *op. cit.*, 70; Charles O'Conor, *Memoirs of Charles O'Conor of Belanagare*, 186.

31 Calandar of State Papers, Dom., 1694-5, 344; TCD MSS N3, 7 f 128; Michael Nugent and Richard Lee, *The Temple and the Lodge*, 184.

32 Charles O'Conor, *op. cit.,*, 157,160,169; O'Conor Don, *The Early Life of Charles O'Conor*, 8.

33 O'Conor Don, *op. cit.*, 9; C. C. and R. E. Ward (eds.), *Letters of Charles O'Conor of Belanagare*, 5,10, 18, 116, 303, 312; Young, *op. cit.*, 69.

5

—

SOME CATHOLIC FAMILIES
IN ULSTER AND LEINSTER

Among the few Catholic landowners in the north-east were the
Whytes, of Saxon or Jutish origin, who had come over with
Strongbow (who must indeed have had a big ship). Charles
Whyte, a former colonel in the Spanish service, had an estate
in County Kildare: by 1689, though an MP in King James's
Parliament and Governor of Kildare, his soldiering days were
over. Crippled with gout, he 'took protection' after the Battle of
the Boyne, pardoned because the Austrian Emperor put in a
good word for him and because of his kindness to Protestants
when he could have been very unkind to them. His son, Captain
John Whyte, who pleaded the Articles of Limerick, was hard
up, but married well, a Mary Purcell whose mother had been
born a Trevor. Through her he inherited an estate, and sold the
place at Leixlip, the family being known henceforth as Whyte
of Loughbrickland, in County Down. They escaped gavelling;
he and his heir Charles were only sons, and of Charles's two sons
the younger was a Knight of the Military Order of St John of
Malta, indifferent to such vanities as an estate in Ulster. It helped
that they were related to two powerful Protestant families, the
Trevors whose head was Viscount Dungannon, and the Hills of
Belvoir, near Belfast. Captain John made what was obviously a
collusive arrangement with Arthur Hill between 1737 and 1751.
When John died, twenty-six leases named them as partners and co-

owners of the estate. No doubt the arrangement continued after the captain's death: and no discoverer challenged it because it would never do to get on the wrong side of Lord Dungannon.[1]

Captain John's grandson, Charles, had difficulty in extracting from his wife's brother, Edward Dunne, the marriage portion of £2,000 plus 5 per cent per annum interest. In 1752 the court gave him judgement for this, but he still could not get his hands on the money. Had he been a Protestant, he could have taken out a mortgage on Dunne's estate; but as both he and Dunne were Catholics, there would be a risk of discovery. The best legal advice was that the mortgage could be camouflaged by having rents from Dunne's estate paid direct to Whyte, who would covenant not to foreclose for the principal so long as he got the annual interest.[2]

The Savages of Portaferry were another Catholic family in County Down. In 1689 they were all Catholics but divided in allegiance between King James and King William. Two brothers, Patrick and Hugh, were on the Williamite side. In 1724, Patrick died, having bequeathed Portaferry to his only surviving son, Edward, who was at Trinity College studying for the Bar. He does not appear on *The Convert Rolls*, but must have been a Protestant. Edward, unmarried, made a will in favour of his uncle, James, a Catholic, entailed for James's son, John, and to John's male heirs. Edward then went abroad for his health, returned to the Catholic faith and died in 1725 after making another will in the same terms as the first.

James's two sons were both Catholics. The law required that the estate be gavelled, unless James or his elder son, John, conformed within six months. James refused, but John thought Portaferry worth more than a Mass, and so inherited the whole estate, his father being only his tenant for life. John died in 1733. His younger brother, Andrew, in the Spanish service, hastened home, conformed and inherited the estate. Thereafter the Savages conformed like ninepins, eleven of them between 1738 and 1770.

Andrew was a bad manager, ran into debt and sold a lot of land but made an advantageous marriage to Margaret Nugent. A certain Billy Savage accused Andrew of complicity in the '45, and Margaret's brother warned her:

> Mr Savage should go to town and inform the government of the attempt made against him, and tell them he came to Dublin on purpose to acquaint them of it, because he would not on any account lie under any suspicion of disaffection to His Majesty or attempts against the law.

But Andrew's eldest son was a pillar of the establishment, High Sheriff of County Down and Colonel of the Ards Volunteers. Other Savages married other Nugents and finally one inherited the Nugent estates in County Meath on conditions that he change his name by deed poll to Nugent. He did so reluctantly, observing that despite the financial advantages, he would far rather be an old savage than a new gent.[3]

He doubtless had in mind Robert Nugent of Carlanstown, County Meath, who in 1762 conformed in order to become a Westminster MP. A cruising predator, he fared well on commissions, bribes, sinecures and jobs, the most lucrative being that of Comptroller to the Household of the Prince of Wales, though it carried the liability of lending money to His Royal Highness. He was reputed to be exceptionally well-endowed in his physique and was notorious for marrying ('Nugentising') rich elderly widows, the third of whom was old enough to be his grandmother. Having flourished like the green bay tree in this world, he insured himself for the next by returning to the Catholic faith shortly before his death in 1788.[4]

Unless their shortcomings in County Roscommon totally escaped the notice of the antiquarian, there was a sad deterioration in the country people's character east of the Shannon. In County Westmeath, reported Arthur Young:

> They steal everything they can lay hands on . . . all sorts of iron hinges, chains, locks, keys etc. Gates will be cut in pieces and conveyed away as fast as built. Trees as big as a man's body, that would require ten men to move, are gone in a night . . . Turnips are stolen by the carload, and two acres of wheat plucked off in a night. How far it is owing to the oppression of laws aimed solely at the religion of the people, how far to the conduct of gentlemen and farmers, and how far to the mischievous disposition of the people themselves, it is impossible for the passing traveller to ascertain.

But in County Louth he was assured by Mr Forster, Chief Baron of the Exchequer, that Catholics in general were honest, sober and industrious people; and the Penal Laws, although very severe in letter, were never executed.

> It is rarely or never (he knew no instance) that a Protestant discoverer gets a lease by proving the land let under two-thirds of their value to a Papist. There were severe penalties for carrying arms or reading Mass [*sic*]* but the first is *never* executed for poaching, and Mass houses are to be seen everywhere.

---

* There were no penalties for reading Mass.

There were weavers' looms in most of the cabins, earning 7s or 8s a week. And in ten years rents had risen from 3s 6d an acre to a guinea, 'which great work was done by the tenants, and lime and fallow the means employed.'[5]

The principal Catholic landowners in County Louth were the Bellews of Barmeath Castle. The family had been transplanted to Galway by Cromwell, but after the Restoration Sir John Bellew returned to Louth as agent to Lord Carlingford. He found the family estates in the hands of soldiers and adventurers, but in the Restoration Settlement he was authorised to eject them, paying compensation: if in any difficulty, he could choose other land nearby. He did, of course, experience considerable difficulty in making them disgorge, but eventually he recovered about 2,280 acres. He also bought from Lord Carlingford Barmeath Castle with its 351 acre demesne, and a further 1,028 acres in hand. On his death in 1679 it passed to his only son, Patrick, created a baronet in 1686. He was outlawed in 1691, but adjudged within the Articles of Limerick, so his estates were returned to him. He died in 1715, leaving three sons between whom the estate should have been gavelled, but it wasn't, perhaps because of the services his heir, John, had performed for King William 'in the enemy's quarters', for which he had his outlawry reversed and was pardoned. Nor was it gavelled when John died in 1734, passing intact to Edward, the third baronet; and from him to his eldest son, John, who having no sons, passed it on intact to his younger brother Patrick, the fifth baronet. There was no particular reason why the land was not gavelled: presumably the younger sons just did not claim their legal rights. Some of the family turned to a 'mercantile career' on very little capital. One, Garrett, having only £400 capital to start him off, chartered a ship and invested the money in a mixed cargo for sale in an Irish port, hoping afterwards to set up in Cadiz. Sir

Patrick, the fifth baronet, approved of commerce but deemed 'trade' somewhat *infra dig*; and when Garrett's brother married the daughter of a Dublin seedsman, Sir Patrick confessed, 'my pride suffers a little on account of the alliance.'

A rather distinguished cousin of Sir Patrick was Dominick, who, after training at the Irish College in Rome, was ordained in 1771 and a year later came as parish priest to Dundalk. He found there a fair degree of tolerance and Papists progressing in numbers, wealth and influence. He also found two rival parish priests with whom he had a rather unseemly power-struggle, each preaching against the other, until he was appointed (very young) Bishop of Killala in 1780.[6]

Masonic emblems, moulded in plaster on the wall of the dining-room, indicate that the Bellews were Freemasons and that Lodge meetings were held at Barmeath. If a Catholic Mason were ever in trouble, as Sir Patrick's son, Francis, was to be, he could count with certainty on help from his Protestant brethren.

Meath, adjoining Louth, was the most prosperous county in the kingdom, Arthur Young, noted:

> The country is cheerful and rich, and if the Irish cabins continue like what I have hitherto seen, I shall not hesitate to pronounce the inhabitants as well off as most English cottagers. They are built of mud walls eighteen inches or two feet thick, and well thatched, which are far warmer than the thin clay walls in England. Here are few cottiers without a cow, and some of them two. A bellyful of potatoes and generally turf for fuel from the bog. It is true they have not always chimneys to their cabins, the door serving for that and window too.

If their eyes are not affected by smoke, it may be
an advantage in warmth. Every cottage swarms
with poultry and most of them have pigs.[7]

Catholic landowning families included those of Viscount
Gormanston (Preston), the Earl of Fingall (Plunkett), Eustace,
Everard, Nugent, Barnewall, Baggot – all names of Norman
origin except Plunkett, which was Danish.

The Gormanston estate was entailed, so was protected
against gavelling. Anthony, the ninth viscount, dying in 1716,
was succeeded by his son, Jenico, who died in 1757 and was
succeeded by *his* son, Anthony, the eleventh viscount, who died
in 1786. So for sixty years the estate had only two owners, a
recipe for stability. Jenico, the tenth viscount, was a keen and
experimental farmer, borrowing a 'plough-drill', the recent
invention of Jethro Tull, to sow a pilot plot with wheat, hemp,
barley and oats, comparing the results with 'the common way'
of hand-sowing, much to the advantage of Tull's method.
Neighbours consulted him on his 'new improvement of rearing
and feeding calves with the help of haywater.' Would it work
with horses? It worked very well with calves, he replied,
'eighteen, nearly all hearty.' In one year he raised the estate's
rent-roll from £1,400 to £1,800 and 'it would soon rise further
by the expiration of leases.' Although as a Catholic he could not
be a member of the Grand Jury which functioned as the local
government of the county, by vigorous lobbying he made his
views known and prevailed in road alignments and turnpikes
'long wished for by all in that part of the country who thought
it hard to pay for a bad road, but now they will travel and pay
with pleasure.' Although a steady Catholic, he arranged for an
English schoolmaster to serve his Protestant tenants. The
Protestant Bishop of Meath wrote that Catholics were making

difficulties about finding the man a house, and he 'would receive Viscount Gormanston's commands if he will do me the honour to eat a bit of mutton with me.'

But Jenico had trouble with his son and heir, Anthony, writing in 1756 to him at college in Paris about his 'very childish idea of marrying' too young. 'I do not know how you think I applied to study after I was married. . . . This wavering about a state for life is no more than is common to young folks.'

Jenico died in 1757 and his widow, Thomasine (*née* Barnewall), thereafter lived mainly in Liège with her three younger sons, one of whom became an Austrian officer and one a priest.

Anthony, the eleventh viscount, seems to have continued a rather difficult character. An aunt warned him in May 1774 that his three younger brothers, 'hot and of your temper', might take advantage of the gavel law, and advised him to act in the 'mildest manner towards them.' (Actually there was no danger of this, as the land was entailed.) In January 1776 a General Plunkett of the Austrian service found them in Brussels, 'all unemployed and requiring as members of the same family a decent income to support the dignity of it.' They would be satisfied with £200 a year each, and 'never the most distant thought of profiting by the Penal Laws.' Would Gormanston write an 'affectionate letter implying your consent?' Anthony replied briefly that he already gave them quite enough.[8]

In 1773 Anthony made an unfortunate marriage to an English lady, Henrietta Robinson, described by a non-admirer as very beautiful but 'attached to every vice that dishonours the sex, with a most violent adherence to the Protestant religion. From the very consummation of their marriage she had an aversion to her husband and an unbounded desire to spend his estates.' Soon the marriage was in trouble. In the summer of 1775 Anthony would have gone over to Brussels to see his brothers, 'but my lady's conduct prevented me'. She fled to her mother in London, taking their son Jenico. To Daniel MacNamara, his lawyer friend in London, Anthony wrote in October 1780 complaining of his lady's conduct 'as a high insult to my feelings as a father and my sentiments as a man. The case has already interested the whole kingdom, as well as me, both Protestant and Catholic.' He tried unsuccessfully to recover Jenico by a writ of *habeas corpus*. Anthony's old school friend, the Duke of Portland, wrote from London, indicating that the only obstacle to recovering his son seemed to be financial: 'You would purchase your own ease at no very high price.' In the end, that is what he did.[9]

In 1786 Anthony died suddenly in London, when Jenico was only twelve. The Robinsons wished to have him declared a ward of court and brought up as a Protestant but his grandmother, Thomasine, the Dowager Lady Gormanston, would have none of this, and to prevent it connived with C. J. Dixon, a young and enterprising priest whom Anthony had solemnly charged with ensuring that 'the baleful steam of Protestantism and heresy be not breathed on the lad's tender mind'. Father Dixon proceeded to Gormanston to abduct Jenico, prepared if necessary to have his preceptor 'gagged and bound'. Fortunately, it was not necessary: abductor and abductee went off happily to a safe house in Dublin. Hearing, however, that the boy's mother was waiting at Holyhead for a fair wind for Ireland, the good Father (himself laid low with fever) shipped Jenico off to Liverpool in charge of a trusty family friend, an ex-officer of the Irish Brigade, and from Liverpool via London to Liège, where his uncles would look after him.

Father Dixon was himself in some danger of being charged with kidnapping and sentenced to be hanged. The vengeful lady's henchmen, each with a brace of pistols, hunted him over Dublin so that he had to escape from roof to roof, and once over a garden wall lacerating his arm on the broken glass on top. Eventually he too got away safely, and arriving at Liège 'knew the happiness to see his labours ended and his young charge advancing in virtue and learning'.[10]

The Gormanston crest is surmounted by a fox. There is a strange tradition, with more supporting evidence than most tales of the supernatural, that whenever a Viscount Gormanston is about to die, foxes from all over the county assemble at the castle. When the Earl of Fingall was hunting his hounds, a countryman said to him, 'You can take your hounds home, my lord. Lord Gormanston is dying, and every fox in Meath is at Gormanston.' When in 1907 the fourteenth viscount died, his coffin was placed in the castle for the burial next day, and his son undertook to keep watch on it. He heard a snuffling at the door, and thinking it was from a litter of wolfhound puppies that had got out of their kennel, went to investigate. Outside the door he saw four or five foxes, and aimed a kick at one, which simply moved further away. More foxes were outside another door.[11]

Luke Plunkett, third Earl of Fingall, was outlawed in 1691 and deprived of his estates, although he had died in 1685. This bureaucratic blunder was rectified in 1697 by a royal pardon and the restoration of the estates to his only son, Peter, who had been too young to fight. Peter, too, had only one son, Justin; and Justin, dying childless in 1734, was succeeded by a distant cousin, Robert, a captain in Berwick's who was an only son. Robert's eldest son, Justin, died in infancy and his other son, Arthur, inherited as the seventh earl, dying in 1793. So for a hundred years the estate could not be gavelled.

Peter, Justin and Robert spent all their lives in France, absentee landlords employing agents of varying quality to run their estates. These were considerable, amounting in 1697 to 5,768 presumably Irish acres, that is to say about 10,000 statute acres. In 1708 these were leased out to fifty-five tenants paying from a few shillings to £270 a year in rent, with a total rent-roll of £2,479. Most of the leases were for thirty-one years, a few for twenty-one years. Going by their names (admittedly an unreliable guide) about a dozen of the tenants seem to have been Protestant.

Justin's cousin Robert, the captain in Berwick's, who succeeded as sixth earl in 1734, seems to have taken little interest in his property. It is possible that he left the overall management of it to Lord Bellew, incidentally a convert, who was the third husband of Justin's widow. Robert's agent, Hugh Reilly Esquire, was hardly a treasure. He lived in the Dower House of the disintegrating Killeen Castle and was supposed to pay rent for it to Lord Bellew, but by 1742, when the arrangement lapsed, he was £704 in arrears. He also allowed many other tenants to fall into arrears, which amounted in all to £987 in 1738, and could see 'no prospect' of getting this money out of them. Furthermore, Robert's first-born son, Justin, died in infancy in 1735 so in that year Robert decided to cut his losses, and put 3,124 (presumably statute) acres up for sale. Three years later he advertised for sale 5,702 profitable acres. How much he actually sold is not clear. It is possible that the 1738 sale was cancelled, for Robert died that year. The estate does not seem to have greatly diminished between 1697 and 1768.

Robert's other son, Arthur, inherited at the age of seven and was brought up as a Catholic, albeit by a Protestant guardian. He had the good sense, or good fortune, to marry in 1755 an English heiress, and spent the first fifteen years of his married life mainly in Berkshire, but visiting Ireland from time to time. Killeen Castle having been repaired, he took up more or less permanent residence there in the late 1770s. The rent-roll which had languished at about £2,000 (less arrears) for the previous thirty years, rose to £2,492 in 1770, £3,068 in 1773 and £3,476 in 1777. There were now only thirty-nine tenants, including half a dozen Protestants; perhaps the worst payers had been evicted. Either Arthur and his English wife were good managers, or the agent they employed, Patrick Dease, was an improvement on Hugh Reilly.[12]

Randall Plunkett, the eleventh Baron Dunsany, preserved his estates under the Articles of Limerick. When he died in 1735 these passed, ungavelled, to his eldest son, Edward. In that year Edward conformed, according to family legend lest he be deprived of a favourite horse. (With any family but the Plunketts, one would discount this as a tall story.) He remained on good terms with his Catholic relatives and seems to have 'held' land for the seventh Earl of Fingall. It is not clear why this was necessary; the Fingall estates were under no threat. Perhaps Fingall used some of his wife's money to buy land or lease it for more than thirty-one years, transactions which would have been discoverable.[13]

The estates of Nicholas, Viscount Barnewall of Kingsland, had been saved by the Articles of Limerick; those of his young kinsman John, 11th Lord Trimleston, by good luck and the good feeling of the Trustees for Forfeited Estates. They and their successors enjoyed their estates, entailed and therefore not gavelled; their younger brothers seeking their fortunes in foreign armies or in the 'mercantile career'. Some were Freemasons. Richard Barnewall, son of the 11th Lord Trimleston, in 1734 established a lodge in Toulouse; the fourth Viscount Barnewall was Grand Master of Ireland in 1733-5. He was refused a seat in the House of Lords because he could not take the oath repudiating the Pope's spiritual authority in the kingdom. In 1757 seven Catholic bishops met in the 12th Lord Trimleston's house to draw up a pastoral address to the faithful.

Father Patrick Barnewall, a Jesuit, left Meath for the English Mission and established at Preston, concealed in a plain building, the first Catholic chapel there since the Reformation. The Barnewalls were *very* Catholic, and felt it keenly when two sons of the 12th Lord Trimleston conformed, to prevent their father playing fast and loose with the estates.[14]

The Everards were another Catholic family with wide acres in county Meath. Colonel Mathias Everard was adjudged under the Articles of Limerick and resumed possession of 3,663 Irish acres near Randlestown. He was also licensed to carry arms. He was a great builder, and whatever he built he added a memorial stone making clear that it was he who built it. He died childless in 1714 and was succeeded by his brother, Christopher, also a compulsive builder – banqueting houses, canal, terrace, bridge, all bear his name and the Everard arms. Clearly the Everards did not feel that safety lay in obscurity. An unidentified Christopher Everard was sentenced to death for high treason during the Jacobite rebellion of 1715; but with a fellow-prisoner, Walter Eustace, he broke out of Kilmainham prison and got clear away.[15]

Alexander Eustace managed to keep his land and his faith through the Interregnum and into the Restoration, quietly amassing wealth by good farming on good land, for which he was known as Alexander of the Corn. He had three sons, all of whom held King James's commission. Maurice, the eldest, raised a regiment of infantry but was able as an Articleman to keep his 1,417 Irish acres. He died childless in 1698. Thomas, the second son, died childless in 1692, owner of about 2,400 acres. James, the youngest, seems not at first to have owned any land in fee simple, but marriage to the widow of the Earl of Strafford brought him a thirty-one-year lease of 1,100 acres at Yeomanstown in County Kildare. As an Articleman, he claimed Thomas's estate; but as Thomas had died in rebellion, not covered by the Articles, his claim was disallowed. However he was not without influence, through Eustace Protestant relations and his family connection with the Straffords; so a special Act of Parliament gave him this estate provided his son conformed. When his wife died in 1702, Protestant trustees in an obviously collusive arrangement leased Yeomanstown to him for three lives renewable forever at a rent of less than two shillings an acre, though its true value was six shillings and sixpence an acre. The lease was too long and the rent too low for a Catholic, but as it was settled before the anti-Popery Act of 1703 it was not discoverable, or at least not discovered. As a further precaution against discovery he mortgaged the land to another Protestant for 500 years, he himself receiving all the rents and profits. So he became the fortunate owner in fee of his two brothers' estates, totalling some 3,800 Irish acres, and the perpetual tenant of 1,100. He farmed 596 acres and set the remainder. He built a fine thatched house of noble proportions and, with a proper sense of priorities, a stable block of even nobler proportions with a slate roof.

In 1703 he was in trouble, having smuggled over from England a book entitled *Memoirs of King James II*, of which he had 500 copies surreptitiously printed in Dublin. The Irish House of Commons enquired into this scandalous affair, and the Attorney General ordered all copies of the book to be publicly burnt by the common hangman. However, as over 440 copies had already been sold, Captain James Eustace took this punishment like a man.

Neither he nor his son Alexander appear in *The Convert Rolls*, so presumably they did not conform. As Alexander was an only son, the estate was not gavelled. Captain James Eustace seems to have got away with a lot, thanks perhaps to the benign influence of his Protestant kinsmen in the county, of whom two became generals and one an MP. His portrait hung at Yeomanstown until 1798 when some rebels, thinking from the red coat that he was in the British army, drove a pike through it.

His daughter Jane married John Mansfield, of a Catholic and Jacobite family in County Waterford. John's grandson inherited half the Eustace estate on the death of Captain James's son in 1783. The estate then remained in Catholic hands for two hundred years.[16]

At Luttrellstown near Dublin resided Colonel Henry Luttrell who, for betraying his comrades at Aughrim, had been given special permission under the 1709 anti-Popery Act to inherit and hold his land free of all encumbrances laid on Papists, just as if he had been one of God's chosen Protestants. He was no credit to Catholicism, making himself conspicuous at Mass by ogling the pretty girls and attracting their attention by tossing at them little pebbles from a supply kept in his pocket. He challenged to a duel his son, Simon, who replied, 'Sir, I will fight you with all my heart, if only you can prevail on any gentleman to be your second.' He was murdered in his sedan chair in 1717. He must have asked for it.

His grandson went over to England, where he found congenial employment in the murky fringe of politics, as the creature of George III's most hated Prime Minister, the Earl of Bute. He kidnapped and debauched a child of twelve, and then hired witnesses to swear that she was already a prostitute; and shocked even the least censorious by appearing at a private masque as a corpse in a coffin bearing a plate stating that the occupant had died of clap contracted in his hostess's house.

But the Ministry was in difficulties, and to extricate itself required the services of 'a man of the firmest virtue, or a ruffian of dauntless prostitution'. Luttrell volunteered as their ruffian.

The Ministry's problem was, as usual in the 1760s, Mr Wilkes.

He had been expelled from the House of Commons for publishing seditious, obscene and impious libels and promptly re-elected for Middlesex, no one daring to oppose him. He was again expelled and declared 'incapable of being elected', again stood for election and was again unanimously elected, his only opponent being unable to find a proposer. Next day the House resolved that the election was null and void. Wilkes, of course, stood a third time for Middlesex. As the Ministry saw it, at all costs – and the costs would be heavy – he must be defeated. Braving the mobs bawling 'Wilkes and Liberty', Luttrell, who did not lack courage, stood against him. At Wilkes's side stood a relation of the Earl of Fermoy, a ferocious swordsman known as 'Tiger' Roche. Wilkes, who needed no lessons in dirty tricks, gave it out that if Luttrell won, his reward was to be Bute's daughter. Wilkes coasted home with 1,143 votes to Luttrell's 296; but the Commons, undaunted, voted that 'Colonel Luttrell ought to have been elected'; and, a few days later, that 'Colonel Luttrell had been elected.' So Luttrell took his seat, the most hated man in the two kingdoms. He did not escape the attention of Junius*:

> There is a certain family in this country in which nature seems to have entailed a hereditary baseness of disposition . . . The son has regularly improved on the vices of his father, and has taken care to transmit them pure and undiluted into the bosom of his successor. In the Senate their abilities have confined them to those humble, sordid services in which the scavengers of the Ministry are usually employed. But in the memoirs of private treachery they stand first and unrivalled.

---

* Junius was the *nom de plume* of a very savage anti-establishment writer in the media during the years 1760–80. His identity is still unknown.

A cartoon showed Luttrell as 'The Irish Arithmetician' proving that 296 votes for the 'Teague' was more than 1,143 for Mr Wilkes. When Luttrell's sister married the king's unattractive uncle, 'Butcher' Cumberland, Junius besought the nation to redouble its prayers for the health of the king and the royal offspring 'lest a Luttrell succeed to the throne of England'.[17]

The Esmondes of Ballystranagh, County Wexford, had followed the Conqueror to England and Strongbow to Ireland, besides producing during the eleventh century a Saint Esmonde of Salisbury. During the sixteenth and seventeenth centuries they had an unfortunate propensity for being on the losing side, and suffered confiscations of land by Henry VIII, Elizabeth, James I and Cromwell. The most noted seventeenth-century Esmonde was Sir Laurence, a professional soldier who turned Protestant. He was made a baron and fought in the civil war on the royalist side. He was married to Elizabeth O'Flaherty, but he 'put her away', or she left him and went back to Connemara, taking with her their son, Thomas, lest he be brought up as a Protestant. Thomas fought in Charles I's army and was made a baronet in his father's lifetime. His father died in 1644 and, blood being thicker than holy water, left the family estates to him, entailed. Thomas scorned to inherit the title but did not disdain the property. This, however, he did not keep for long; he resisted Cromwell and in 1652 lost his whole estate. In the Restoration Settlement he got back, as an 'innocent papist', a niggardly 2,000 acres out of 30,000.

But he held only a fraction of those 2,000 acres, and the recovery of the remainder necessitated a protracted and complicated legal battle. Cromwell had granted the estate to his New Model Army general, George Monck. Under the Restoration Settlement, Sir Thomas Esmonde had been granted instead lands in Clare and Connaught, which he did not in the least want. There was, however, an acknowledgement of the right of his son Laurence, as an 'innocent Papist', to recover the Wexford lands, if he could, by legal action. This was easier said than done. Monck, as commander of the army, had done more than anyone to restore Charles II to the throne, for which he was created Duke of Albemarle. He had immense influence. However, nothing daunted, in 1676 Laurence Esmonde took out a suit of ejectment against the second duke, Christopher, and won it. But this was only the first step of litigation which would drag on for over thirty years.

Albemarle promptly got the Exchequer Court's judgement reversed on a Writ of Error, moved in and occupied the property by force. In 1688 Laurence Esmonde returned to the charge, persuaded the court to reaffirm his right and got possession. He died in that year, and was succeeded by his eldest son, also named Laurence, who was a minor and was educated in France from 1689 to 1692. This caused him to be indicted for foreign treason, but on the intervention of Queen Mary the indictment was stayed. However, taking advantage of his youth, inexperience and political embarrassments, the Earl of Bath, who had inherited Albemarle's interest 'by surprise and contrary to the apparent truth of the case', obtained possession of a moiety (half) of the property and, to hold it, pleaded that privilege of Parliament protected him against civil suits.

In 1699 Laurence Esmonde was again indicted for treason but one juryman withdrew so there was no verdict. The time limit for treason prosecutions having expired, he was troubled no more on that score; but in 1699 he had to break the entail of the estate in order to sell land to cover the costs of so much litigation. In 1703, however, no doubt in consequence of a tip-off and some good legal advice, he re-entailed the estate just before the first reading in the Commons of the anti-Popery Bill with its gavelling clauses. The estate was thus protected ever after from gavelling.

Bath died in 1701 and his interest passed to the Duke of Beaufort – more heavy metal for a plain country baronet to contend with. The duke also pleaded privilege of Parliament, to circumvent which in 1709 Esmonde persuaded a Protestant friend, Henry Brownrigge, to purchase on his behalf Beaufort's moiety, as well as other parts of the estate which had been sold in 1699. Brownrigge basely decided to hang on to them himself. What, Esmonde asked Sir Toby Butler, should he do now? Sir Toby advised:

> I think the best way is to bring a new ejectment [suit against Brownrigge] and it may be brought for the whole or for a moiety, and when Sir Laurence is in as of his ancient right, he may to fortify his ancient right get a release from Brownrigge . . . And I think taking such a release is not contrary to the Act against the Growth of Popery, for it is no new buying or purchasing, since Sir Laurence's title appears of record by a recovery he had formerly [in 1688] and was never since evicted in any legal trial.
>
> As for the lands which are not Sir Laurence's ancient right [i.e. those sold in 1699] all that can be done is that Brownrigge may make a lease of thirty-one years to Sir Laurence, at two-thirds the yearly rent of them, and then Sir Laurence will be entitled to the possession.

Sir Laurence seems in the end, after thirty-three years' litigation, to have prevailed, but at a cost which crippled his family for generations, forcing the sale of a great part of the estates.

He died in 1720 and his son, also Laurence, the fourth baronet, died unmarried in 1738. The estate then passed to an uncle, John, serving in the Spanish army, who died in the same year: then to another uncle, Walter, who died without issue.

From Walter it passed to James, a first cousin once removed, the seventh baronet. As a young man he had served in the Irish Brigade in France, but when his father was killed at the age of eighty-four by a fall when hunting, he had returned to Ireland to find a wife. He married the only daughter of a Colonel White, of Cromwellian descent, thereby recovering Esmonde land which had been forfeited a century earlier.

The family is remarkable, if not unique, in that no male and only one female Esmonde appears in the eighteenth century *Convert Rolls*.[18]

Wexford was a corn-growing county of smallish farms (forty acres was considered a comfortable holding) and no very large estates. It produced the best malting barley in Europe. In the early 1790s there were 242 malting houses in the county, nearly all run by Catholics; a hundred ships kept the Dublin distilleries supplied, and more plied to Britain and the Continent. With the Continent the Catholic gentry had strong links. The O'Tooles passed generation after generation into the French service: at one time seven O'Tooles were serving in the Irish Brigade. The Hays, Waddings and Suttons were deeply involved in commerce in France. Because farms were mainly tillage, there was none of the Whiteboy violence prevalent in Tipperary, one cause of which was the preference of landlords for large grazing farms which employed little labour and accommodated fewer tenants.[19]

It was a county of hard-fought elections, the fighting taking the form of endless challenges to would-be voters on the ground that they were not really Protestants. In an election for Wexford of Leigh *v.* Ram a voter named Percival was asked by Leigh's counsel, 'Are you a Protestant?' To which Percival replied, 'I look more like a Protestant than you do.' At this Leigh's counsel complained that he had been insulted (by the implication that he looked like a Papist): whereupon all the Leigh supporters walked out of the courthouse. They were persuaded next day to return, and evidence was given that Percival's deceased wife had been a Papist but that it 'had been doubted whether Percival was married or not'. Percival's vote was disallowed.

Next came John Goodall whose vote was also challenged on the ground that he had a Catholic wife. He said she had conformed before he married her, some eight years earlier. He was then asked if there had been earlier nuptials when she was still a Catholic.

'There was,' he replied in some confusion, 'a ceremony, or a sort of ceremony, but I did not look upon it as a marriage, and there was no consummation in consequence of it, nor even a ceremony of marriage, for I was drinking all the time.' The lady's honour was upheld by disallowing his vote.

John Devereux protested that he had been a Protestant churchgoer for fifty years; but his namesake Walter Devereux testified that he had known John for forty-five years, and had been at school with him, and had often seen him at Mass but never at church. So frequently did Walter give similar evidence that suspicion arises that he was on Leigh's payroll.

In the case of Thomas Rath, Leigh's counsel called a witness who deposed that Thomas and his brother Joseph were Papists married to Papists: he had often seen them at Mass. But Ram's counsel called the Reverend Andrew Hamilton who swore that the Raths were his parishioners, that he regarded them as Protestants and had often seen them at Holy Communion, 'though not as often as he would have wished.' But the same applied to all his parishioners: none were as regular communicants as he would have wished. So Rath was allowed to vote.

The gossipmongers must have enjoyed elections.[20]

The only Wexford family with pretensions to grandeur was that of Colclough (pronounced Cokelee), descended from a Staffordshire gentleman who for his military services to the Tudors was rewarded with the dissolved abbey of Tintern in the south-west of the county. His son, Sir Thomas Colclough, married twice – first to a Protestant whose Protestant children inherited Tintern; then to a Catholic for whose Catholic children he bought the 14,000 acre Duffry estate in the north of the county. Colcloughs fought on opposite sides in 1641 and the Duffry estate was confiscated by Cromwell, but over half was restored under Charles II. No Colclough took part in the Williamite war, being either too old or too young to fight.

The Protestant branch of the family ended with Sir Thomas's childless great-granddaughter Margaret. From her Tintern passed to Caesar Colclough of the Catholic Duffry line, whose mother was a Barnewall. As a Catholic he could not inherit Tintern from a Protestant, but he *did* inherit; he does not appear on *The Convert Rolls* and his younger brother remained Catholic. Presumably at his birth in 1696 it was assumed that Margaret, after twenty-three years of childless marriage, would have no children, and he was reared a Protestant so that he could add Tintern to Duffry.

Known as 'The Great Caesar', he was a very wealthy man. Obviously he was a Protestant with fingers crossed: he built a Catholic church and a school for both religions; in the early years of the eighteenth century when priests returning from Continental seminaries had better be inconspicuous, he provided many with discreet cover, in jobs about the Duffry estate.

As a landlord he was wildly popular, not least because of his enthusiasm for Gaelic games. He took a hurley team to England for an exhibition match before George III, wearing yellow sashes as their colours. The king got highly excited, exclaiming, 'Come on, the yellow-bellies!' – a term still applied to Wexford men.[21]

County Kilkenny was Butler country. In a list of landowners in 1775, the Catholic Robert Butler of Ballyragget drew £7,000 a year in rent, and other Catholic Butlers £5,500, out of a total rent-roll for the county of £134,000. It contained the best agricultural land in Ireland, and the Catholic interest was not so much in the gentry (apart from the Butlers) as in strong farmers. There was little Protestant settlement: even the Ponsonbys, pillars of the Protestant Ascendancy, had few Protestant tenants.[22] Neither the Whiteboys nor the rebels of 1798 had any success in County Kilkenny.

---

1   Calendar of State Papers, Dom., 1694-5, 135; RIA MSS, G 340; Annesley papers in PRONI (Public Record Office of Northern Ireland).

2   *Ibid.*

3   Nugent papers in PRONI.

4   Ida Grehan, *Irish Family Histories*, 146.

5   Arthur Young, *A Tour in Ireland*, 16-17, 37.

6   J. G. Simms, *Williamite Confiscations*, 76; Maureen Wall, *Catholic Ireland in the Eighteenth Century*, 80; Bellew family papers at Barmeath Castle.

7   Young, *op. cit.*, 9.

8   NLA, MS 13765, correspondence of ninth, tenth and eleventh Viscounts Gormanston.

9   Aubrey Gwynn, 'Gormanston Castle in Irish History', in *Studies*, 1942, 63.

10 Aubrey Gwynn, *op. cit.*; *A Short but Interesting History*, apparently by Father C. J. Dixon, in Gormanston family papers.

11 Countess of Fingall, *Seventy Years Young*, 245; *The Gormanston Foxes*, pamphlet in Gormanston family papers.

12 Simms, *Williamite Confiscations*, 75; Simms, *Irish Jacobites*, 133; Burke, *Peerage, Baronetage and Knightage*, 731-2; TCD MSS N 1, 3, 77-100; NLA MSS 8024 (1)-(6); Mary Rose Carty, *History of Killeen Castle*, 21-3; Countess of Fingall, *op. cit.*, 104.

13 Dalton, *King James's Irish Army List,* I, 24.

14 Simms, *Williamite Confiscations,* 138-9; Calendar of State Papers, Dom., 1697, 501; 1699-1700, 168; 1701-2, 148; Wall, *op. cit.,* 59; R. E. Parkinson, *History of the Grand Lodge of Ireland,* II, 315; Thomas Wyse, *Historical Sketch of the Late Catholic Association,* II, 63-76.

15 R. H. A. J. Everard, 'The Family of Everard', Part III, 23; Part IV, 33-41, in Patrick Melvin, *The Irish Genealogist,* VIII; TCD MSS N1 3.

16 Simms, *Williamite Confiscations,* 129; Eustace family papers in the possession of Mr Patrick Mansfield; Dalton, *op. cit.,* II, 413-4; TCD MSS N1 3.

17 8 Anne, Ch. 13, XXXVIII; TCD MSS N1 3; E. J. Bourke, 'The Luttrells of Luttrellstown', in *Journal of the Cork Historical and Archaeological Society,* 1921, XXVII, 65-9; Charles Chenevix Trench, *Portrait of a Patriot,* (Edinburgh, 1962), 246-9.

18 Esmonde family papers; NLI MSS 8516 (1), (3).

19 Kevin Whelan in T. P. Power and Kevin Whelan (eds.), *Endurance and Emergence,* 130-5, 147-8; Nicholas Furlong in Kevin Whelan, *Tintern Abbey, County Wexford,* 170-1.

20 David Goodall, 'All the Cooking that could be used: a County Wexford Election in 1754', in *The Past,* (Journal of the Céinsealaigh Historical Society of Wexford), 16-21.

21 Sean Cloney in Whelan, *op. cit.,* 19-25.

22 W. Nolan and Kevin Whelan (eds.), *Kilkenny History and Society,* 273-4.

6

Some Catholic Families in Munster

In contrast to Wexford, Tipperary was a county of big grazing estates. In 1775, of ninety-one estates with rent-rolls of over £1,000 a year, twenty-two were owned by Catholics, including some of the largest. (These did not include Kilcash, which by 1775 was no longer in Catholic hands.)

Theobald Butler, seventh Lord Cahir, having complied with William's first invitation to surrender in February 1689, had after sundry vicissitudes recovered his 10,724 profitable Irish acres by 'royal favour'. These passed intact to his only son, Thomas. Thomas had six sons, four of whom died young. James, the eldest, enjoyed the whole estate, with a rent-roll of £13,000 a year, for forty-two years. When the Catholic Relief Act of 1778 enabled Catholics to hold land on 999-year leases, he divided his estate into large farms on sixty-one-year leases, with provisos against sub-letting, and departed to live in France.

He died in 1786, succeeded briefly by a younger brother who died two years later; and then by a cousin, James, who was living on £30 a year in India; plus if, as seems probable, he was in the service of the East India Company, a substantial income from private trade and commissions and perks of all kinds. But James also died a few months after succeeding to title and estates, without even knowing his good fortune. He was succeeded, as twelfth Lord Cahir, by his distant cousin Richard, a Protestant.[1]

Another Catholic Butler landowner in Tipperary was the

sixteenth Baron Dunboyne, who recovered his 1,107 profitable Irish acres (nearly 2,000 statute acres) under the Articles of Limerick. He owned more land round Dunboyne in County Meath, but this was probably held for him by Protestant Butlers because it does not appear in the list of forfeited and restored estates. However, his grandson, Pierce, twentieth Lord Dunboyne, on his retirement from the French army, settled there in 1768.[2]

The Butlers of Kilcash were descended from the first Duke of Ormond's younger and Catholic brother, whose grandson Thomas was a colonel in King James's army, but thanks to the Articles of Limerick kept his castle with 8,000 acres on the southern slopes of Slievenamon. His wife, a daughter of the Earl of Clanrickard, known as Lady Iva, was famous for her beauty, her generosity and her courage in sheltering from the authorities sundry bishops and priests on the run. It must have been a grief to his parents when their son John conformed in 1739, thereby acquiring the whole estate and relegating his aged father to the position of tenant-for-life.

With this Kilcash ceased to be a Catholic-owned estate, occasioning the famous Irish poem *Caoine Cill Cais,* 'Lament for Kilcash', by Father John Lane, a protégé of Lady Iva. Translated by Frank O'Connor, two stanzas read:

> What shall we do for timber?
> The last of the woods is down.
> Kilcash and the house of its glory
> And the bell of the house are gone,
> The spot where that lady waited
> Who shamed all women for grace
> When earls came sailing to greet her,
> And Mass was said in the place.
> I beseech you of Mary and Jesus

That the great come home again,
With long dances danced in the garden
Fiddle music and mirth among men,
That Kilcash, the home of our fathers,
Be lifted on high again,
And from that to the deluge of waters
In bounty and peace remain.

In 1758 the third Duke of Ormond died childless. The dukedom became extinct, but the earldom of Ormond and the estates, including Kilkenny Castle, passed to John of Kilcash. He died childless in 1766. As he died a Protestant, a Catholic could not inherit land from him; but his heir, his first cousin John Butler of Garryricken in County Kilkenny, had prudently conformed two years earlier. John of Garryricken and his Catholic father, Walter, moved into Kilkenny Castle in 1766. Probably John was the owner: he was known as 'Jack of the Castle' and his father as a Catholic could not have inherited it from a Protestant. The castle was ripe for restoration, and in 1769 Jack of the Castle married a Protestant heiress with money to restore it. Clearly Jack was one of those Catholics who 'pretended heresy for worldly reason.' He and his wife attended Holy Communion in St Canice's Protestant cathedral twice a year, and he accompanied his father to Mass in the castle chapel on the other fifty Sundays. He lived it up, drinking and gambling, and died at the age of fifty-five.[3] His sister, Lady Eleanor Butler, was one of the 'Ladies of Llangollen'.*

---

*   Lady Eleanor Butler and Miss Sarah Ponsonby created a great scandal in 1781 by eloping and living together. They survived the scandal and their relationship became generally accepted by a wide circle of friends, including the Duke of Wellington. They were known as 'the ladies of Llangollen' after the village in which they lived in Wales.

The Catholic Butlers were no less prominent in ecclesiastical affairs, and the eighteenth century has been called 'the Butler era' in the Archdioceses of Cashel and Emly. Dr Christopher Butler of Kilcash was Archbishop from 1712 to 1757, a very long innings, seeing many changes from creeping about in disguise to being recognised and honoured by all. He was followed by Dr James Butler of the Dunboyne branch of the family from 1757 to 1774, and by another Dr James Butler of the Ballyragget branch in County Kilkenny, from 1774 to 1791. All three were strong supporters of the government and frequently denounced the Whiteboys from their pulpits. John Butler was Bishop of Cork from 1767 to 1790, a tall, lean, piratical-looking man with a patch over one eye and a tight black wig, a rather formidable figure. At the age of nearly seventy, through the early death of a twelve-year-old nephew, he unexpectedly became the twenty-second Baron Dunboyne. The Dunboyne branch had run out of young male heirs, and his duty to his family required that he beget some, and quickly too; while his duty to the church required that he do nothing of the kind. Family loyalty prevailed: he conformed and promptly married. The Pope was terribly put out, as well he might be. But despite the former bishop's best endeavours, no heir was produced; and he died again a Catholic in 1800. In his will he left the Dunboyne estates in County Meath to Maynooth College for the education of Catholic priests.[4]

The Mathew family were Welsh and first came to Ireland in the fifteenth century. They were much intermarried with the Butlers, and acquired three estates in County Tipperary, at Thomastown (near Tipperary town), Thurles and Annfield (near Thurles). Most of them were called George or Thomas or Theobald, which makes for great confusion.

George Mathew of Thurles married the Catholic widow of

Viscount Thurles, mother of the first Duke of Ormond. She brought up all her ten children as Catholics, except the eldest, who became duke. Their son George Mathew, described as an 'obstinate Papist', was thus half-brother to the Protestant Duke of Ormond whose Tipperary estates he managed. He married the well-endowed widow of the sixth Lord Cahir. Doubtless with the help for his half-brother, he acquired under the Restoration Settlement some 6,000 acres at Thomastown, built a commodious house and died in 1689 from a surfeit of claret. His elder son had died young, so the only other son, Theobald (Toby), inherited the whole estate. Having been commissioned into Sutherland's Horse, Toby was outlawed; but he was adjudged under the Articles of Limerick and recovered his estates. He died in 1711, leaving them to his son who became famous or notorious as Grand George.

He was very grand, on an income from rents of £8,000 a year. He enlarged the house and surrounded it with a 1,500 acre park complete with arboretum, a herd of deer and 'water brought at no small charge from a great distance.' His hobby was hospitality. His house could accommodate forty guests, and it was his foible that each should do his own thing in his own time. He showed each guest on arrival to his apartment:

> This is your castle. Here you are to command as absolutely as in your own house; you may breakfast, dine and sup here whenever you please, and invite such guests as may be most agreeable to you.

There was a large dining-room where guests could eat if they desired company; a coffee-house; and a detached building furnished as a tavern, complete with waiter and buxom barmaids. There was a system of bells to summon whichever servant a guest required. The only amusement banned was gambling, of which Grand George had a horror. Jonathan Swift stayed four months. One hopes his host found this equally enjoyable.

In 1709 Grand George conformed, probably lest he be obliged to gavel his estate with two younger brothers. His son, Theobald, married a cousin, Mary Ann Mathew of Thurles. Theobald died in 1736 leaving a three-year-old son whose guardian was his maternal uncle, George Mathew of Thurles. Two years later the little boy was drowned in the Thomastown lake on Holy Innocents' Day. There were ugly rumours that a wicked uncle might have had something to do with it, since with his nephew's death the Thomastown estate passed to him. The boy's mother (the uncle's sister) is said to have laid a curse on the Thurles branch of the family, that no male would ever inherit. And none did.

Theobald Mathew of Thurles – elder brother of the George who had built Thomastown – got only 800 acres under the Restoration Settlement. He does not seem to have been outlawed (but the lists for the county are incomplete), and died in 1699. He was succeeded by his eldest son, known as Major George Mathew. He is not listed by Dalton in *King James's Irish Army List*, but according to family tradition had been King James's High Sheriff for Tipperary and had raised a troop of dragoons quartered at Thurles. He was not attainted, perhaps because of the Ormond influence. He was constantly under suspicion of Jacobite goings-on, twice arrested and released, but still licensed to bear arms. During the Jacobite rebellion of 1715 he was lodged, without trial, in Clonmel jail with his son-in-law, John Ryan of Inch. In 1699 he inherited the Thurles estates, ungavelled: they passed to his only son, George, in 1725; and to George's only son, also George, in 1734; and in 1738 there was added to them the much larger Thomastown estate when the last George's ward was drowned.

The last George died without issue in 1760 and the Thurles estate, plus the Thomastown estate, all went to his second cousin Thomas, owner of an estate at Annfield, whose wife had brought him £40,000 in a marriage settlement. Thomas of Annfield was a Freemason, becoming Provincial Grand Master in 1757. He was an extremely rich man and determined to remain so, conforming in 1755 rather than gavel with three younger brothers. Of these, George joined the Irish Brigade and fought at Fontenoy. He then sailed off to join Prince Charles Edward in Scotland but was captured at sea. He would probably have been hanged for treason had he not been able to show King Louis XV's commission.[5]

In 1761 Thomas Mathew stood for the county at the general election, his opponent being an evangelical Protestant whose name, Sir Thomas Maude, was a by-word for bigotry. Mathew won, but Maude made the routine appeal of a defeated candidate to the High Sheriff. He alleged that Mathew's agent, Thomas Prendergast, was unqualified to vote since his wife was a Catholic and he had been seen to pray with Father Hennessy of Clonmel. This led to a duel between Prendergast and Maude's agent in which Prendergast was killed. Maude also alleged that 'many Papists assembled from different parts of the country and greatly intimidated my voters.' Many of Mathew's voters, he alleged, were unqualified because they were Papists or of dubious conformity, or under the influence of Papist landlords. The High Sheriff cravenly returned both candidates, leaving it to the House of Commons to decide which of them was properly elected. Inevitably the Commons decided for Maude. But Francis Mathew, Thomas's son, who was said to have 'come in by Papist influence', retained his seat for Tipperary borough.[6] Thomas's crypto-Catholicism is further indicated by the fact that his granddaughter was Nano Nagle, foundress of the

Presentation Order of nuns.

The Ryans of Inch, near Thurles, owned about 1,000 acres in 1691 which by prudent purchases had been increased to 5,000 before the anti-Popery Act of 1704 made it illegal for Catholics to buy land. The money for the purchases came from commerce and from shares in a privateer. Inch House, built by John Ryan in the seventeenth century, was the first in the county with a slate roof, small slates held together by oak pegs set in mortar. They kept clear of the Williamite war − Daniel, who died in 1692, was probably too old for it, and his son John, born in 1690, was certainly too young, so none of their land was confiscated. Since the Ryans' own Inch estate of about 5,000 acres had been entailed before 1703, it was safe from gavelling. But there was another, slightly larger property leased from Thomas Mathew of Annfield − for 999 years which made it highly discoverable. The easy solution to the difficulty would have been for the second Daniel Ryan, born in 1720, to conform; but he preferred to lay up for himself treasures in heaven while taking prudent steps for the safeguarding of those on earth. This he did with the collusion of a powerful and trusty Protestant friend, Amyas Bushe, High Sheriff of Kilkenny. Daniel Ryan took from Bushe a short-term loan on the security of the estate, and defaulted on the repayment. Bushe then took him to court and gained possession of the estate, on which, however, the Ryans continued to live, farm and take all rents and profits. It was indeed a gentlemen's agreement and, like a gentleman, Bushe's heir returned it to Ryan's heir as soon as the relaxation of the Penal Laws made it possible for Catholics to hold land on 999-year leases.

That is the Ryan family legend − supported by some indirect evidence. In his long and detailed will Daniel Ryan makes no mention of any real estate. Why should he? Part of his land was entailed and so could not be left to anyone but his eldest son;

the rest of it belonged to Amyas Bushe. But his son, John, making a will in 1777 directed that his interest in the 999-year Mathew lease be sold 'as soon as may be' – which surely means as soon as it was safe for a Catholic to own to such a long lease, which it was a year later. Moreover Daniel Ryan left to his younger sons, one in the Spanish and one in the Austrian army, £800 and £500 respectively to be forfeit if they 'molest or disturb' John 'for any further fortune, estate or interest'; that is to say, if they attempted to discover this arrangement. Finally, a portrait of Amyas Bushe hung in Inch House until 1982, and now hangs in Arthur Ryan's house in New Zealand.

Unfortunately Daniel Ryan was extravagant and a bad manager, and seems to have handed over the running of the place, several years before he died, to his eldest son, John, who was worse. John sold £3,000 of trees, and in his will directed that all his livestock, as well as his interest in the Mathew lease, be sold to clear his debts. He died childless and his brother George, a colonel in the Spanish service, came home from Peru to enjoy the fatted calf, but found it all skin and bone. The leased land had been sold, and of the £1,400 a year rentals from the Inch estate, after payment of debts, annuities, jointures and dowries, he was left with a miserable £194 a year. As for Inch House, the contents included:

17^1/2 leather bottom and other old chairs;
six darned table cloths;
sixteen china plates and dishes, all cracked;
fourteen wine glasses worm fashion and three broken decanters;
twenty-one china bowls in five pieces and two spoutless teapots;
nine useless candle moulds;

half a barrel of feathers and some yarn;

a rotten plover-net and tackling;

an air-pump and a microscope both out of order;

a string stram without strings;

a close-stool chair and two white chamberpots, cracked;

the adventures of Moll Hackabout in four prints glazed and framed;

a stand with several books in English and French;

an old saddle.

Stock

an old cur-bitch and nine pups in the stables;

an old carpenter in the workhouse;

an old woman and a greyhound in the kitchen;

seven unmerciful widows on my back and a lawsuit about the widow's dowry or thirds.

Clearly the gallant colonel had to marry money, without delay; which he did.[7]

The Everards of Fethard were not quite as grand as the Butlers with whom they were much intermarried, but grander than the *arrivistes*, Mathews. Sir John Everard, a captain in Purcell's Horse, fought at the Boyne and was killed at Aughrim, being unable to claim benefit of the Articles. His wife, a daughter of Lord Cahir, died soon after him, leaving their only child, Redmond, the fourth baronet, aged two. He was brought up by a Protestant Butler relative as a Protestant. In 1702 a private Act of Parliament restored to trustees for the twelve-year-old boy his father's forfeited estates, 5,901 statue acres worth £1,307 a year in rents. At the ripe age of twenty-one he became an MP, first for Kilkenny, then for Fethard.

After Queen Anne's death in 1714, Sir Redmond became an

ardent Jacobite, and spent most of the rest of his life in France, in and out of the Old Pretender's court at St Germaine, on the fringe of every Jacobite plot for the next twenty-seven years. 'The little knight' as he was called (though he was a baronet) was never really trusted as he could not hold his tongue. He was also hopelessly unbusinesslike and, a permanent absentee landlord, frittered away nearly all his estate. He may well have become a Catholic, but of that there is no evidence. There was something essentially silly and feckless about the little knight. After his death without issue in 1742, the Everards of Fethard were of little account – small Catholic landowners, French officers, even a glazier, an apothecary and sundry householders in Fethard town.[8] A branch of the Everard family emigrated to Holland and are still there, still Catholic, and keenly interested in their Irish roots.

The McCarthys of Spring House, Kilshane, near Tipperary town, and the Keatings of Garanlad, were described by Arthur Young as 'two of the greatest farmers that ever were in Ireland.' Denis McCarthy farmed 10,000 good acres stocked with 8,000 sheep, 2,000 lambs, 550 bullocks, 80 fat cows, 180 horses and a labour force of 150-200. Only 200 acres were tillage. He owned little land: most of his vast farm was on thirty-one-year leases, renewed again and again.

Sir Denis McCarthy had settled at Kilshane and built Spring House in the late seventeenth century. The land seems to have belonged to his forebears but had passed in the Restoration Settlement to the Duke of Ormond, from whom he leased it. In the early eighteenth century he leased a lot more, building the estate up. His son, Justin, was father-in-law of Daniel Ryan of Inch, with whom he had many business dealings over the years, buying and selling hundreds of sheep and cattle.

Justin's son, Denis, was the McCarthy whose farming Arthur Young admired. Another English visitor, Thomas Campbell, admired no less his hospitality:

> There was no constraint in the article of wine, nor
> indeed in any other. There was as much ease as in
> the house of an English duke. The eldest daughter
> is married to a colonel in the Imperial [Austrian]
> service, the eldest son is an officer in the same
> service . . . At meals we were regaled with bag-
> pipes . . . After supper I for the first time drank
> whiskey-punch, the taste of which is harsh and
> austere, and the smell worse than the taste. The
> spirit is very fierce and wild, requiring seven times
> water to tame and subdue it.

Two of Denis's nephews were captains in the service of the
Honourable East India Company under Clive and Warren
Hastings. Neither returned home as nabobs, dying in their
thirties, whether of malaria, blackwater fever, dysentery, typhus,
cirrhosis of the liver, surfeit of claret or the pestilential climate
of Bengal.[9]

The head of this great sept, Donogh McCarthy, fourth Earl
of Clancarty, fared less well. He was born in 1669. While he was
still a boy, his father died and his mother, a Protestant, sent him
to Oxford to be brought up as a Protestant by Dr Fell, Dean
of Christ Church. His uncle Justin, Lord Mountcashel, evidently
subscribed to the contemporary jingle:

> I do not love thee, doctor Fell,
> The reason why I cannot tell.
> But this alone I know full well,
> I do not love thee, doctor Fell.

He extracted his nephew from Oxford and married him, aged not quite sixteen, to the eleven-year-old Lady Elizabeth Spencer, daughter of Charles II's Secretary of State the Earl of Sunderland. The happy couple settled down at Macroom until 1689 when James II, having fled from England, landed at Kinsale. The earl became a Catholic and raised Lord Clancarty's regiment of foot for the king's service. He or his men were alleged to have allowed Jacobite zeal to overcome discretion: not only did he lend his castles at Blarney and Macroom to be used as prisons for interned Protestants (fair enough, they had to be put somewhere), but they unlawfully commandeered a horse from a butcher in Mallow. The judge of assize ordered the animal to be restored to its owner, whereupon the earl and a section of his men tossed the butcher in a blanket till he fell on the pavement and fatally cracked his skull – an outrage that would cost his lordship dear.

Clancarty was captured at the fall of Cork and imprisoned in the Tower of London. In 1694 he escaped, leaving in his bed a periwig-block with his wig on it and a paper pinned to the wig: 'The block must answer for me.' He got away to France and commanded a troop of Horse Guards for King James until the Treaty of Ryswick in 1697.

In 1698 he ventured to London to see his wife after their long separation, but was arrested and again imprisoned. Six months later the king pardoned him but his 81,000 acre estate in County Cork with a rent-roll of £9,000 had been forfeited, subject to annuities for his wife and brother. He did not lack influence, and great efforts were made by his father-in-law and others to have this forfeiture reversed; but he was damned by the Grand Jury of County Cork, who protested against any leniency being shown him; for, they said, he hated the English, had treated Protestants abominably and there was no chance of Cork being planted with English so long as he was at large there: 'The people swear that they will go to the Indies.' Clancarty's pardon was made conditional on his leaving the country and swearing never to take up arms against the Protestant succession. Sustained by a pension of £300 a year, he and his wife retired to Hamburg and lived in a modest way on an island at the mouth of the Elbe. He died in 1734.

Clancarty's eldest son was a commodore in the British navy. He should have inherited the family estates since they were entailed and only his father's life-interest could be forfeited for 'treason'. But the estates had been divided among so many people that the Ministry, while privately recognising the justice of his claim, found that removing the present proprietors after forty years' occupancy was too difficult. He was told to seek his own legal remedy; but when he did so, the British House of Commons passed a resolution declaring all lawyers acting for him to be public enemies. His case had to be abandoned. He remained in the navy for several years, bitterly resentful, and was made captain of a first rate ship of the line, when war broke out in 1741. He then threw up his command, went to France, and pledged his support to the Pretender. On a pension of £1,000 a year from Louis XV, he vegetated for the next fifty-five years at Boulogne, 'within sight of the cliffs of the country where he could never set foot.' He gave weekly parties for British people passing through, at which he spread the good word and denounced the government for its treatment of him. The Duchess of Marlborough left him a legacy of £20,000. As he could not himself go to England, he sent his wife to claim it for him; and that was the last he saw of his wife and his legacy.[10]

The Keatings, of Garranlad north-west of Clonmel, farmed on an even bigger scale than the McCarthys, having about 17,000 acres of leased land stocked with 3,000 cattle, 16,300 sheep and 300 horses. By the 1770s they had conformed, but their kinsmen of Knockogh, west of Cahir, remained staunchly Catholic. Robert Keating of Knockogh, whose grandfather had been adjudged under the Articles of Limerick, was a big landowner and farmer and a close friend of Lord Cahir. Four of his brothers were priests, and his brother-in-law was a Father Nicholas Sheehy.

Geoffrey Keating, whose two brothers were killed at the Boyne and Aughrim, went to France with Sarsfield and rose to be a major in Walsh's. His wife, a daughter of Thady Quinn of Adare in County Limerick remained in Ireland. In 1696 he took leave to go and see her. Travelling through London in disguise, he was spotted and imprisoned in the Tower; but was then allowed to visit his wife on parole. Having reached Adare, he resigned his French commission and decided to stay on land which was his wife's share of the Quinn estates. But one day there arrived a lieutenant and a squad of soldiers with many apologies and a warrant for his arrest for involvement in a Jacobite plot. Geoffrey followed the young officer to Limerick, on parole, and then to Dublin, where the case against him fell through because all the prosecution witnesses retracted their evidence. So he lived and farmed at Baybush in County Limerick until his death in 1741. Of his four sons, one stayed at Baybush, farming the estate, and the others went off to the Irish Brigade. Others of the family went sugar-planting in Mauritius and St Domingue (Haiti). One, who was a Freemason, prospered as a silk merchant in Dublin.[11]

The fertile country round Nenagh in north Tipperary was owned mainly by Cromwellian magnificoes – de Warrenne Waller, Sadleir, Minchin, Bailly. The only Catholic landowners of note were the O'Mearas. Thady O'Meara's estate was forfeited in 1690 but he pleaded the Articles of Limerick and the Trustees of Forfeited Estates restored Lissiniskey, with 2,254 profitable

Richard Talbot, Earl and Duke of Tyrconnell
English School, seventeenth century
(National Gallery of Ireland)

*Thomas Butler
of Kilcash
Portrait by James
Latham in Kilkenny
Castle
(By kind permission of
the Office of Public
Works and GPA* Irish
Arts Review)

*Sir Charles Whyte
of Leixlip
Portrait by Garret
Morphy
(Private Collection)*

Captain Henry MacDermot, of the Irish Brigade in the British army
and the Connaught Rangers in the Peninsular War
Photograph by Mr Patrick Glynn
(By kind permission of Felicity, Madam MacDermot)

Myles MacDermot, of Coolavin
Photograph by Mr Patrick Glynn
(By kind permission of Felicity, Madam MacDermot)

Patrick Nagle, of Annakissy, County Cork. He was the nephew of Nano Nagle, founder of the Presentation Order of nuns, pioneer of women's education; and cousin of Edmund Burke. He evidently does not take very seriously the Penal Law prohibiting Catholics from carrying arms.
Portrait by Hunter; photographed by Pádraig Ó Flannabhra, Nenagh
(By kind permission of Brigadier W. S. Hickie)

Charles O'Conor of Belanagare, 'The Antiquarian' Photograph by Mr Patrick Glynn (By kind permission of Mr Pyers O'Conor Nash)

Hugh O'Conor, of the Spanish Army, Knight of Calatrava Photograph by Mr Patrick Glynn (By kind permission of Mr Pyers O'Conor Nash)

Carolan's Harp
Photograph by Mr Patrick Glynn

*Maurice 'Hunting Cap'
O'Connell
(By kind permission of
Sir Maurice James
O'Connell, Bart., and
the Office of Public
Works)*

*Daniel Charles,
Count O'Connell
The last Colonel of the
Irish Brigade
(By kind permission of
Sir Maurice James
O'Connell, Bart., and
the Office of Public
Works)*

acres, to his son Daniel. At the same time William Meara and John Meara, perhaps his brothers, had their estates restored at Kylemore and Lisbony, near Nenagh. Lissiniskey remained in O'Meara hands all through the penal days, but the family seems to have succumbed to insolvency near the end of the eighteenth century. The root of their financial problems may perhaps be guessed from a remark by a visitor in 1778 that O'Meara 'was not inferior in hospitality to any of his ancestors.'[12]

Increasing Catholic confidence and the economic miracle after mid-century produced a new Catholic interest, strong tenant farmers, prosperous and upwardly mobile, of which the Scullys of Kilfeakle in County Tipperary are an example. Jeremiah Scully from County Longford settled near Cashel in the 1690s. His son Roger leased in all about 4,000 acres near Tipperary town. He bequeathed £6,000 in cash and £14,000 worth of leased land to his son James, who by 1782 had acquired a further 1,855 acres and a fine house, on leases of thirty-one years, three lives and 999 years. His livestock were valued at £14,000 (including Bakewell rams imported from England), his personal property at £40,000. He sowed rye-grass and clover, drained bogs, hunted, raced and steeplechased. His son Denys was a close friend of Daniel O'Connell, his grandson High Sheriff of the county. And his grandfather had started from nothing, a blow-in from County Longford.[13]

Tipperary, Limerick and Cork were the counties where Jacobitism lingered longest: many of Sarsfield's Wild Geese came from there. About the last practising Irish Jacobite was Sir John Cotter, of Anngrove near Thurles, a relation by marriage of the Mathews. His Jacobitism was not very dangerous: he had not the nature of a plotter but delighted in tirades against the House of Hanover and in publicly baiting sheriffs, magistrates and the like. He went too far and in 1720 he was executed. The ostensible crime for which he suffered was not treason, but the rape of his own mistress, a fair Quakeress named Betsy Squibb. But it was widely believed that he could have raped her to his heart's content had he not been a practising Jacobite.[14]

The failure of the '45 reduced Jacobitism from deadly danger to romantic lost cause. The death of the 'Old Pretender' in 1766, the Pope's refusal to recognise his son as King of England and Bonnie Prince Charlie's slide into drink-sodden disillusion gave it the *coup de grâce*. Catholics were now free in conscience to recognise George III as their king, as most men of property, the bishops and the clergy did. But the Jacobite danger was replaced by what amounted to almost a rural insurrection in south Tipperary.

The Whiteboys' grievances were economic. In the 1750s, with the removal of export duties on beef and pork products and on wool, livestock farming boomed. There was a widespread shift from tillage to pasture, and as tillage farms became scarcer, the small farmers who wanted them had to pay more in rent. When leases ran out, landowners tended to renew them by 'cant' (auction), regardless of the merit and circumstances of the outgoing tenant. So long as there was plenty of common land, this was a safety valve; but when landlords (as in England) enclosed common land, the cottier had nowhere to keep his cow or a couple of pigs. Finally there was the grievance of Catholics having to pay tithes to the Church of Ireland rector, and pay them not on pasture but on tillage, which bore more heavily on the small farmer than on the well-to-do. Except for the monstrous inequity of tithes, there was no sectarian element in Whiteboyism. Indeed, among the first victims of the Whiteboys were large Catholic tenant farmers on the estates of Lord Cahir. There were Protestant Whiteboys.[15]

The troubles started in 1761 with the Whiteboys, wearing

over their clothes the uniform of a white shirt which gave them their name, threatening tithe proctors (collectors) with death, flogging and house-burning, levelling the walls and fences of enclosed land, maiming horses and cattle, destroying tithe crops and administering oaths of secrecy. Intimidation was emphasised by the erection of gallows and the digging of graves. A centre of Whiteboy activity was the parish of Clogheen, the priest of which was a gentleman of good family and comfortable means, Father Nicholas Sheehy.

The reaction of Protestant zealots such as Sir Thomas Maude was predictably paranoid. The Whiteboy terror, they insisted, was Jacobitism and Popery militant, bent on destroying the Protestant religion, the authority of the magistrates, the very constitution of the kingdom. The Reverend John Hewetson, a magistrate very active in the cause of law and order, described one of their operations:

> for the most part mounted on horses pressed or stolen from their neighbours, headed by officers decked with white sashes and hats fringed with white ribbon, armed with guns, swords and pistols, marching in a military form through the country always preceded by the music of bagpipes or the sounding of horns.

Such a degree of military organisation suggested, nay *proved* the presence of French officers among them. Whatever the Catholic hierarchy might say – and the Butler bishops were particularly strong in their denunciation of these villains – depend upon it, Popish priests inspired and organised them. Catholic-owned cattle and horses might be houghed (ham-strung), Catholic-owned walls pulled down and crops destroyed, but Whiteboyism, they insisted, was a *Papist* terror. The county was awash with arms; they 'expected a person from abroad to lead them . . . Nothing less than an absolute rising was fully intended.' And the Romish priest most guilty was Father Sheehy of Clogheen.

In 1762 zealous magistrates crammed the jails with suspects, and three were hanged for houghing cattle. Others were publicly whipped on little or no evidence, including a gentleman, George Everard, at Clogheen. The Whiteboys reacted with greater violence – whipping a tithe-proctor, cropping one man's ears, slitting the tongue of another for speaking up against them, attacking the houses of those who paid tithes. A farmer was 'terribly abused' for taking the lease of a farm by cant. 300 Whiteboys attacked a troop of Light Dragoons taking a prisoner to jail.[16]

To what extent, if at all, Father Sheehy was involved is not known. Probably he thought, and even spoke, like the citizens of Cashel whom Thomas Campbell questioned on the subject:

> They did not, without an artful and wily address, discover their sentiments on the Whiteboys. They always took care to say that they were wrong in what they were about, at the same time they were insinuating that others were more at fault than they.

Dr John Curry, one of the founders of the Catholic Committee, wrote of Sheehy:

> The man was giddy and officious, but not ill-meaning, with something of a Quixotic cast of mind towards relieving all those within his district whom he fancied to be injured or oppressed.

Over the centuries he is instantly recognisable as the socially-concerned clergyman whom crusty Establishment figures find so irritating. The authorities, therefore, and notably Sir Thomas Maude, resolved to bring him to book. He had already been indicted for unlawful assembly, for tendering unlawful oaths, for intending to levy insurrection, and for assaulting John Bridge; but had not surrendered himself for trial. In February 1765 he was indicted for high treason and £300 offered for his arrest.

He wrote to the Secretary of State offering to surrender himself for trial in Dublin, as he could not expect justice in County Tipperary. This was agreed. In Dublin he was well treated and released on bail until his trial, which did not take place until February 1766. The prosecution evidence was so conflicting and unconvincing that he was acquitted. He was then re-arrested on a charge by Maude, Parson Hewetson and John Bagwell, MP, for murdering John Bridge who, they asserted, was a Whiteboy informer who had threatened to implicate him. Sheehy was brought back to Clonmel, bound on horseback, and the same disreputable witnesses testified to these new absurdities. The preposterous tenor of the prosecution evidence was that the Whiteboys would 'serve the French king, conquer Ireland and make it their own.' Bridge had been murdered as an informer and 'enemy to the French king.' Robert Keating of Knockogh, Father Sheehy's brother-in-law, a much respected Catholic landowner, was prepared to testify that Sheehy had spent the whole night of Bridge's murder at his house at Knockogh; but he was disposed of by a trumped-up charge of murder during the 'battle of Newmarket' when the Light Dragoons were attacked. For this he was taken to Kilkenny for trial and acquitted because there was no evidence whatsoever against him – but by that time Father Sheehy had been hanged, his head stuck on a spear over Clonmel jail gate. If ever there was a judicial murder, it was this. Three months later three equally innocent Catholic gentlemen, including Father Sheehy's cousin Edward ('Buck') Sheehy, were also executed for the murder of Bridge.[17]

Popular tradition always pointed to Sir Thomas Maude as the principal persecutor of Father Sheehy. Local legend told of an unbearable stench coming from Maude's deathbed, and his screams of physical and mental agony – obviously the devil claiming his own.

What made Tipperary, or rather south Tipperary, so different from other counties was the bitterness between Catholic and Protestant gentry. The Maudes and Bagwells regarded Father Sheehy and his cousin Buck Sheehy and Robert Keating not merely as traitors, but as traitors to their class. Lord Cahir was supposed to be sympathetic to the Whiteboys, an absurd accusation; Lord Dunboyne and Robert Butler of Ballyragget had to go to Dublin and tender bail on Whiteboy-related charges. Bagwell and Parson Hewetson compiled a black list based on 'information sworn to against all the leading Catholic gentry of the county.' This persecution resulted in a marked increase in conversions in the 1760s.

In 1774 Catholics were permitted to swear allegiance to George III and, advised by Archbishop James Butler of Cashel, most of the Tipperary gentry did so. This had an effect on Protestant attitudes, as did Dr Butler's excommunication of Whiteboys for 'drawing on us and on our holy religion the odium of a mild government.' It was observed that the Catholic clergy were attacked for levying marriage fees, and this too had a good effect even on the Maudes and Bagwells.

The whole atmosphere in County Kilkenny, fertile agricultural land held by strong Catholic farmers, was inimicable to Whiteboyism. It was regarded as an alien import, and Whiteboys were known disparagingly as 'Munstermen'. 500 of them attacked the house and estate village of Robert Butler of Ballyragget, and were driven off by the spirited defence of the villagers, Catholics to a man. Sometimes known as 'Rightboys', the Whiteboys were not entirely eliminated in south Tipperary; but by the 1780s they were reduced from near rebellion to mere nuisance.

They made little impact on County Waterford, base of the large and powerful Power (or De la Poer) family, generally Catholics. The Powers had mixed fortunes in the seventeenth century. Richard, first Earl of Tyrone and sixth Baron Poer of Corochmore, was brought up by his guardian as a Protestant. He none the less raised for King James a regiment of foot which defended Waterford, but not very well. With him was his younger son, James, who afterwards claimed to have been held there by parental authority though his heart was with William and Mary. When Waterford surrendered and the garrison was allowed to march off to Cork, James went over to the Williamite camp. At Cork the earl, a military tyro, had the misfortune to confront the greatest soldier of his day, the future Duke of Marlborough. His defence did not last long, and when the garrison surrendered, he was taken off to London and lodged in the Tower, where he died in 1690. His outlawry was reversed by royal pardon to save the estate for his elder son, John, who also took the Williamite side and died unmarried in 1693. The next earl was the younger brother, James, who died in 1694 leaving all his property to his only child, Catherine. For lack of male heirs, the earldom became extinct.

The barony, however, passed to a distant cousin, John Power of Monylargy, whose father Piers had been outlawed in 1641 for rebellion against Charles I. John, 'known as Lord Power', was an ardent Jacobite, a colonel in the army and Mayor of Limerick. He went with Sarsfield to France and distinguished himself in the Irish Brigade. Over the years, however, his Jacobitism became less ardent; and when William made overtures to him in 1702 he had half a mind (despite the promise of promotion to Major General in the French army) to go home and make friends with the mammon of unrighteousness. The death of the king in 1703 'retarded his interest', but he petitioned Queen Anne for the reversal of his outlawry and was supported in this by the Duke of Ormond on the grounds that 'during the late calamitous times he had been kind and serviceable to divers Protestants, especially in Limerick during the siege, he being Mayor there.' His outlawry was not reversed, but he was given a pension of £300 a year and employment under the King of Portugal, Britain's ally; while his son Henry was brought up by Ormond as a Protestant and kept beyond reach of want by a pension of £550 a year. John was murdered by his footman in Paris in 1721.

In 1717 Henry petitioned George I to the effect that he was entitled by entail to the estates of the Earl of Tyrone. Resolved 'to remain true both to the Protestant religion and to the succession of the illustrious house of Hanover,' he was not barred, as his father had been, by his religion from inheriting land from a Protestant. The king passed his petition to the Lord Lieutenant for investigation. Immediately there was a terrific uproar from Catherine, daughter of the last Earl of Tyrone, whose estates she had inherited, and from her husband, Sir Marcus Beresford. They pointed out that Henry Power's father John and grandfather Piers had both been attainted for treason. They opined that Henry's design was obviously to reverse these attainders:

> Whereby others in the same circumstances may be
> encouraged to make the like attempts which . . .

would very much tend to weaken the title of the Protestants of the kingdom who hold their estates under the Acts of Settlement and Explanation and the sales of the late Trustees [of Forfeited Estates], and prove of dangerous consequences to the Protestant interests.

The Irish Parliament thought likewise, making the point in an address to the king that:

the greater part of the titles which your British and Protestant subjects have to their estates are derived from the attainders in 1641 and 1688 . . . And this was so well understood that no outlawry of any person guilty of the rebellion of 1641 was reversed until the government of the late Earl of Tyrconnell, about the year 1687, when the design to extirpate the British and Protestant interests, and to establish Popery as the national religion, was openly and avowedly declared.

So although the estate should have passed to Henry under the entail, because whatever his father and grandfather had done he was guiltless of treason, his claim never had a fair hearing.[18]

There was, however, one branch of the Power family which remained Catholic and prosperous. Piers Power and his brother Richard, remote untitled cousins of earls and barons, had been transplanted by Cromwell to Galway and granted an estate of 4,000 fairly barren acres at Ballydrinny. In 1678 Richard's son, Edmund, returned to Waterford and leased from the Duke of Ormond, for three lives, the 3,000 acre estate of Gurteen, good land just five miles downstream from Clonmel and across the river Suir. (The duke retained the game rights and timber.) Although this was Power country, Gurteen itself had never been a Power property. It was a far better proposition than the Galway estate which, however, the Powers did not sell until 1775. Edmund died in 1686 and his son John, who as a Catholic was no doubt Jacobite at heart, remained neutral during the war, as was only prudent since he held his land from the second Duke of Ormond who took the Williamite side. When the lease for three lives expired, it was renewed, again and again, for thirty-one years. As tenants rather than landowners, the Powers of Gurteen were saved a lot of worries: the question of gavelling did not arise, and they need fear no discoverer. Moreover they seem to have been Freemasons: a foundation stone of Gurteen House is dated by the masonic year. It is probable (not certain) that Lord Arran, brother of the second Duke of Ormond, was also a Mason, Grand Master of the Lodge in Paris. This would have further safeguarded their position. By more leases they had increased their estate to about 10,800 acres by 1782 when the Catholic Relief Act enabled them to buy it.[19]

At Ballyvonare near Mallow in County Cork lived another Catholic landowning family, Harold-Barry. (Harold was a Dubliner of Danish extraction who married a Barry.) They owed their survival largely to being Freemasons. They were close friends for generations with the St Legers of Doneraile Court, grandest of the Protestant Ascendancy families who in their frequent sojourns in England moved in royal, or at least princely, circles. They were also Freemasons, and Lodge meetings were held at Doneraile. It was there that Lady Mary Aldworth, curious to learn what the men were up to on these mysterious occasions, hid to watch. She was detected, and the safest way to silence her was to swear her in, the only female Mason in history. A popular masonic toast was 'To our sister, Aldworth.'[20]

Nearer to Cork, and friendly with the Harold-Barrys, were the Nagles of Annakissy. Pierce Nagle was High Sheriff of County Cork in 1689, the last Catholic to hold that office for 140 years. His younger brother Sir Richard was twisted and bitter about the shabby treatment of Catholics in the Restoration Settlement. He wrote a pamphlet attacking Charles II in such terms that he thought it prudent to deny authorship and threaten legal action against anyone who attributed it to him. On James II's accession, he continued his campaign against the Settlement, with more hope but no more result until 1689 when the Irish Parliament, with him as Speaker, confiscated most of the land granted in the Settlement to Protestants. Both Pierce and Richard, and a third brother, David, were outlawed in 1690. A fourth brother became a monk. Sir Richard went to France with Sarsfield and became James II's Secretary of State at St Germaine; Pierce and David pleaded the Articles of Limerick. David was adjudged within them, but Pierce's claim was one of the few rejected on the grounds that he rejoined the Jacobite army after taking protection: he offered the principal witness against him half his estate to keep silent, but in vain.

Nevertheless his son, James, born in 1679, was allowed back some of the estate after Pierce's death in about 1730. Seeing that he had been brought up in France, was a Page of Honour to James II, and a Gentleman Usher to James's Queen, Mary of Modena, the Trustees of Forfeited Estates must have been in a benign mood when they considered his case. So he recovered enough of the family land to call himself 'of Annakissy', to live there and even give a Grand Ball. As he was an only son, the question of gavelling did not arise. He lived to the ripe age of ninety-four, and the estate passed to his eldest son, Pierce. There were six others, of which only two can be traced. Stephen was given by Pierce £90 a year, possibly on condition of not insisting on gavelling. Garrett, the youngest son, sought his fortune with the Irish Brigade, joining Lally's in 1742. He probably fought at Fontenoy and then went with Lally to India, being one of the garrison of Pondicherry when it was captured in 1760. He became a Chevalier of the Military Order of St Louis, and in his retirement settled down at Cambrai.

The next James Nagle, born in 1756, was the Chevalier's nephew. He might have followed his uncle into the French service, but joined instead that of the East India Company. Soon after arrival in India in 1780, when serving under Sir Eyre Coote against the Sultan Hyder Ali of Mysore, he was captured and imprisoned at Seringapatam. His name is not among the British officers released when the war was over, so he was probably able to take advantage of his family's French connections (Hyder Ali being an ally of France) to be released on parole, or handed over to the French, thereby escaping the horrid fate of prisoners chained two-in-two for years on end. (Said the mother of the not-tempered David Baird, 'I'm sorry for the man that's chained to our Davie.') He may have been returned to Europe on a French ship, for surely he would not have qualified for leave by 1787 when he was in Europe, visiting his uncle at Cambrai and exchanging Indian reminiscences.

He returned to India in 1788 and thereafter was almost continuously on active service. With the Third Native Infantry he was at the capture of Seringapatam and (for the second time) of Pondicherry, at the invasion of Ceylon and on expeditions to the Isle de France (Mauritius) and Manila. He commanded the regiment at Sir Arthur Wellesley's bloody victory at Assaye: 'On with you,' was Sir Arthur's order to the Third to charge; and he received the rare compliment of a mention in the future Duke of Wellington's despatches. In command of a force of irregular Mysore Horse (his recent enemies and jailors) he captured a thousand bullock loads of grain, which must have earned him a brief, frosty encomium from Sir Arthur. Although only a Company officer, he was given command of a flying column which included detachments of two king's regiments, the Seventy-Fourth Highlanders and the Nineteenth Light Dragoons, and sent to run down a large body of pillaging Pindaris. In a country where no force took the field without ponderous and chaotic impedimenta of bullock carts and elephants and camels, tents and cases of wine and furniture, servants and provision vendors, water-carriers and sweepers and *femmes de campagne*, Colonel James Nagle raced after the enemy night and day, without even tents, and brought them to battle, taking all their guns and plunder. In 1805 he returned to County Cork, his health broken but his bank balance mended, and lived there for twenty-five more years. His half-brother, Patrick, was noted mainly for his lack of business acumen. Investing much of the family money in France, he 'lost it on the surface and then chased it underground,' on some coal-mining venture.[21]

The most distinguished Nagle was neither the Chevalier of the Military Order of St Louis nor the paladin of the Honourable East India Company. Nano Nagle, of that branch of the family whose seat was Ballygriffin near Cork, whose mother was Ann Mathew of Annfield, in her youth was a social butterfly who greatly enjoyed a Paris season. Returning home one morning after an all-night party, she was stricken in her conscience by the sight of pious Parisians hurrying to Mass, and forthwith resolved to mend her ways. She became a nun, and founded the Presentation Order, pioneers of female education in Ireland.[22]

Thirty-five miles west of Limerick lay the castle and demesne of the Knight of Glin. Desmond FitzGerald, the knight in 1689, a major in Sir John FitzGerald's regiment of foot, was killed outside the walls of Derry, gasping out a dying wish that he be buried at Glin 'where the accursed tongue of the Sassenach would never be heard.' There were 8,000 acres at stake, which were ordered in 1696 to be forfeited because he had died in rebellion. But because it had been entailed in 1672 and he was only tenant for life, his widow was allowed to hold it in trust during the minority of his eldest son Thomas, to whom it passed.[23]

Thomas, known ironically as Tomas Geancach ('snub-nosed') because of his hawk-like beak, thus inherited 8,000 acres; and in 1701 obtained a certificate that neither he nor his younger brother John had taken part in the war. In 1705 there arose a dispute over the boundary between the Glin estates and those of O'Connor Kerry which had been granted to Trinity College. There were clashes between the retainers of the two parties, raids and cattle thefts. The row simmered on until 1711 when Thomas was in trouble for insulting Colonel Richard Southwell MP, brother of the Member for Trinity College. A reward of £100 was offered for his apprehension, but with the help of influential friends, the feud was patched up; and in 1713 Thomas was, rather surprisingly, among the Catholics licensed to carry a sword, case of pistols and gun. His younger brother John was a noted duellist, known as Sean na gComhrac (John of the Combats). In a fight on the Kerry boundary he wounded Richard Southwell and two others, all good swordsmen. The College got an order for sequestration against Thomas, but none dared serve it 'because of the said knight's universal and powerful influence over the whole county.' Also, perhaps, because of his brother John's reputation.

Glin was often the hiding-place of an unregistered priest, Father Butler. One day a priest-hunter, George Green, arrived, hot on Father Butler's trail. He asked John if the priest was there, and John replied quite truly that he wasn't. Green made the mistake of calling John a liar, and was tarred and feathered for his indiscretion.

John was not a man to be annoyed with impunity. In Dublin there was a lady whose amorous advances he had repelled. (He never married, and was apparently not a ladies' man.) Ear-cropping being in vogue, she demanded his ears and taunted guests at her dinner-table with being afraid to get them for her. One promised them in half an hour, and went off. In less than half an hour there was a furious hammering at the door and in strode John FitzGerald, intact, and flung her champion's ears in the lady's face, shouting, 'Here they are, you strumpet!'

Thomas's wife had eloped with him, her family opposing the match because he was quarrelsome and trouble-prone. She came to Glin in 1701 after which 'no one knew hunger or poverty in the district.' In the famine of 1739-40, when she was old enough to know better, she and her retainers even raided west Limerick and the College estates in Kerry for cattle to feed her people, who knew her as *bean tighearna* ('woman chieftain'). She was probably the first wife of the Knight of Glin to be known as 'Madam' or 'Dame' FitzGerald.[24]

Thomas had five sons of whom the eldest died young. He was succeeded as knight by the second son, John, who conformed in 1730 but (according to local tradition) it was a false conversion because he remained a Catholic until he died in 1737, the day after his wedding. The next knight was the third son, Edmund, very untypical of the family. He was a quiet, scholarly man, not very practical, and a Freemason while still a Catholic. This, however, did him little good: he married a Protestant heiress and conformed in 1741, but died childless and bankrupt twenty-one years later.

His heir was his extrovert brother Richard who reacted violently to Edmund's somewhat passive lifestyle. He married twice, kept a prominent local mistress and begat innumerable children on both sides of the blanket, but no legitimate son. He too was a great duellist, equally deadly with a pistol at twenty paces or a sword in a ten-foot ring. Whenever he entered a public assembly he would call out, 'Is there a Moriarty here?' – a reference to a family feud dating back to 1582. When a middleman named Studdert was in arrears with his rent, Richard rounded up his cattle, destroyed his house, staved his boat, battered his orchard, and stole a hayrick. The sheriff's bailiff went to recover the cattle and Richard's younger brother Thomas told him the sheriff's order would not be obeyed and 'he valued it not a fart.' Richard publicly caned Studdert.

The Limerick Protestant gentry were incensed by the veneration paid at local patterns (semi-religious fairs) to a neo-raparee named Donal O'Brien, whom they threatened to flog. The knight, a kinsman of O'Brien, sent them all individual invitations to the pattern as he wished to watch the flogging. That ended the matter. In one of Richard's duels his Spanish opponent wore under his clothes a mail shirt, most ungentlemanly behaviour. Richard could not understand why his thrusts had no effect until a spectator called out in Irish, 'Stick him where they stick the pigs!' so he ran the Spaniard through the throat.* Richard conformed in 1740 and died in the family tradition, intestate and bankrupt, in 1775.

The next knight was the fifth brother, another Thomas, who married a Protestant heiress of Cromwellian stock. He, or perhaps she, kept their finances under control. He conformed in every sense of the word and died wealthy and conventional. Thereafter all Knights of Glin were pillars of the Protestant Ascendancy.[25]

---

* The story is also told of Daniel O'Connell, who fought only one duel, and that with pistols.

Valentine Browne, the third Viscount Kenmare, succeeded to the Kenmare estates in 1720 on the death of his father, Nicholas, from whom they had been forfeited. During the father's lifetime they had been held in trust for the son, a child during the war, by the Trustees of Forfeited Estates who appointed an agent, John Asgill, to manage them and enjoy the revenues less £400 a year allowed to Nicholas's wife. On this, the viscount and viscountess had lived in a modest way, relieved from time to time by handouts from Major George Mathew. The estates in Counties Kerry and Cork were enormous, though largely bog and mountain. To them were added, by marriage to a family short of sons, thousands of much better acres round Hospital, in County Limerick. In all there were over 135,000 acres, preserved from gavelling by the good fortune that in each of three generations only one son survived the father and had issue.[26]

When Valentine came into his inheritance at the age of twenty-six he found it engulfed in debt, the egregious Asgill having mismanaged and plundered his charge. Nothing could be extracted from Asgill who took up permanent residence in Fleet debtors' prison, and thousands of acres of forestry had to be sold to clear debts. But there were still over 120,000 acres left. Valentine was generally an absentee in London, while his agent, Daniel Cronin, tried to collect rents from 'the mean jades whose pulse he tried by driving [away their cattle], ejectment and persuasion.' Valentine gave up the unequal struggle and died in 1736.

His only surviving son, Thomas, the fourth viscount, was no ball of fire, but he was scrupulously honest, much respected and took a genuine interest in pulling together his huge, encumbered inheritance. Above all, from 1747, when he came of age, he lived on his estate.

His first problem was his agent Daniel Cronin, who was also

tenant of several farms which Thomas's father had set to him at a rent far below two-thirds of their market value, a transaction which was discoverable. Indeed, a neighbour, Arthur Herbert, quarrelled with Cronin and threatened to discover it. Thomas wrote:

> As Cronin was extremely alarmed by this threat,
> he applied to me to take out an ejectment which
> he would not oppose, and that he would afterwards
> agree with me to advance the rent so high as to put
> it out of the power of malice.

The viscount might be new to estate management, but he knew how to arrange a neat and discovery-proof collusion.[27]

However, when he tried to introduce a linen industry to benefit the poor on his estates, he meant well but was naive enough to be conned by a plausible rogue:

> On my first coming to the estate in 1747 I found
> it a large barren waste with monstrous great farms,
> few or no substantial tenants, and a general spirit
> of dirty poverty and indolence. [I decided to
> introduce a linen industry.] The public granted me
> four spinning wheels and every assistance.
>
> As I was myself an utter stranger to the business,
> I was informed it would be necessary to bring
> weavers from the north and to that end I applied
> to John Murphy who was employed in building a
> bridge in the north . . . He like a true knave
> pretended to me that he had bred his younger son,
> Martin, for some years before that to the trade,
> which he was a perfect master of; that if I brought

down the said northerners at my own suit, I would never have peace from their pretensions and clamour, but if I would [employ his son to supervise them] he should fix twenty families of them, build slated houses for them, keep a bleachyard and manufacture a thousand yards of linen yearly. [My ignorance made me think that a great quantity.] We entered into an agreement. He built five houses and put looms in each of them. Instead of bringing families from the north, he picked up five vagabond deserters and broken weavers and established them as masters . . . The spinning school he employed to procure him thread for nothing. The looms the Board paid for have mostly been kept idle, the bleachyards ill-supplied with bleachers and worse with materials. His roguery and neglect of the spinning school made them to be struck off . . . Instead of answering my intention of promoting industry and the welfare of the poor, I see myself cheated on it above £100 a year by a rogue to the sole use of providing for one of his sons . . . Time will furnish the remedy, but the linen manufacture is still a very sensible object.[28]

As tenants for his farms, he preferred working farmers: 'the farm should be set to people who will occupy it, not gentlemen.' But he drew the line at the 'indolence and bad payments of the Moriartys.' Owen Moriarty was:

one of the toughest to get rent from . . . though I would always choose to encourage resident tenants, yet these being the most wicked, quarrelsome and

profligate people in my mountains, care must be
taken when the lease expires not to set it to any
of the family . . . Michael Riordan is one of the
most wrangling, beggarly vagabonds on the estate.
The rent is very ill paid and no improvements
made . . . The present tenant is by no means
punctual in his rents, and a coxcomb. [The trouble
was] a common practice with farmers in these parts
to take all the land they can possibly get without
considering their sufficiency to stock or improve
them.[29]

But there were good tenants as well as bad:

Cooper is a man of little substance but is an active,
laborious man. As he is of an industrious family
of Protestants settled about Mr Orpen's in Glen-
erough, the dealing with him may be a means of
procuring more of the same stamp.

(Protestant tenants were invaluable at elections, since they had
the vote but would use it as directed.)

James Mahony has built a good house on the
premises, made many good ditches and other
improvements, and is a young man of good
substance. The land will rise in its value in 1763.
[When the current thirty-one-year lease would
have expired.]

Some gentleman tenants were all right:
Doonemark. Set by myself to Richard Mellefont

Esquire for three lives at £39.18.0 per annum. The farm has been vastly improved and divided into fields of proper size with the best ditches well planned. He is a very genteel and worthy man.

But on the whole gentlemen were not satisfactory tenants:

Arthur Sanders is very slow in paying my rent, is become a gentleman and a JP and of the kindred and clan of the Herberts whose nephew he is. [Shehene was] set by my father to Ed. Herbert, senior, Esquire for a rent of £26.5.0 during lives of Thomas, Edward and Nicholas his sons. He now gets if for £70 a year, which it will be at least worth when it expires, and then it will be in the interest of my family to set it to people of less consequence.[30]

Worst of all as tenants were the not-quiet-gentry middlemen, the half-sirs:

Pride, ignorance and sloth mark the middling sort of Irish. Everyone of them thinks himself too great for any sort of industry except taking farms. When they happen to get them, they screw enormous rents from some beggarly dairyman and spend their whole time in the alehouses . . . If they have sons, they are all to be priests, physicians or French officers.

As for the lower sort of Irish, the viscount lamented the impossibility of ever 'imprinting any idea of industry and amendment among them.'

With the Ryans of Ballyvistea he had a somewhat turbulent relationship, railing at John Ryan's shortcomings (and shorter payments of rent) but renewing his lease again and again. John was the son or more probably grandson of Thady Ryan who built Ballyvistea House at Oldtown, County Limerick, and died in 1740 at the age of ninety-eight. Thady Ryan is not named in Dalton's *King James's Irish Army List*, nor among those outlawed for domestic treason. (Lists from Limerick are incomplete.) But he is included in O'Hart's list of forfeiting proprietors, and family legend insists that he was in the Jacobite army.[31] He may have been a volunteer or, at the age of fifty, employed on some staff job for which he was qualified by experience of soldiering in the Polish army at the relief of Vienna.

Kenmare writes of Oldtown Farm, set to John Ryan for thirty-one years from 1725 at a rent of £119.5.10 a year:

> This was held by the tenant's family for many generations and most of them, particularly his grandfather, were remarkably faithful and attached to mine.
>
> The tenant ran deeply in arrears in my minority, though he paid scarce half the present rent which I was content to take in small amounts, and after forgave him £300 for improvements he made on the [adjoining] Logh farm. [The improvements were considerable: John Ryan drained the land] by blasting rocks in the river and running several judicious drains effectively to it . . .
>
> After in 1756 when his lease expired I set it him at 20s per acre for all the good land and 6s per acre for some few acres of bog. He was so remiss in his

payments I was compelled to eject him out of Logh farm, and after out of this [Oldtown] ... Upon great protests of amendment I forgave him and set him the present lease on the same terms as before ... He is skilful farmer and as well capable of making rent as any man in the country, but spoilt by keeping company with rakish gentry, horseracing etc. which has rendered him a most unpunctual tenant.[32]

One of the rakish gentlemen was Thomas FitzGerald whom John Ryan assisted in a most discreditable escapade. FitzGerald and fourteen armed men broke into the house of the White family near Cappagh in County Tipperary, grabbed Rebecca White (an heiress) and, while one held up her family at pistol point, dumped her shrieking, 'Murder! Murder!' onto the horse of John Ryan of Ballyvistea and galloped off with her into County Limerick, where a priest was waiting at an empty house to marry the ardent swain and the heiress. The marriage does not seem to have been a success, except perhaps financially for Thomas FitzGerald: the lady spent the rest of her life in Dublin.[33]

John Ryan's neighbours seem to have been addicted to the abduction of heiresses. Some years later Henry Grady and some friends entered the Protestant church at Tipperary town during morning service, carried out Miss Susannah Grove, locked the door behind them to impede pursuit, and rode off with her to Oola near Oldtown, where the pair were united in Holy Matrimony by Father Daniel O'Neill, probably a 'regular' priest. Father O'Neill was arrested and taken by sixty soldiers for trial in Limerick. The High Sheriff reported:

> A very great number of people pelted them with
> stones in such a manner that the soldiers were
> rendered incapable of charging their pieces after
> they had made some shots . . . I must observe that
> five times that number of soldiers could not take
> a priest to a gaol through that country.

It is unlikely that John Ryan, in his fifties and busy farming about 300 acres, was involved in these unseemly disturbances but his son, known as 'Jack the Devil', may well have taken a leading part in them. Among his escapades was a fight with a peer of the realm at the races, for which he was sentenced to a fine; but when the bailiffs came to collect it, he drove them off with a whip.[34]

It remains to be said that Thady Ryan, and his son John, and John's more reputable son Thady, were master of a pack of hounds of a peculiar colour, bred from Kerry beagles, with good noses, good tongues and terrific drive. Ryans directly descended from Thady still hunt the Black and Tans, one of the most famous packs of foxhounds in the world.[35]

Another Catholic family of strong farmers or modest landowners (600 acres at Croom in County Limerick) were the Hedermans. The name sounds German, but is an anglicisation of an Irish name. They must have been under some sort of official protection: according to family tradition, the castellations in front of their house were a warning to troops that the owners of the house were 'special'. They were also, of course, an indication to 'regular' priests on the run that this was a 'safe' house. They, like the Ryans of Ballyvistea, hunted their own pack of hounds, which probably made them well liked by the Protestant gentry and safe from harassment.[36]

1 L. M. Cullen, *The Emergence of Modern Ireland*, 122; Maurice J. Bric, *Tipperary History and Society*, 113, 279; information from Lord Dunboyne; *Gentleman's Magazine*, (1788), 562.

2 Information from Lord Dunboyne.

3 Katherine M. Lanigan, 'Kilcash and the Butlers', in *Journal of the Butler Society*, 1985, II, no. 4, 292-8.

4 'George Butler', in 'Butler Archbishops of Cashel' in *Journal of the Butler Society*, 1978-9, I, no., 8, 626-30; Lord Dunboyne, *Butler Family History* (pamphlet), 27-8; *Gentleman's Magazine*, (1788), 562.

5 Dalton, *King James's Irish Army List*, I, 240; Maria Liddy (ed.), *The Diary of Mary Mathew*, Introduction iv-vii; The Most Rev. David Mathew, 'Father Mathew's Family' in *Capuchin Annual*, 1956-7, 143-52; D. G. Marnane, *Land and Violence, A History of West Tipperary from 1660*, 22.

6 Bric, *op. cit.*, 149-50.

7 Ryan family papers in the County Library, Thurles.

8 R. H. A. J. Everard, 'The Family of Everard', II, *in* Patrick Melvin, *The Irish Genealogist*, 1988, VII, no. 4, 524-30.

9 Arthur Young, *A Tour in Ireland*, 154; T. Campbell, *A Philosophical Survey of the South of Ireland*, 141-2; Burke, *Landed Gentry of Ireland.*, 535.

10 S. T. McCarthy, *The McCarthys of Munster*, 210-17.

11 Young, *op. cit.*, 154; G. F. Keating, *The Keating Family*, MSS in Genealogical Office of NLI, 55-7.

12 Hardinge, *Transactions, RIA*, (1865), XXIV, Pt. 3, 294.

13 James O'Donoghue, 'The Scullys of Kilfeakle', *Tipperary Historical Journal*, 1989, 38-57.

14 L. M. Cullen, 'Catholics under the Penal Laws', in Andrew Carpenter (ed.), *Eighteenth Century Ireland*, I, 32; Cullen, *The Emergence of Modern Ireland*, 199.

15 Bric, *op. cit.*, 155-7; Andrew Carpenter, *op. cit.*, I, 32.

16 Bric, *op. cit.*, 153-7; Patrick Corish, *The Catholic Community in the Seventeenth and Eighteenth Centuries*, 122-4.

17 Bric, *op. cit.*, 157-60; Campbell, *op. cit.*, 155.

18 Simms, *Williamite Confiscations*, 75-6; *The Gentleman's Magazine*, Aug. 1897, 13; Dalton, *op. cit.*, II, 209-10; G. O'C. Redmond, *The Power and Corroghmore Peerage Claim*, (privately printed), 56; Appendix 32, 51; Appendices 27, 28.

19 *Ibid*, 95; Appendix 56, 92; Appendix 54.

20 Family tradition related by Mr Peter Harold-Barry; Brother Laurence Dern, *Ahimon Rezon, or Help to a Brother;* William Begemann, *Freemasonry in Ireland* (MSS), 2.

21 Dalton, *op. cit.*, I, 162-3; Basil O'Connell, 'The Nagles of Annakissy' in Melvin, *The Irish Genealogist*, III, No. 1, 338-43.

22 *Dictionary of National Biography*.

23 Simms, *op. cit.*, 141.

24 Father J. Anthony Gaughan, *The Knights of Glin*, 57-64.

25 *Ibid.*, 64-73.

26 Dalton, *op. cit.*, II, 638; Kenmare papers X, XI, 10-1, 322.

27 *Ibid.*, 51, 185-6.

28 *Ibid.*, 214.

29 *Ibid.*, 179, 181, 213, 192.

30 *Ibid.*, 204, 215, 218-31.

31 Michael MacEwan, *The Ryan Family and the Scarteen Hounds*, 35; John O'Hart, *Irish Landed Gentry*, (1887), 514.

32 Kenmare papers, 242, 245.

33 Marnane, *op. cit.*, 21.

34 *Ibid.*, 26; MacEwan, *op. cit.*, 37.

35 *Ibid.*, 37.

36 *Some Historical Facts about the Hedermans* (privately printed).

7

KERRYMEN

In Kerry relations between the Catholic and Protestant gentry were pretty good, though many Protestants of the lower orders, known as 'shoneens', were insufferable bigots.

The Orpens of Killowen were English royalists who after the English civil war moved to Ireland. In 1688 Richard Orpen received into his house scores of Protestants who felt threatened, and stood a siege by 3,000 Jacobite troops under Captain Phelim McCarthy. Forced at last to surrender, he managed to escape to England where he joined the Williamite army as a captain. When the war was over, he returned to Kerry, naturally expecting to find his estate in ruins. On the contrary, it was in excellent shape, having been looked after by Catholic neighbours. Thereafter, when his party was in the ascendant, he was always ready to 'hold' land for them or help in any other way.[1]

So was Maurice FitzGerald, Knight of Kerry, who had narrowly escaped outlawry after the Boyne because the jury took pity on his extreme youth. He conformed in 1703 on marrying a Protestant Crosby. But when James FitzGerald of Liscarney, a Catholic, no relation, was in trouble, he confidently looked to the knight for help by 'holding' his lands on a bogus lease:

> At the time of making the lease it was apprehended
> that the inheritance of the said lands may be lost
> by my son's being in foreign service, to evade which

the above lease was made to the Knight of Kerry
as the known and most particular friend to the
family with the intent that he may protect them
from any evils consequent on my son's being in
foreign services.[2]

The knight's father-in-law, Sir Thomas Crosby, was a Protestant
who had served in King James's army. It was alleged, on rather
doubtful authority, that the Crosby family papers included a
commission from King James to execute martial law in Kerry,
and a certificate from Kerry Protestants addressed to King
William testifying to Crosby's loyalty to him. He was in any case
no bigot.[3]

The knight's main concern was not Popery but the problem
of maintaining Dingle as a pocket borough in the face of Lady
Ann FitzGerald's determination to swamp the voters' roll with
her own creatures from Carberry. (She was known in the family
as Alecto, after one of the furies.) In 1773 Robert, Knight of
Kerry, wrote to the Reverend John Day:

> The presence of Alecto I should not fear much, but
> I should always wish such a fiend at a hundred
> miles distance. The presence of Carberians demand-
> ing to be sworn would be troublesome, and is
> better avoided. Therefore the task of intercepting
> expresses and letters is one of the most essential
> importance, and for this I wholly rely on [your son]
> Ned. Castlemaine and Cahirmoran bridges are the
> places to watch for expresses . . . sure you will keep
> Ned tight to this business. The persons instructed
> to intercept the expresses must be instructed to use
> all discretion, to practise artifice, nor force, and

Ned and Arthur Herbert will take care of the post
office . . . The blow must be struck on the twenty-
ninth which is to save a borough in the family.[4]

For Catholic families it was vital to keep on good terms with
the Protestant gentry who, as MPs, JPs, and Grand Jurymen, ran
the country. They were all known as 'colonel', however tender
their age or meagre their military experience. When 'Colonel'
Blennerhasset's lady was brought to bed of a baby boy, a
neighbour called to ask after her, and also about the colonel's
health. 'Do you mean the young colonel or the old colonel?' she
was asked. The 'young colonel' was less than a week old.

  Much of the forfeited land in Kerry had gone not to
individuals but to institutions, notably to Trinity College,
Dublin. Trinity seems to have been a good and considerate
landlord. Morrogh O'Connor, evicted from Trinity land, appealed
against the eviction, and wrote an eclogue on the outcome:

> What could I do but to the college run,
> And well I did, or I should be undone.
> There did I see a venerable Board,
> Provost and Fellows, men that keep their word,
> Sincere and just, honest and fair and true,
> Their only rule is to give all their due,
> No bribes, no interest can corrupt their minds,
> Unbiased laws the rich and poor man finds:
> Alike to all their charity extends,
> E'en I, a stranger, found them all my friends.
> Such were the Saints who once possessed this isle
> And drew down blessings on this happy soil.
> They soon (for Justice here knows no delay)
> Gave their short answer, 'Morrogh, go thy way,

Return, improve your farm as heretofore,
Begone, you shall not be molested more.

Well, perhaps Morrogh gilded the lily, but it was a praiseworthy effort, deserving even a reduction in his rent.

Others who acquired huge areas of bog and mountain were Baron Shelburne and the Earl of Cork. Neither, of course, wished to reside in so barbarous and remote a land, in daily contact with hostile and unintimidated tenants, so they put in intermediate tenants to lease from them what was in many a case the middleman's ancient patrimony, pay them rent and set the land to farmers.

Among the middlemen were the O'Connells of Iveragh, who had played an honourable part in the war, four holding King James's commission of whom two were killed. When it was over Captain John O'Connell, who had fought in all the battles but had been able to plead the Articles of Limerick, settled down at Derrynane on land leased from the Earl of Cork, and there built a sound, plain, two storeyed, slate-roofed house. He kept some acres in hand, and set the rest to farmers who often paid their rent in labour or in kind.[5]

He died in 1741 and was succeeded by his eldest son Daniel, known as Dónal Mór (big Daniel), who had five sons, John, Maurice, Morgan, Connell and Daniel Charles*, and five daughters. Maurice, born in 1726, was a vague dreamy young man who at twenty-three was told by his elder brother John to pull himself together:

---

*   He was generally called Daniel, but in this book is called Daniel Charles to distinguish him from the Liberator Daniel O'Connell.

You do nothing but read from morning to night,
nor exercise in any way . . . a mere recluse, caring
for nothing but your room and reading . . . [You
must learn to manage] dry and milk cattle, how got
and how disposed of; how the ground is tilled and
managed. . . Go visit the workmen; go fish of a fair
day in the boat; sometimes ride and see the
herdsmen and cattle. See waste grass and corn, and
sometimes rush, leap, play ball, etc. By this you'll
inform yourself and do your family a service, you'll
exercise yourself and, which is more than all, you'll
please your father.[6]

Two years after issuing this reprimand, John died. But Maurice
seems to have taken it to heart, for he developed into a most
formidable man, hard and tightfisted. He ruled his estates
(which were never gavelled) like an absolute monarch, his orders
being exactly obeyed especially when reinforced by the token of
a little crooked pruning-knife, the symbol of his authority. He
was known as 'Hunting Cap', because he always wore one rather
than pay the tax on beaver-hats. Like most of the Os and Macs
at the beginning of the century, he anglicised his name to
Connell to avoid drawing attention to himself, until the relaxation
of the Penal Laws made it safe to resume the name O'Connell.

It was advisable for a Catholic to keep a low profile. Dr
Smith, a traveller and antiquarian, during a visit to Derrynane
wished to buy a good hill pony and offered in return to give the
Connell family a write-up. Hunting Cap was horrified. 'For
God's sake take the pony for nothing, and leave us in the
obscurity which is our safeguard.' Yet he was consulted by the
'colonels' on such matters as re-aligning and improving the
abominable Kerry roads, and provided labour and tools for that

purpose. He was on friendly terms with the local Protestant rector, who in Lent invited him to dine, with a delicate understanding of Popish traditions: 'If you can spare time to help us in farming, you shall have salt herrings and oysters in plenty.'[7]

He had two beautiful sisters. The first, Eileen (Eibhlín) fell precipitately in love with Arthur O'Leary, a fair-haired, smashing, dashing, hard-riding major of the Hungarian Hussars. He was a duellist, a sportsman and a notable athlete whose most remarkable feat was to stand upright and keep his footing on a large hogshead as it rolled down a steep hill. When Eileen announced her intention of marrying him, the O'Connells were appalled, for O'Leary, although undoubtedly a gentleman, with a fine house near Macroom, seemed unlikely to make a steady husband. However, marry him she did. He owned a famous dark bay racing mare, a great jumper, on which one day he hunted with the Muskerry, and was the only man up at the kill. Riding along behind him with the rest of the field was a Protestant landowner, Arthur Morris, who arriving at the scene of the kill, demanded to buy O'Leary's mare for five pounds, as was his right under the Act of 1696 for disarming Papists.

O'Leary furiously refused to sell. Angry words were exchanged, and both gentlemen lashed out with their whips. O'Leary challenged Morris, who refused to fight, but afterwards used his position as magistrate to have O'Leary indicted (presumably for assault) and, when he failed to present himself for trial, outlawed. Soldiers attacked O'Leary's house and he beat them off by firing from the windows, his wife loading for him. Eventually he was ambushed and shot dead. The first she knew of it was when she saw the mare galloping home without him. She pursued the soldiers who had killed him through the law courts and succeeded in having two transported. Morris was put on trial for causing O'Leary's murder but was acquitted. Some months later he was shot and mortally wounded in Cork by O'Leary's brother, who made his escape to America.

There were several versions of the story; and some questions about it. Would, indeed *could* Morris have had O'Leary outlawed for what was merely contempt of court arising out of a common assault and a challenge? (Local gossip linked the dashing hussar with Morris's wife.) If he was outlawed, why should the soldiers who shot him be transported? However, of his killing there is no doubt. His widow wrote in Irish the classic poem *A Lament for Art O'Leary*.[8]

Hunting Cap's other sister, Mary, was as beautiful as Eileen, but fair where Eileen was dark, and less headstrong. She fell in love with a young Englishman named Herbert, a relative of the Earl of Powis, whom she met while he was on a visit to the family estates in Kerry. Having won Mary's heart, he very properly addressed her mother, who emphatically refused her permission to the match. His family, she was sure, would regard it as a shocking misalliance – a relative of an earl marrying the daughter of an ordinary country gentleman, an Irish Catholic at that. She would not consider it unless he produced his father's and the earl's consent in writing. So young Herbert departed with a flea in his ear, and Mary was married off to a Mr Baldwin who lived in Macroom. He was of a family which had come to Ireland in the sixteenth century as Protestants, but had been converted to Catholicism by a Catholic tutor. He was a good man, but middle-aged, lanky and spindle-shanked, hardly one to make a girl's heart beat faster. At the wedding breakfast there arrived a letter from young Herbert, saying that he had obtained the required permission from his father and from the Earl of Powis. But it was too late: the ring was on Mary's finger. As things turned out, she had an excellent husband, and her brothers Maurice, Morgan, Connell and Daniel Charles had great liking for 'brother Baldwin'. But on the not infrequent occasions when she wished to put him down, she had only to say, 'But for you, Mr Baldwin, I might be Countess of Powis.'[9]

Since Iveragh was far too rough and steep for horses, the local form of hunting was beagling, hunting on foot the strong mountain hares with the black and tan Kerry beagles, foundation stock of the Ballyvistea Ryans' foxhounds. It was a rough and dangerous sport, toiling uphill and bounding over boulders and scree, risking a broken ankle with every stride, vaulting or clambering over drystone walls. Morgan's eldest son Daniel was an enthusiastic beagler: in later life, when he was famous as 'The Liberator', it gave him an annual holiday free from the strain of politics and the evading of creditors.

Kerry in the eighteenth century was a lawless place. In the 1760s, when south Tipperary was plagued by the Whiteboys, Iveragh had its 'Loders'. Whiteboys had an undeniable economic grievance, but Loder gangs were purely predatory, out for protection money from landowners. In 1767, said a witness in court, a gang of nine armed with:

> guns, pistols and cutlasses fired several shots to the terror of the inhabitants . . . extorting victuals, drink and all other necessaries; also frightening them to such a degree that they durst not follow their lawful occupations . . . and when they arrived at Derrynane declared they would bring some of the gentlemen of the county under an annual contribution, particularly Messrs Maurice and Morgan O'Connell whom on refusal they intended to rob, murder and do bodily harm to. [They attacked Keane Maloney, a kinsman of Hunting Cap] on the high road, on his return from divine

service, wounded him with scimitars, cut two of his
fingers and laid open his head in several places.[10]

Hunting Cap and his brother Morgan were not men to be
blackmailed. They were against crime – from which term
smuggling was, of course, excluded. Not all their relatives were
so particular. The O'Sullivans of the Bere Peninsular, kin by
several marriages of the O'Connells, in the first half of the
century had been lawless petty gentry who in smuggling would
draw the line at nothing. In 1733 Morty Oge O'Sullivan, an ex-
Austrian officer, had recaptured a cargo of contraband seized by
the revenue officers. In 1754 he shot dead his smuggling partner,
John Puxley, a Protestant landlord, and sauntered into Mass
advising Puxley's friends to go and cry by the corpse. He was
himself hunted down and killed by troops. But his nephew
Daniel was a captain in the Berehaven Yeomanry and so active
against the French fleet in Bantry Bay in 1796 that he was made
a Freeman of the City of Cork, the first Catholic to be so
honoured for nearly a hundred years. By that time the O'Sullivans
had become most respectable, with social vanities which a
French visitor found ridiculous.[11]

Hunting Cap's aunt, Siobhán O'Donoghue, known in Irish
as 'a bite of the devil's belt', was married to a McCarthy out west.
Near her house was a mill where lived a young Protestant miller
and his sister to whom she had always been very kind. The young
man repaid her kindness by filing a discovery against her
husband. Siobhán had timely warning of his intentions and sent
a trusted messenger to Glenesk, where the wildest of wild men
defied law and order but were as docile as sheep to the
O'Donoghues. He told them that his lady wanted the young
miller silenced, but not killed. So they cut out his tongue.[12]

Hunting Cap built up his estate by leases and discreet

purchases through his Protestant cousin, Hugh Falvey. At one time he wanted to buy an estate on the shore of the lake of Killarney, but one of the Herbert family gave him fair warning that if he did so, a discovery would be filed against him. Herbert eventually bought the estate for much less than Hunting Cap had offered. Singularly enough, Hunting Cap had no resentment against Herbert, who, he said, had acted honourably: he could have waited till Hunting Cap had bought the place, and then got it for nothing.[13]

Besides estate and family management, and public duties performed *sub rosa*, Hunting Cap managed the 'free trade' of south Kerry. Derrynane harbour was a blind one, sheltered behind a headland and invisible from the sea. With deep water right up to the jetty, it was an ideal smugglers' hole. Into it came French, Spanish and Irish vessels laden with brandy, rum, claret, green and bohea tea, silks, velvets, great French mirrors and tobacco. They carried away to France and Spain, in defiance of the Navigation Acts, beef, wool, hides, butter and the item listed as 'Wild Geese', recruits for the French and Spanish Irish Brigades. His lieutenant in this was his younger brother Morgan who lived twenty miles away (their wives did not hit it off) at Carhen, farming on land leased from Trinity College and Lord Lansdowne, running profitable salt-pans and a general store where one could buy anything from an anchor to a button. He was a big bluff man, a great snuff-taker and backgammon player, ideal as lieutenant but without Hunting Cap's organising ability. All the colonels, all the Grand Jurymen, were involved in the free trade, but it was Hunting Cap who ran it on proper, businesslike lines, instructing his agent, Owen McCrohan, in Cork in 1754:

The *Alexander*, Captain John FitzGerald on board, has shipped 5 large sacks of wool: 58 firkins butter and 65 salted hides; all of which you are to insure as follows: on the wool, £18; on the butter, £48; on the hides, £24; and on the vessel, £68. In all, £158 . . .

The whole proceeds are to be invested for tea, half green and half bohea. As to the last commodity, it promises pretty well. Brandy is in no demand, nor is there a likelihood that there will be a call on it for some considerable time.

I mentioned to you to send thirteen ankers brandy, three of which cherry, a cask powder sugar and three tierces good claret for private consumption . . . and am ordered to direct you to send two quarter casks small white St Martin of Rhenish wine (for my father).

The price of the looking glass (for my mother) deduct from the proceeds of the above mentioned butter.

Your brother Jemmy has shipped himself [as a Wild Goose] according to your directions. I fancy my brother will ere now have advised you of his arrival in Caen.[14]

Free trade was extremely profitable, and one item in Hunting Cap's accounts indicates how minor revenue officials were taken care of: 'To the boatmen who came seeking a prey, 5s/5p.'

For many years the business ran like clockwork, giving great satisfaction to the whole county. But in 1782 there was posted to Waterville as revenue officer for south Kerry, Captain Whitwell Butler, a former naval officer, who was not bribable. On 5 September he came swooping into Derrynane harbour while

Hunting Cap, Morgan, sundry cousins and a gang of peasants were busy unloading a cargo. It was a fair cop. All Hunting Cap could do was to invite Butler to breakfast, mentioning at the same time that the cargo included a silk dress for his wife.

'You shall have it free, madam,' Butler gallantly replied, 'if it costs me my commission.'

After breakfast Butler said he would return to Waterville on foot, cutting across the peninsula, with a small escort. Hunting Cap, knowing how furious the peasants would be at the loss of their profit, handed to an O'Sullivan nephew the little crooked pruning-knife and told him to accompany Butler and see him safely home. In the village of Cahirdaniel they noticed glowering faces and heard angry words; but the sight of the pruning knife made the villagers draw back. Some time afterwards, Butler sent O'Sullivan home, thinking that he was by now quite safe. He wasn't. He was ambushed, his small escort routed and he beaten almost to death.

Three months later Hunting Cap was warned that Butler was out for his blood. The warning came from Owen McCrohan, who had paid Butler a friendly visit, smuggler to revenue officer, and learned that Butler had procured from Lord Chief Justice Annaly a warrant for the arrest of Hunting Cap, his brother Morgan, and cousin Daniel O'Connell of Tarmons, on a charge of instigating the barbarous attack on him. An informer, Kelly, had also alleged that Daniel O'Connell had offered a reward of £100 for Butler's murder. The only evidence against them was the word of Kelly, and the fact that most of Butler's assailants had been Hunting Cap's tenants. But since the warrant was signed by the Lord Chief Justice, only he could order the accused to be released on bail; and they would have to stand trial not in Kerry where the jury, knowing the situation and Kelly's unsavoury reputation, would surely acquit them, but in Dublin where they might well be convicted and hanged.

Hunting Cap wrote an indignant letter to his legal adviser, Counsellor Dominic Trant, a Kerryman who had conformed in order to practise as a barrister:

> I beg leave to communicate a most horrid and base attack that has been made on my brother and me and Mr Daniel Connell by Mr Whitwell Butler. . .
>
> The warrant sets forth that we are charged in information on oath before his lordship [Annaly] as being the persons who raised the mob that assembled and beat Mr Butler after making a seizure, and that Mr Daniel Connell has at different times offered a reward of £100 stg to any person who would assassinate Mr Butler . . . that my brother and I have repeatedly uttered words to the same effect . . .
>
> Conscious of our innocence and of our just abhorrence of such barbarous, inhuman and un-Christian practices, we are ready to meet these abominable charges in open court, in the face of our country, at the next Assizes. . . What I would take the liberty to request from you is you would move my Lord Annaly and prevail with him to admit us to bail in the country . . . and that you would be our counsel at the next Assizes . . . and you'll see we shall baffle Mr Butler's plotting and poisonous machinations.

Annaly's great friend John FitzGibbon abominated Popery but as Trant's brother-in-law took the point, and persuaded Annaly, that unless they were tried soon, in Kerry, these gentlemen of irreproachable character (smuggling being no reproach):

> must either be out on their keeping like Whiteboys
> or, if taken, lie in the worst jail in Europe, that of
> Tralee, among felons and malefactors.

Lord Annaly granted the request for trial in Kerry, and at the next Assizes the colonels on the Grand Jury rallied round and decided that the O'Connells had no case to answer so they left the court without a stain on their characters.

Congratulating Hunting Cap on the happy outcome of the case, Trant added:

> My brother-in-law, Mr FitzGibbon, has declared
> himself a candidate for the County of Limerick at
> the next election. May I request that you be kind
> enough to exert yourself for him, as I flatter myself
> you would for me in a similar situation.[15]

Dominic Trant was the grandson of Sir Patrick Trant, Bart, who had been attainted in 1691 and lost most of his estates, though his widow and son were allowed to retain a small portion. Dominic's elder brother, John, was established on this at Dovea in County Kerry. Although a Protestant, Dominic had written a pamphlet supporting Catholic claims, which resulted in a challenge from Sir George Colthurst whom Dominic shot dead, departing immediately to France until the matter blew over. Another branch of the family, which remained Catholic, was established in business in Cork.

While Hunting Cap and Morgan stayed at home, the next brother, Connell, learned seamanship and navigation at Nantes but then elected, on the outbreak of the Seven Years War against

France, to sail as second mate of an English privateer. (A Catholic, he could not hold a British navy commission.)

> I sailed from Falmouth second mate in a letter of marque bound to Cape Breton and Rhode Island . . . but having the misfortune to lose our rudder in high seas . . . we bore away, with a kind of rudder we knocked up, for New Providence, one of the Bahama islands where we arrived with only 25 lbs bread, half a barrel of beef and one cask of water aboard . . . Having got a new rudder and everything else in proper repair, we sailed for Cape Breton where we arrived after a passage of thirty-two days during which nothing occurred. From Louisburg we sailed for Newport in Rhode Island when, to complete the voyage, the merchants refused paying the wages which amounted to near £500. We, however, libelled the vessel [seized it for debt]. . . I quitted the island for New York. When I got there I accidentally met cousin Denis McGillicuddy who was fitting out in a snow, cousin Denis being shipped chief mate . . . I concluded to come second mate to him. We are bound from here to York and shall, God willing, drop down the river in a day or two.
>
> I am glad to her that brother Morgan is become attentive to his and my father's business, but sorry to think Daniel is wasting away his time in that idle country. I request, dear brother, you may urge my father to put him to some business and that speedily.

Five years and several voyages later Connell was washed overboard in a gale and drowned.[16]

The 'idle country' in which the youngest brother, Daniel Charles, was 'wasting away his time' was France, where he had gone to obtain a commission in the Irish Brigade. (Neither brother commented in his letters on the singularity of their fighting on opposite sides. Indeed there was nothing very singular about it: each one was following his chosen profession, and if this led to them shooting at one another, so be it.) As no Irish regiment then had a vacancy for a cadet, Daniel Charles was posted to another regiment of foreigners in the French army, the Royal Swedes, in which he spent most of his service. He was soon engaged in the bitter winter campaign which started in February 1761, fighting alongside his cousin Morty O'Connell of Tarmons, who had joined the Austrian army at the same time as Daniel joined the French.

His military career in the French army was dogged by penury. Pay was low, promotion slow, uniform and equipment expensive. His elder brother helped from time to time, but Derrynane was far away. His mentor and financial standby in France was the Chevalier de Fagan, a Kerryman, captain in a cavalry regiment. Even when he became assistant adjutant, he could not live on his pay. What Daniel Charles really wanted was 'if possible to get into the English service without injury to my religion.' Meanwhile he was quite happy to fight the English.[17]

In 1768, when the war was over, he and his colonel crossed the Channel to spend a few days' leave in London. Arriving at the height of the Wilkite riots, he was terribly shocked at what he saw:

> My eyes, unused to the licentiousness that the
> English call Liberty, see with horror, nay contempt
> for the nation, their mistaken sense and notion of

things. Royalty despised, subordination unknown, and unbounded pride and contempt for other nations. Inhumanity, ferocity – in a word, a barbarism unknown to the rest of Europe render the inhabitants, I mean the lower sort of people in England, the most odious. I believe the better sort of people well bred in all countries, so don't comprehend them in the above critique.[18]

Hunting Cap had visited London three years earlier, and recorded his impressions of the royal family:

First was the king, a tall, ruddy, fair-haired, sandy-complexioned, smooth-faced but soft-countenanced man, inclined to be fleshy, discursive and harmless, good-humoured but of a weak, injudicious turn. Next was the queen, a low, pale-faced mean-looking woman, large mouth and nose a little turned-up, on the whole rather ordinary, not in the least majestic.

But London was *very* majestic: 'innumerable are the magnificent buildings of the very great city.'[19]

In 1769 Daniel Charles was posted to Clare's in the Irish Brigade – more expense in uniforms, etc. the Chevalier de Fagan must have smarted for it – in which he served in the East Indies. From the Isle de France (Mauritius) he wrote:

It is with the utmost trouble that we support life here. We are a numerous corps of troops and provisions very scarce. No money at all. War alone can make our lot better, worse it can't be . . . Our

soldiers are good and willing, but poor, the greater
the misery, the more intrepid when questions of
plunder arise.[20]

Back in Europe, he was much troubled by young kinsmen who
came as cadets to his regiment. Himself an abstemious, methodical
man, he lamented their utter lack of these qualities. They drank,
they gambled, they got into debt, they overstayed their leave in
Ireland, they never arrived in time for the beginning of the term
in the military college where he had with such pains secured
their vacancies. 'Why cannot you Kerry gentlemen be more
punctual?' was his refrain. Two out of three of the officers in the
Brigade were Kerrymen.[21]

I have some expectation of getting a commission
for Eugene [McCarthy] in Walsh's. I would wish
to be rid of him for between us I fear he'll prove
Daddy's own child, particularly if he should remain
in this regiment where there's the very worst
example for young men. He discovers the strongest
propensity to gambling and is not averse to the
bottle. . . I should have had him in a dungeon on
bread and water to pay his debts, was I not apprehen-
sive that it may prevent [Walsh, Comte de] Serrant
from giving him employment in that regiment.[22]

But the profligate Eugene made good in the Irish Brigade and
ended his career as a colonel in the British army. That remained
Daniel Charles O'Connell's ambition, despite the impression
that the London lower orders had made on him. When the Penal
Laws against Catholics were relaxed in 1778 he wrote exultingly
to Hunting Cap:

A revolution so unexpected and so long wished for
must needs procure an accession to the power and
prosperity of the Kingdom of Ireland and unite in
one common sentiment of loyalty the hearts of that
long oppressed and unfortunate nation. One step
more still remains to be made – I mean the liberty
of spilling their blood in defence of their king and
country. I doubt not 'twill soon be granted, though
no motive could ever induce me to bear arms
against France where I found an asylum when
refused one at home.[23]

One of his protégés in the Brigade was Rickard O'Connell, of
the Clare branch of the family, who went to France in his mid-
twenties, older than most cadets, to escape the vengeance of the
relatives of a young lady with whom he had trifled, and of priests
censorious of the trifling: 'in spite of my reverence for the
religion of which they are ministers, I abhor the selfishness of
this ungenerous, hypocritical tribe'. As for the English, he wrote
in 1779 to his friend Maurice Leyne, *étudiant en médicine au
College des Lombards:*

Would to God we were at this moment 200,000
strong in Ireland, and that I had command of one
single company in Oak Park. I would kick the
Members and their Volunteers and their Unions
and their Societies to the Devil! I would make the
rascally spawn of that damned Cromwell curse the
hour of his birth. Oh heaven! Can there be such
brutes in human form? But our dear country
swarms with them.[24]

In 1780 Daniel Charles was back with the Royal Swedes as their lieutenant colonel. If he was not yet to be allowed to fight for the King of Great Britain and Ireland, the next best thing was to fight against him. This he did, with great distinction – he was made a Chevalier of the Military Order of St Louis – at the capture of Minorca and the siege of Gibraltar. In the last action he commanded a floating battery manned by volunteers from his regiment. It was believed, erroneously, to be unsinkable and non-inflammable, being constructed of very heavy timbers protected by armour made of timber and cork soaked a long time in water, with the space between filled with sand, and roofed with wet hides. He himself was sceptical of the efficacy of these ponderous contrivances and was proved right, after fighting his valiantly and being wounded by red-hot shot as he brought his sinking battery to safety.[25]

He rose to Court favour, and hence to general's rank, through the patronage of the Polignacs – a corrupt crowd, but when you are a penniless soldier of fortune in a foreign land you do not choose your patrons, but hope they will choose you.

His last appointment under Louis XVI was that of Inspector General of Infantry, in which he devised a new system of battle drill of which the ultimate beneficiary was Napoleon. He did not at first anticipate the horrors of the French Revolution and the Terror, and ill-advisedly arranged for Morgan's two boys, Daniel and Maurice, to be educated at Dr Stapleton's school at St Omer, and then at the English College at Douai, from which he organised their escape when things became too hot for them.[26]

Allied by marriage to the Nagles, Trants and O'Connells were the Hickies of Kilelton in north Kerry. The Hickie (Hickey, O'Hickey) sept was long established in County Clare where by tradition they provided physicians to the O'Briens and MacNamaras. In the fourteenth and fifteenth centuries O'Hickeys wrote, and translated from Latin into Irish, several medical treatises. Apart from their hereditary calling, the principal O'Hickeys were men of consequence, counsellors in peace and chieftains in war. As Gaels took to Anglo-Norman practices in land tenure, they became substantial landowners in County Clare. As such they suffered Cromwellian confiscations. Many, leaving home, more or less adapted to the new circumstances. Some made good in the commercial world of Limerick and Dublin. Joseph Hickey, a friend of Edmund Burke, became a successful attorney in London; his son William, also an attorney, wrote a famous diary, racy and indecorous, of life in London and Calcutta.

What was, or became, the senior branch of the family stemmed from James Hickie, whose estates in the barony of Tulla in County Clare were confiscated in 1652. His son, William, crossed the Shannon and settled in County Kerry. William's son, also William, made an advantageous marriage in 1682 to Pomel Edmunds, co-heiress of the O'Connor Kerry estates at Asdee on the shore of the Shannon in north Kerry. In the mid-nineteenth century these comprised 3,368 acres with a rent-roll of £1,120, plus valuable fishing rights, enough to confer on the family a modest prosperity. Since there is no record of their buying or selling land during the previous 150 years, it is reasonable to suppose that the estate was of about that size through the eighteenth century. It sufficed to rebuild a more modest house at Kilelton as a large Georgian mansion, probably in about 1800.

During the nineteenth century the Hickies of Kilelton served generation after generation in the British army, commanding regiments, brigades, even a division against Russians, Sepoy mutineers, Boers and Germans. But for the whole of the eighteenth century they stayed at Kilelton, prosperous, much respected, inconspicuous and never deviating from their Catholicism.

This they were able to do because their estate was never gavelled. It couldn't be, for the second William who married Pomel Edmunds had only one son, also William, who married Phillis Trant of Dingle. Their elder son, William , died in 1766, three years before his father's death; so the younger, Michael, inherited the undivided estate in 1769. Michael, by his wife, Margaret Nagle, had three sons, but lived until 1809, long after the gavelling law was repealed. Under no pressure to conform, having no younger sons to place (and support) in foreign armies or in the 'mercantile career', the Hickies of Kilelton were quiet, comfortable country gentry, inconspicuous but much respected. Their status can be inferred from a letter written by Michael's son, William, who was in France being given a French polish shortly before the French Revolution. There he was befriended by a distant cousin, Countess Watters, born a Rice of County Kerry.

Few young men have seen more of the world than I have on the sum allowed me. Countess Watters is astonished at it, and does me the honour to say that I must have a great deal of cleverness and economy. It is true, both one and the other is requisite to bring both ends of the year about with my allowance. If I spend too much in one month, I must bring it up in the next. However, Countess Watters would have me remain another year in France. She continues as usual very polite to me. I am to dine there tomorrow. There is to be a crowd of Marquises, Counts and Countesses there. It is probable that I shall be the only person without a title, but still I shall feel myself as much at my ease as if I was still at Kilelton; pride and that stiffness peculiar to the Irish nobility not being known in this country. No fuss about going out of the room to dinner, no ceremony about sitting down to table, no healths drunk; in short, these matters are accidental, not ceremonious.[27]

---

1   Mary Ann Hickson, *Old Kerry Records*, 271.
2   Knight of Kerry papers, 1/1/4.
3   Dalton, *King James's Irish Army List*, 1, 442.
4   Knight of Kerry papers, 1/3/98.
5   Basil O'Connell, *O'Connell Family Tracts*; Mrs M. J. O'Connell, *The Last Colonel of the Irish Brigade*, I, 2.
6   *Ibid.*, I, 22.
7   *Ibid.*, I, 3, 22, 39.
8   John T. Collins, 'Arthur O'Leary, the Outlaw', in *Journal of the Cork Historical and Archaeological Society*, IV, Pt I, no. 174, Jan-June 1949, 1-3, 21-3; Mrs M. J. O'Connell, *op. cit.*, I, 171.
9   *Ibid.*, I, 163.
10 *Ibid.*, I, 113-4.
11 John McVeagh (ed.), *Richard Pocock's Irish Tours*, ed. John McVeagh, (Dublin, 1995), 162.
12 Mrs M. J. O'Connell, *op. cit.*, I 137.
13 *Ibid.*, I, 269-70.
14 *Ibid.*, I, 46-7.
15 *Ibid.*, I, 304-12.
16 *Ibid.*, I, 86-8.
17 *Ibid.*, I, 93.
18 *Ibid.*, I, 119-20.
19 *Ibid.*, I, 143.
20 *Ibid.*, I, 155.
21 *Ibid.*, II, 33, 216.
22 *Ibid.*, I, 194.
23 *Ibid.*, I, 207.
24 *Ibid.*, I, 223.
25 *Ibid.*, I,. 286-93.
26 *Ibid.*, I, 293.
27 Thomas Pierce, 'Hickie of Kilelton' in *The Shannonside Annual*, 1947; Hickie family records.

8

THE YOUNGER SONS

In terms of prestige the finest career for the younger son of a
Catholic landowner was that of a 'French officer'. About 6,500
Irishmen went to the French army with Mountcashel in 1690,
and 12,000 with Sarsfield in 1691. In the war of 1688-97 of
England, Holland and the Empire against France, some 6,000
Irishmen died, including Sarsfield, or were crippled. At the
Peace of Ryswick Mountcashel's original Irish Brigade was
retained in the French army, but the regiments from Limerick
were disbanded, and the men turned loose, many to become
highwaymen. (One named O'Neill was broken on the wheel for
murder and highway robbery.) After four years of peace the War
of the Spanish Succession started in 1701, and such of the
Limerick men as could be found were re-formed into five
regiments of foot and one of horse. Irish regiments won great
renown in north Italy at Cremona, and at Blenheim, Ramilles,
Oudenarde and Malplaquet where their desperate counterattack almost saved the day for France. By the end of the war
in 1715 there remained only 3,300 Irishmen in the French
service. They were formed into the new Irish Brigade, of five
single-battalion regiments – Dillon's, Berwick's, Clare's, Lee's,
and Dorington's (later Walsh's) and Nugent's Horse. Each was
named after its 'Colonel Proprietor', but was commanded in the
field by a lieutenant colonel.

In 1703 two Spanish regiments had been raised for the

Spanish service, which in 1715 were joined by one from France, making the King of Spain's Irish Brigade of three regiments – Irlanda, Hibernia and Ultona.

There were no Irish regiments in the Imperial service, but many Irish officers. The advantages of joining this, rather than the French of Spanish services, were quicker promotion and the fact that the Emperor was generally in alliance with Britain, so it was easier for Austrian officers to go back and forth on leave or on retirement – not that French or Spanish officers found that difficult. As Austria and France were generally at war with each other, Irishmen often fought on opposite sides.

Among Irishmen who served the King of Spain, Hugh, grandson of O'Conor Don, had a career of extraordinary distinction. After service in Cuba, 'Captain Colorado' (redhead) was appointed Inspector of the northern frontier of the Spanish empire which stretched from Texas to California. It was plagued by raids of the Apaches, fiercest of the Plains Indians, who in thirty years had scalped thousands of settlers and ruined hundreds of ranchers. His troops, badly mounted, badly armed and low in morale, were dispersed in garrisons too small to do anything but protect themselves: San Antonio, the most important settlement, had a garrison of only twenty-two. He concentrated his 2,300 men in twenty-two forts and by aggressive patrolling, and doubtless harsh reprisals, put an end to the Apache menace. He died in 1779, aged forty-five, a brigadier-general and Knight of Calatrava.[1]

In peacetime the government did little to discourage foreign recruiting, being only too glad to get rid of 'idle swordsmen'. But in 1745, after the battle of Fontenoy, the Irish Parliament enacted[2] that no one who served France or Spain could hold property in Ireland. It does not seem to have been very effective: most officers in foreign service were younger sons who owned or would inherit no land. Of those who did, Captain 'Billy' Chevers, a Spanish officer, resigned his commission, came straight home and did not even try to regularise his position for a year. His former commanding officer wrote, 'You did ill to admit being in the Spanish service. They could never have proved it of you.' But he got a pardon all the same, although Britain and Spain were at war, and duly inherited.

Pierce, twentieth Lord Dunboyne, succeeded to the title and estates of his elder brother who died unmarried in 1768. But he had served twenty-six years in France, retiring in 1769 as a lieutenant colonel, and promptly a discoverer raked this up against him, claiming his estates in County Tipperary and around Dunboyne castle in County Meath. Dunboyne, however, could produce a royal pardon for his French service and won his case, settling down at Dunboyne for the rest of his life.[3]

The prestige of King Louis's commission was its principal reward. Financially, the 'French' officer, until he reached high rank, was a drain on his family. 'Whatever the rank of a military man,' wrote Captain Daniel Charles O'Connell in 1775, 'the mediocrity of his pay keeps him in continual distress.' His outfit cost him at least £200; promotion to captain was slow, and even a captain's pay was only £100 a year, less than the income from an intermediate tenancy. The 200 or so officers in the Irish Brigade had a high turnover rate. Even some who left with Sarsfield made their peace with the government and came back. Captain Philip Roche returned in 1703 and started a flint-glass factory near Dublin, an early example of Catholic gentry taking to trade. Lieutenant Colonel Edmund Morris had persuaded Luttrell's Horse to go over to King William's service after the surrender of Limerick; but when, shortly afterwards, it was disbanded, he, being 'reduced to a low condition, was necessitated, contrary to his own inclination, to enter the French king's service in order to obtain subsistence for himself and his family.' However in 1701, thoroughly disillusioned, he changed sides yet again and 'humbly prayed for license to return,' which was granted. He then turned Protestant and his Catholic father threatened to disinherit him. But Morris was a survivor; he got Parliament to pass a private Act securing him against this.[4]

Occasionally the British government tried to win over prominent Jacobites whose ardour might have waned. Such a one was Colonel John Power who, disgusted with France and the French, returned home in 1703, and was found employment with Britain's ally, the King of Portugal. In 1720 Henry O'Brien, the Protestant, anti-Jacobite Earl of Thomond, persuaded his Catholic, Jacobite cousin Charles O'Brien, Viscount Clare, to leave his regiment for a while and come to London for an audience with George I. The king promised Clare a pardon and the restoration of his estates if he would come home and conform. No deal. Clare went back to his regiment, his exile sweetened by a legacy from Thomond of £20,000. His son commanded the Brigade at Fontenoy.[5]

The French officer who had returned home on leave or retirement, was far more a man of the world than his stay-at-home elder brother, on the lookout for a well-endowed heiress, sporting slightly part-worn Parisian fashions, interlarding his speech with French expressions and his conversation with anecdotes of soldiering in Flanders, Italy and the Indies. He was a familiar figure in Ireland and the object of dark suspicions by the authorities, who saw his fell hand in every enterprise without relish of salvation.

Many officers left the Brigade to better themselves in other armies. One of the first to do so was Owen O'Rourke from County Leitrim who after the Treaty of Ryswick entered the Imperial service and finished his career as ambassador of Prince

James Edward (the Old Pretender) to the Emperor Charles VI. Another was Peter de Lacy who joined the service of the Czar, spent many years fighting Swedes and Turks and ended up as a field marshal and Governor of Courland. Others managed plantations in the West Indies, or embarked on 'the mercantile career.'[6]

Officers of the Brigade were sometimes selected for political and diplomatic missions which had nothing to do with soldiering. Charles Wogan of County Kildare had taken part in the Jacobite rebellion of 1715, was captured at Preston and imprisoned in Newgate, from which he escaped and made his way to France. In 1719 he was sent to Russia to negotiate a marriage of James Edward to a daughter of the Czar. The Czar, however, was not impressed with the match, so Wogan made his own choice of a bride for his king – Princess Maria Clementina Sobieska, daughter of John Sobieski, King of Poland. Unfortunately the Austrian Emperor, Britain's ally in the recent war, thought this a very bad idea and had the lady locked up in Innsbruck. Wogan, an expert in these matters, organised her escape, and took her to be married in Rome. For this he was created the Chevalier de Wogan. Bored with garrison soldiering, he joined the Spanish service to fight the Moors.

After the first great flight of the Wild Geese in 1691, there were no more major migrations but a trickle year by year. In wartime the British government did its best to stop recruitment for the enemy; and in peacetime the Irish Brigade did not need many recruits. Archbishop King wrote in 1722, 'The country is disturbed by the sort of people called the Wild Geese, and some thousands of them have been enlisted for the services of the Pretender.' He probably exaggerated: the French and Spanish Irish Brigades could not have absorbed anything like that number.[7]

When the War of the Austrian Succession started in 1740

they were in action again. Spain's Irish Brigade won fame and suffered shocking casualties in Italy, but were eventually defeated by the Austrian General Maximilian Browne, whose father had left Ireland with Mountcashel. The French Irish Brigade's great day was at Fontenoy in 1745. The British broke the French front and were on the verge of a great victory when Marshal Saxe threw in the Irish under Viscount Clare in a counterattack on the British right flank. To the stirring strains of *The White Cockade* on bagpipes, fifes and drums, with the officers shouting 'Remember Limerick and Saxon perfidy!', they advanced in their scarlet uniforms to bayonet-thrusts without firing a shot, and flung back the English regiments in confusion. Marshal Saxe exclaimed, 'What finer reserve than five battalions of Wild Geese!' And the British commander, 'Butcher' Cumberland, in a remark more generous than those usually attributed to him, said, 'God's curse on the laws that made these men our enemies.'

In the following year 400 men of the Brigade under Lieutenant Colonel Stapleton took part in the Jacobite rebellion and fought at Falkirk and Culloden. Those who survived were treated correctly as prisoners of war, and repatriated to France. By that time, however, although their officers were Irish, most of the rank-and-file might have Irish names but were French-speaking and half or three quarters French in blood.

Many rustic Irish lads were sent to France very young to acquire a little French polish before joining their regiments as cadets. An unknown priest writes in 1739 to Denis O'Conor from Brussels that his nephew must learn the French language, dancing and 'the usages of the world'. He recommended that the boy be placed in Dillon's:

> Leaving that of drinking aside, which can easily be
> avoided with a little care, Dillon's of all the Irish

regiments is the best composed and speaks the best French, and is very cheap in its present garrison.

Those who joined the Irish Brigade with romantic notions were apt to be disappointed. As the newly-joined Daniel O'Conor wrote to his brother, Charles of Belanagare, on 3 September 1754:

> A regiment is a sort of world in miniature, and abridged composition of all the follies, all the stupidities and all the knaveries and vices of mankind. We have in it [Clare's] all sorts of characters, fools, knaves, half-fools, half-knaves, half-honest and some few who *pass* for being entirely honest.[8]

A cadet had a hard time. Socially he was the equal of the officers, but he drilled with a firelock and bayonet and marched with private soldiers. 'There is,' wrote Rickard O'Connell of Walsh's, 'no great amusement in stalking under a firelock opposite to a sentry-box for eight hours in the twenty-four.' He described a training exercise while he was still under instruction:

> We were divided into two parties. One represented the English who were supposed to make a descent; the other to beat them back to their ships. Though I have been only five days learning the exercise, Captain O'Conor permits me to march in the ranks and carry a gun. I fired seventy cartridges and the next most dexterous member of my party fired but fifty, upon my honour . . . Our second colonel who happened to pass by and saw us

charge, fire, and jump over hedges and ditches, and
was told by Barry, our officer, how many cartridges
I had fired, talked with admiration of the dexterity
of so fresh a soldier.[9]

In the Imperial army too, cadets had to do duty as private
soldiers. Morty O'Connell was on sentry duty at the palace when
the Empress Maria Theresa asked him the time. Standing
motionless, eyes fixed above her, he replied that he had no watch.
With a motherly smile, she dropped one into the deep pocket
of his tunic.[10]

By the 1760s it was reckoned that barely half the other ranks
of the French Irish Brigade were even of Irish descent.
Recruitment was increasingly difficult. In 1776 Clare's was
allotted a recruiting district in French Flanders 'so that the Irish
Brigade,' wrote Captain Daniel Charles O'Connell, 'may be on
a much more respectable and solid footing than these many years
past.' But four years later Captain Daniel O'Conor wrote to his
brother Charles, the Belanagare antiquarian, calling the rank-
and-file of the Brigade 'a band of ruffians and cut-throats . . .
a vile mob of hirelings, a medley of all the nations of Europe,
the excrement of the human race . . . Perhaps there is not a tenth
part of us genuine Irish.'[11]

To command such men the officers had to be very tough, and
cadet training was robust. Rickard O'Connell wrote in 1779:

> We have a great many English recruits . . . I have
> been appointed to teach them the exercise . . .
> This employment of Exercise Master is of a very
> tiresome sort. It requires a great deal of patience,
> and very much application both rough and smooth
> to transform a peasant, as dull as the clod he treads

on into a smart soldier. But the most grievous task I ever had imposed on me was to lick that bear's cub I brought with me from Ireland into a soldier. Captain O'Conor requested me to take the ungracious burden on my shoulders. Captain O'Conor's request, together with my very great regard and esteem for his respectable family, induced me to spare no pains. I endeavoured to work on his temper by soothing, together with a show of confidence and reward; then severity, when milder means proved unsuccessful to keep him out of harm's way. But on the route hither he gave full scope to his temper and one day at dinner . . . according to our rules I took him on my back and, for want of sufficient number of cadets, got nine sub-lieutenants to thrash him while he was able to roar. When the discipline was over and he recovered breath enough to curse, he became worse than ever, and swore the most execrable oaths – he would murder every one of us . . . Captain O'Conor begged I would teach him at least as much of the exercises as would give him the gait and air of a soldier. Before we were many days at this work, Harry took the sulk and refused to obey my command, and that too in the same rank with my Englishmen, the most of whom are as wicked dogs as ever trod the deck of a privateer. Though under arms, they laughed aloud and 'damned their eyes, but the lad had spirit.' Lest the contagion spread among those so apt to catch it, I ordered Harry to prison, but upon his peremptory refusal was obliged to seize him and clap him in the dungeon where

> I prescribed for him the cool regimen of bread and
> water . . . Having played the devil after his enlarge-
> ment from the dungeon, he is now, thank God,
> gone and I am rid of him.[12]

But under the right sort of Irish officers, the 'excrement of the human race' could still fight like fiends. In the War of American Independence a company under Lieutenants Eugene McCarthy and Stack volunteered to serve as marines in John Paul Jones's privateer *Le Bonhomme Richard.* They manned the tops in his fight with the British frigate *Serapis*, and were the first to board the enemy ship. McCarthy got permission to go to America with Lafayette. On the way they put in at Derrynane, and some officers went ashore to recruit Kerrymen for the American army. All were captured by troops lying in wait for them, but they managed to shout a message in Irish to Daniel Charles O'Connell's mother that he was safe and well.[13]

Walsh's fought in the West Indies and won Tobago from the British in 1781. One of its officers, Thomas Trant of Cork, also won the eighteen-year-old daughter of the Governor of Curaçao with a dowry of £30,000. After a triumphant tour of the newly independent United States, the happy couple went to France where Trant was made a Chevalier of the Military Order of St Louis, Queen Marie Antoinette herself handing him the Star of the Order with a lock of her hair in it. His brother Dominick died in Washington's army.[14]

Freemasonry thrived in the Irish Brigade, especially in Walsh's which was credited with establishing the first Lodge in France. Dillon's too, had a regimental Lodge, as probably did other corps. From the Irish, Masonry spread. In 1732 Captain Martin Kelly established a Lodge in Bordeaux in which Captain Dickson was raised to the Third Degree and the list of masters included the names Stanton, Madden, Quinn, Black and Byrne. A Toulouse Lodge was formed in 1731 by Richard and John Barnewall, younger sons of the eleventh Lord Trimleston, on the authority of Viscount Barnewall of Kingsland, Grand Master of Ireland. Most Irish officers would have been appalled to learn that Masonry is thought to have been an influence undermining the French throne and promoting revolution.[15]

Career officers were obsessed with their pedigrees. This was not mere snobbery. In order to attain high rank, one must have the ear of the king and the court. This meant having *les honeurs du Louvre* which entitled an officer to ride in one of the king's carriages when he went for a drive; to follow him hunting on one's own horse; and to sit at card-table with the queen and dauphin. For this one had to show written proof of unblemished noble descent since 1399, which was very difficult for old Irish families whose pedigrees were meticulously preserved by bards but not in writing. When Charles McCarthy Mór, an officer in the English footguards, died, his younger brother in the French service claimed to succeed him as McCarthy Mór, chief of the sept. O'Connell and Hunting Cap organised a group of Protestant magnates and a Catholic bishop into drawing up a certificate in support of this rebel, witnessed by the Notary Public. When O'Connell himself required proof of his nobility, the Chevalier O'Gorman, an ornament of the French court and an authority in these matters, warned:

> A mere genealogy from the Herald's Office in Ireland is not sufficient proof to qualify him for his presentation at court and for his entrance into the king's coaches. Two literal acts or deeds to each descent proving filiation, profession and a noble maintenance are required in support of the gen-

ealogy . . . It will require at least £300 to make out
this matter.[16]

But within a few months of this letter being written, the whole
charade had become irrelevant. The Bastille had fallen.

An alternative to the Irish Brigades, less prestigious but more
financially rewarding, was service in the Spanish navy. A young
man of some education and seamanship could serve before the
mast for eighteen very tough months, and then be appointed
'pilot', that is to say sailing master, of a Spanish warship, drawing
more pay than the captain. Several O'Sullivans chose this option
and recommended it. If one had the influence to be appointed
pilot to a ship in the 'Flota', the annual treasure-fleet from Santa
Cruz, one could make a fortune. Without influence, however,
one could be left penniless, waiting for a ship, for months or
years on the Cadiz beach, which was not recommendable.[17]

For those who had a taste for the sea and were not
overburdened with scruples, there was privateering. Luke Ryan,
formerly of Dillon's, commanded the privateer *Black Prince*
during the American war, bearing French letters of marque. The
borderline between privateer and pirate, clear enough in theory,
(a privateer carried letters of marque from a belligerent
government authorising him to capture enemy shipping for his
own profit) was sometimes blurred in practice. Ryan was
captured and tried as a pirate at the Old Bailey in 1782. He was
condemned to death, but reprieved no less than three times, and
on the conclusion of peace was released through the mediation
of the French government. So instead of swinging in chains from
Execution Dock at Wapping, he returned to France to enjoy his
gains, some £70,000. Alas, they were all embezzled by bankers
in Brittany, and he died a debtor in the King's Bench prison.[18]

Catholics were not barred from the civil and military services of the Honourable East India Company. In the Calcutta journals of William Hickey, a Protestant Irishman, dozens of Irishmen are mentioned, many of them presumably Catholics. McCarthys, Bellews, MacDermots, Nagles and many more could write H.E.I.C.S. after their names. The potential rewards of Indian service were fabulous, not in salaries which were meagre but in private trade and all sorts of perks and commissions – provided one survived into middle age. The difficulty for an Irishman in getting a job was that he needed influence with the Court of Directors, which was in London. It is curious to find Mr John Halinan of Limerick asking Dr Plunkett, Catholic Bishop of Meath, for help in securing an appointment with the Honourable Company.

Laurence Sulivan from County Cork served in Bombay from 1740 to 1752 and then retired for reasons of health to England where he became increasingly powerful in the company's management. As Chairman of the Court of Directors for most of the time (by rotation) from 1758 to 1782, he was notorious for his zeal in promoting the interest of his family and friends and managed to get his son and three other County Cork Sulivans onto the company's payroll.

One Catholic who gave the pagoda tree a hearty shake was Thomas Trant of Cork. He arrived in Calcutta a thirty-year-old army cadet, but having been 'reared in a counting house', was persuaded by Hickey's chum Bob Pott to resign from the army and become Pott's business manager. The business was prodigious. Pott was resident to the court of the Nawab of Bengal, and all the Nawab's allowances from the company passed through his hands, less what stuck to his fingers. He was agent for the Nawab's extravagant purchases in Europe and Calcutta, for which he drew a fat commission; and collector of customs for the Nawab's territories, a most lucrative post. A generous man, he showered presents on his friends (including, for Hickey, 'a very pretty little native girl whom he recommended for my personal use'); so one can assume that Trant prospered in his employ. But by the end of the eighteenth century this riotous free-for-all had been brought to an end: company servants had to live on their not inadequate salaries and pensions.[19]

Of learned professions, the law was generally, between 1727 and 1792, for Protestants only: Catholics could not be barristers, solicitors or attorneys. One who managed to breach the barrier was the celebrated Daniel MacNamara, who practised in London under the modest title of 'conveyancer'. But he was so profound and well-read a lawyer that many Irish Catholics and Protestants paid him retainers, including a large number of MPs and Viscount Gormanston who consulted him on his marital problems. He was the London agent of the Catholic Association. Lord Chancellor Thurlow said that he owed his position solely to the Penal Laws: but for these, Dan MacNamara would be chancellor. He also moved in exalted social and political circles: he was friendly with Burke and other leading Whig politicians, and the Prince of Wales often dined at his villa in Streatham, declaring that nowhere in London could one dine better. (He should know.) With his influence, MacNamara's nephew got a job with the East India Company, but was killed in a riding accident in Madras.[20]

The Catholic church was a career option for the younger sons of landowning families. One required, of course, a dedication to a religious life and an acceptance of celibacy. One also required ample financial backing, for the would-be priest, having acquired a good knowledge of the classics at home or in a Catholic school in Dublin, Limerick or Cork, then had to study for several years at a seminary in Rome, France, Spain or the Netherlands. The parish priest did not have, like the Church of Ireland rector, an assured income from tithes; but nor did he have a wife and family to support. His income was about the same as that of a lieutenant or captain in the Irish Brigade, £50 to £100 a year from offertories, marriage and funeral fees, etc.; but to this could be added in many cases the profits of a small farm, fees for tutoring the sons of Catholic gentry, gifts in kind from his parishioners and hospitality (not only from Catholics) which he would not be expected to return. The parish priest was not affluent, nor was he impoverished. If he became chaplain and tutor to some Catholic family, he had a very comfortable way of life. Nevertheless, his earthly reward was not financial but in job satisfaction and the respect in which he was generally held.[21]

A somewhat atypical parish priest was Dr Patrick M'Dermot who had been chaplain to the Irish Brigade at Fontenoy. He returned to Ireland in the 1760s and worked in Meath until he died in 1814 at the age of 111 years. 'Dr Mac' was a 'character', and a great favourite with the Protestant gentry: 'every respectable family in the neighbourhood ambitioned his society.'[22]

Some priests, having trained abroad, stayed abroad, many in slightly out-of-the-ordinary jobs such as chaplains to the French fleet or to the French East India Company. Louis XVI was attended on the scaffold by an Irish priest, the Abbé Edgworth.

Throughout the eighteenth century many Catholic landed families contributed a son or two in every generation to the priesthood. The problem, in so far as there was one, of going abroad for a priest's education was neatly solved by Patrick Joseph Plunkett, son of James Plunkett, Esquire, of County Meath, who in 1752 at the age of fourteen felt a vocation. His father apprenticed him to a Dublin merchant and had him sent to France 'as if on mercantile business, but in reality to evade the Penal Laws.' He was to become Bishop of Meath, greatly respected both by Catholics and Protestants.[23]

In 1795 the government, alarmed at the prospect of priests trained abroad being infected with republican notions, founded the College of Saint Patrick at Maynooth for the training of Catholic priests. Many continued to go abroad for training; but among those who studied at Maynooth the proportion from gentry families declined: the typical Maynooth product was the son of a strong farmer, with perhaps a lawyer or doctor brother, whose sisters were genteelly educated.

The medical profession was open to Catholics. Traditionally certain septs were physicians to their overlords – O'Meara to Ormonds, O'Leys to O'Flahertys, O'Sheils to MacMahons, O'Hickeys to O'Briens. This continued well into the seventeenth century and probably many traditional doctors were skilled practitioners but not such as would be regarded as professionally qualified in an increasingly scientific profession. By the middle of the century there were three recognised grades of medicos, apothecaries, surgeons and physicians. Apothecaries were not unlike modern GPs: they not only dispensed but prescribed medicines. In the worlds of Jane Austen and Maria Edgeworth, if a servant fell ill the apothecary was summoned; if a member of the family was indisposed, the physician was asked to call. Surgeons, bizarrely connected with barbers and wigmakers, were somewhat lowered in public esteem by association with 'resurrectionists' who exhumed recently buried corpses for examination and dissection by anatomy students. A young man could qualify as an apothecary or a surgeon by serving a six- or seven-year apprenticeship.

To qualify as a physician was much harder. An O'Hickey or an O'Ley might learn a great deal from his father or uncle: one O'Hickey, his land in Clare having been forfeited in 1691, set up as a physician in Limerick and prospered. It was doubtful, however, if he could write MD after his name; and it was probably with an eye to such practitioners that the Royal College of Physicians in Ireland was given a charter by Charles II in 1667 and by William and Mary in 1692 'to stamp out the daily abuse of the most necessary and laudable art of physics ... by the practice of mountebanks and empirics and other ignorant and illiterate persons.' An MD had to be a university graduate and to be licensed to practise by the Royal College of Physicians which was affiliated to Trinity College, the Protestant Holy of Holies. A few crypto-Catholic converts may have gained entry to Trinity, but they cannot have been many. In 1687 James II granted a charter to found a College of Physicians in Kilkenny, but it does not seem to have survived his downfall. But Edmund O'Meara, a Catholic, a graduate of Rheims and physician to the Duke of Ormond was elected an Honorary Fellow of the Royal College of Physicians; and when he died in 1681 his son William followed in his footsteps. We do not know how or where William qualified to be an MD but certainly his father must have ensured that his training and qualifications were adequate.

So how did a Catholic become a physician? As early as 1728 private medical schools were advertised in the Dublin *Weekly Journal*. James Brennan, MD and his brother Peter, a surgeon, Catholics from Kerry, kept such a school in Dublin; and there was another in Omagh. James was a prominent Freemason, which may have helped. But they seem to have taught anatomy and surgery rather than physics. So a Catholic who wanted to be a physician had first to obtain a degree at a university outside Ireland, and then be licensed to practise by the college in Dublin. Most took their degrees in France, some in Britain where, according to Dr William Drennan who studied in Edinburgh, 'A student of medicine is a term of contempt, but an Irish student of medicine is the very highest compilation of disgrace.' But in France an officer of the Irish Brigade felt it no shame to be a friend of Maurice Leyne, *étudiant en médecine.*

Dr Terence MacDermot and his nephew Hugh studied medicine in Paris and took their degrees at Rheims. In 1781 Hugh MacDermot, finishing his course in anatomy and chemistry, wrote to his father:

> Still there remain the study of practical medicine and the immediate cure of disorders for which there are no professors established at this university... Many physicians, perfect masters in theory, yet when first brought to the bedside of a patient, find themselves embarrassed and at a loss how to proceed.

With the support of his uncle, Dr Terence, and his grandfather, Charles O'Conor of Belanagare, he proposed to complete his studies in Edinburgh, cost what it may, and his father somewhat grudgingly agreed. He matriculated in December 1782 and seems to have practised in London, no doubt as a junior partner, until 1788 when he returned to Ireland and put up his plate at Belanagare, moving to Coolavin when his father died.[24]

Almost the first of Dublin's hospitals was the Charitable Infirmary, founded by six doctors, apparently Catholics, in 1721. The best known Catholic Irish physician in the eighteenth century was Dr John Curry, the friend of Charles O'Conor of Belanagare. His grandfather was a Jacobite cavalry officer from County Cavan who died at Aughrim, his father a successful Dublin merchant. Born about 1715 he studied medicine in Paris, took his degree in Rheims and put up his plate in Dublin in the early 1740s, duly licensed by the Royal College. He specialised in fevers, writing *An Essay on Ordinary Fevers* (London, 1743) and *Some Thoughts on the Nature of Fevers* (London, 1774). He attributed most fevers to 'cold taken' and observed that more people died of colds than by 'fire, sword, pestilence or famine'. His cure for the common fever was to keep the patient warm in bed, bleed him and make him drink plenty of liquids 'without drops of any kind.' 'It is Nature cures disorders', was his maxim.

One day in 1746 – that day of the year on which Protestants were regaled in church with 'anniversary invectives' on the rebellion of 1641 – he happened to encounter two ladies and a lively little girl who, setting eyes on him, raised her hands in horror and asked, 'Are there any of those bloody Papists in Dublin?' Curry determined to set the record straight and published next year his *Brief Account from the most Authentic Protestant Writers of the Irish Rebellion, 1641*, followed by *An Historical and Critical Review of the Civil War in Ireland*. Over the next thirty years he churned out booklets and pamphlets urging the repeal of the Penal Laws and the recognition of Catholic loyalty to the Crown. His last work, written with great satisfaction, was *The State of the Catholics in Ireland from the Settlement under King William to the Relaxation of the Popery Laws in 1778*. He corresponded regularly with Charles O'Conor, the antiquarian, with whom he founded in 1760 the Catholic Committee, a pressure group to better the position of Irish Catholics. He died in 1780, leaving two sons in the Imperial Austrian service.[25]

Sylvester O'Halloran came from a Catholic landowning family in County Clare. Born in 1720, he studied medicine in Leyden, Paris and London. While in London in 1745, he seriously considered making his way to Scotland to join Prince Charles Edward, but fortunately thought the better of it. He set up in practice in Limerick in 1747, 'a tall, thin doctor in his quaint French dress, with his gold-headed cane, beautiful Parisian wig and cocked hat'. His medical writings included work on cataract, on a new method of amputation, on *Proposals for the Advancement of Surgery in Ireland*, and on disorders arising from injuries to the head. (In the latter, he did not lack practice, faction fights being very prevalent.) He also wrote *A General History of Ireland* and *An Introduction to the Antiquities of Ireland*, a critic of which advised him to stick to subjects of which he knew something. He was also involved in all kinds of public work – advising on the Shannon navigation, founding a debating society, running the Limerick Medical Society and the Royal College of Surgeons which was established to raise the standards and prestige of that profession. He agitated for Catholic Emancipation; his correspondents included Charles O'Conor, Colonel Vallancey and Edmund Burke. He was a very well-known, highly respected man.

He had four sons. The eldest married into the family of John FitzGibbon. The second fought in the War of American Independence in an American Loyalist regiment, and was awarded 800 acres on Long Island which he presumably forfeited when his side lost. The youngest sailed to India in 1781 as a midshipman in an East India Company sloop of war. He transferred to the Bengal army in which he served for over fifty years, and was knighted on his retirement.[26]

The Penthenys (or Pentonys) were a Catholic family in County Meath. Their estates were confiscated during the Interregnum, but at the Restoration just enough was restored to them 'for the little exigencies of obscurity.' Christopher Pentheny, born in 1682, married a wife with West Indian property. His son Peter became a doctor in the West Indies where malaria, yellow fever and other tropical diseases ensured that he would not lack patients. He and his brother Augustine, who ran the family plantations, made a lot of money and, returning to Ireland after the Catholic Relief Act of 1782, bought estates in Counties

Meath, Westmeath, Kildare and Dublin. When he died Daniel
O'Connell referred respectfully to 'old Pentony's fortune,
£100,000.' Two Kerrymen, Dr Jeremy Leyne, a graduate of Avignon
University and his son Maurice, a graduate of Paris University,
practised at Tralee from 1759 until the end of the century.

James Magan, a younger son of the Westmeath Catholic
landed family, qualified as a physician and practised in Dublin.
It was probably his son who took to the 'mercantile career' and
opened a wool shop which enjoyed royal patronage.[27]

Arthur Young noted that trade was held in contempt by
Protestants who 'call themselves gentry' and that 'commercial
people are quitting trade and manufactures when they have made
five or ten thousand pounds to become gentlemen.'[28] Protestants
could afford to hold themselves aloof from the marketplace and
counting-house, for their younger sons could enter the armed
services, the law and politics, which were closed to Catholics.
But to Catholic gentry, except perhaps the grandest houses of
the Pale, a mercantile career was more than socially acceptable.
Some moved into towns and resorted to trade when their estates
had been forfeited; others who had retained their estates invested
spare capital in commerce because the Penal Laws did not allow
them to buy land with it. Moreover it was not advisable for the
affluent Papist to draw attention to himself by building a
mansion or flaunting an extravagant lifestyle; nor could he pour
out his money on elections, which ruined many Protestants.
Capital accumulation by investment in commerce was both more
prudent and more profitable. Finally, the mercantile career for
his younger sons was an alternative to the Church, the medical
profession or foreign military service. There was a co-relation
between landownership and commerce, particularly among
Galway families.

It has been estimated that to apprentice a son to an export

house cost about £200, and to set him up in an independent business in Ireland, £400 to £600 – much the same as the cost in his early years in the Irish Brigade or his education to be a priest or physician. The wills of many landowners show such sums left to the younger sons while the eldest son, despite the gavel law, inherited the estate.[29]

Yet it was difficult for Catholics to become full members of Guilds, without which they could hardly prosper in trade. It looked as though they might be squeezed out of business altogether, but in the first half of the eighteenth century they markedly increased their share of the population, and of business, in every seaport outside Ulster.

The process was most marked – or at least best documented – in Cork. As early as 1694 the Corporation took note of a complaint by the Society of Wholesaling and Retailing Merchants that 'several persons not qualified, Roman Catholics and others, do keep open shops and expose their goods for sale.' Three years later it was found necessary to forbid Protestants to take Popish apprentices. In 1704 the Corporation resolved that:

> An application be made to Parliament next session setting out the grievance the English lie under by the encroachments of the Irish into their respective trades, and also setting forth the great number of Irish flocking into this city to the great damage and danger of the Protestant inhabitants.

In 1706 the Corporation received a complaint by the master of the Company of Coopers:

> that divers others, Irish Papists, who have no right to their freedom [of the Guild] have lately come

and set up and drive the coopering trade within this city . . . and take as many apprentices as they please, and employ as many journeymen as their occasions require who, being Papists, flock to them, which if not prevented will tend to the impoverishing of several of the Protestant coopers.

Coopers, to be sure, were of no great consequence, but in 1709 the Corporation felt compelled to:

demand that Papists be debarred from carrying on any foreign trade . . . which they will in likelihood engross to themselves to the unspeakable prejudices of the Protestant merchants.

In 1718 Archbishop King sounded the alarm:

I may further observe that the Papists being made incapable to purchase land have turned to trade, and already engrossed almost all the trade of the Kingdom.[30]

A Protestant polemicist writing in Cork in 1737 under the name of Alexander the Coppersmith took up the same theme. Not that he was a bigot: indeed he was a model of broadminded tolerance:

I no more condemn a Papist for the crookedness of his thoughts than I do for the crookedness of his legs, provided he extends them not to the annoyance of his neighbours. But if he labours under this natural infirmity, he should not wear white stockings to expose it . . .

Men who have a claim to compassion and a
relaxation of the laws ought to express poverty, and
should think themselves happy were they admitted
to such a share of the trade as would provide a
comfortable maintenance . . . But through the flow-
ing of wealth and the swelling of pride, Protestant
indolence and Papist vigilance, the trade of this
city has been forced out of its natural course into
another channel . . . For the French in galleys of
four or five hundred tons come hither, always
consigned to a Popish factor.

He was deeply disturbed by the Catholic work ethic, potentially
ruinous to honest Protestants. Papists

whose diligence being more and luxury being less
than the Protestants will at last swallow up the
trade and suck the marrow from the city . . . How
secure do men of that religion live, in despite of
the law, while Protestants look idly on, and by an
easiness of temper peculiar to themselves suspend
the execution of the laws.

As for the way in which Papists dealt only with one another,
iniquitous!

If a Papist at the gallows would want an ounce of
hemp, he'll skip the Protestant shops and run to
Mallow Lane to secure it . . . They poison all
things they touch; they consider nothing but the
present; their schemes are always big with cunning.

Let them be warned! A set of men 'living under the frowns of the law' should conduct themselves humbly lest worse befall:

> The parliament to restrain Papist power and suppress clans has incapacitated them from purchasing estates; it would therefore be too hard as well as imprudent to exclude them from the benefit of employing their money in trade. But they should be cautious how they extend the reign of policy and by a vehement impulse of interest raise themselves into object of Protestant jealousy . . . Their bold monopoly of foreign trade will create such popular clamour that at last they will be controlled by parliamentary restraint.[31]

It was not only in Cork city. The Corporation of Youghal in County Cork petitioned Parliament in 1766 that Popish tradesmen were boasting that 'they had more correspondents in foreign countries than Protestants' and that they would not allow Protestants 'to get a morcel of bread in Youghal.'[32]

Alexander the Coppersmith and his ilk overestimated the emergency which so stirred them. The population of Cork city in his day was two-thirds Catholic, but only about a quarter of the export houses were Catholic. But even this represented a remarkable recovery from the disasters of 1691.

The higher ranks of Cork Catholic mercantile families were typified by the Trants, who originated in County Kerry where much of their land had been forfeited, Sir Patrick Trant having been a prominent Jacobite; but his widow and family had been allowed to retain a small portion of it. Ignatius Trant had moved to Cork to better himself, and in the early 1750s he was joined in Mallow Lane by Thomas Trant from Dingle. From their offices and warehouses on Trant's Quay they exported to France beef, butter, hides, tallow, and coarse wool, and imported silk, tea, tobacco and wine. That they traded also with the West Indies is suggested by a newspaper advertisement in 1762:

> To be sold for the account of D.F. a black negro
> boy aged about fourteen, remarkably free from
> vice, a very handy willing servant. Apply Ignatius
> or Thomas Trant in Mallow Lane where the boy
> can be seen.

An exporter on a small scale, or just setting up in business, chartered a ship, filled it with goods and travelled with it as supercargo to France where he sold his goods, filled the ship with French products and returned aboard it to Ireland. But the Trants were exporters on a big scale, and bigger as the Seven Years War brought them naval victualling contracts. They had their own ships, their own quay, their own contacts and agents in Nantes, Bordeaux and Dunkirk, and had no need to sail as supercargoes. They soon moved out of Mallow Lane, except for business, and resided in a grand house, Myrtleville, in the outskirts of Cork.[33]

Thomas Trant's daughter married Andrew O'Shea, another Catholic merchant prince of Cork, and presented him with no less than eighteen little merchant princes and princesses. A Yankee visitor to the O'Sheas was introduced to 'the best Roman Catholic families' and recorded his impressions:

> They dine late (at least to us Americans), their
> entertainments are by no means magnificent, but
> good, and I am happy to find that the bottle is by
> no means pushed to excess, as was formerly the

case when there was no such thing as dining with
them without coming away drunk . . . The evening
societies are very agreeable; a man may either play
cards (Whist, Quadrille and Linskinet are their
favourite games) or enter into conversation, for as
their drums [tea parties] are generally large, some
are always disengaged at play. The women in
general seem fond of sporting a little; their drums
break up at about 12 o'clock, but at suppers a
person can seldom get away before one or two.
Sometimes cards are introduced after supper.

There was a theatre open three months in the year where the
visitor saw Mrs Abington perform as Lady Teazle in Sheridan's
School for Scandal; and there were also concerts of high quality,
and of course balls.[34]

O'Sullivans opened five paper mills in Cork in the 1790s, and
also produced sailcloth, flax and ironware. At Middleton in
County Cork Marcus Lynch built the first woollen mill operated
by water-power.[35]

The anti-Popery Act of 1704 severely restricted Catholic
residence in Limerick and Galway; but by 1762, according to
the Limerick historian Father James White, the bulk of the trade
was in their hands. The two wealthiest families were Catholic,
the Arthurs and the Roches. Patrick Arthur built Arthur's Quay
in 1770; and the Roches owned a huge warehouse and several
ships engaged on the West Indies trade and armed with cannon
against pirates and privateers. Because as Catholics they could
not own the land on which their warehouses stood, it was 'held'
for them by their friend Dr Perry, Protestant Bishop of Limerick.[36]

As for Galway, of a total population of 14,000 in 1762, only
350 were Protestants. Galway was rather a special case, being

the 'City of the Tribes' who had for centuries been involved in commerce. In the mercantile enterprises of the Catholic landed gentry, Galway men, especially tribesmen, were always prominent.[37]

Some set up in business at home; the Burkes of Marble Hill, for instance, as transport contractors. Christopher Bellew of Mount Bellew left the real estate to his eldest son, Michael; and to the three younger sons, Luke, Patrick and Francis, £840, £430 and £430 respectively – enough to pay for their apprenticeships and establish them in mercantile careers well away from home. He himself and Michael set up as flour millers and prospered exceedingly after mid-century when rising grain prices, parliamentary bounties on grain and swelling markets made this line very profitable. The rents of the estate paid for the building of mills, costing from £1,000 to £7,000 each, and profits from the mills paid for expanding the estate by leaseholds and, after 1782, purchases.[38]

There seems to have been something in the Galway air, or in tribal genes, which instilled commercial acumen even into gentlemen totally devoid of commercial experience. Less successful was Thomas Wyse of Waterford who set up a hardware factory in the 1750s. Despite a somewhat surprising development grant of £4,000 from Parliament, it failed. Myles Kean of County Leitrim was confident of making his fortune as a wine merchant in Dublin. He didn't.[39]

Scarcity of coin, the risks and inconveniences of transporting it, and lack of banks, created a need for bills of exchange to finance trade on any large scale. Since these depended on trust, it was convenient for a landed family engaged in commerce to have in Dublin or further afield younger sons and other reliable contacts. Thus Christopher Bellew's sons Luke in Bordeaux and Patrick, first in Cadiz and later in Dublin, could be very helpful to the family milling business. In the 1770s, Isidore Blake of

Tower Hill near Tuam was deeply involved in deals in wool, hides, livestock and butter with his uncle John Blake in Dublin, who also bought the produce of other Galway landowners, including flour from the Bellews, sold them brandy and claret, and collected rents from an absentee landlord's estate in Mayo and remitted them to Bath. The Blakes of Ballyglunin used to sell their wool to Alexander Bodkin, another tribesman, in Dublin. There were compact groups of Galway merchants in Dublin, London, Nantes and Bordeaux, all trading with each other and with Galway landowners by means of bills of exchange.[40]

Further afield the Catholic Irish interest was predominant in the smaller West Indian islands (Jamaica was mainly Scottish and Protestant). In Montserrat and Antigua, Blakes of Menlo were established in the mid-seventeenth century, and after the Williamite war they were joined there by Bodkins, Butlers, Skeretts, Frenchs, McCarthys and Trants. In 1729 half of Monserrat's thirty plantations, including the six biggest, were owned by Irish Catholics. According to climate and soil they grew coffee, tobacco, sugar and cotton. Coffee required least land and labour: Christopher Bellew's youngest son, Francis, had only about seventy acres and sixteen slaves; he might have bought more, but died young. Sugar and cotton were the most labour-intensive: a Butler sugar plantation required 189 slaves, eighty-eight mulattos and sixteen horses to work it. Irish plantations were established, mainly by ex-officers of the Irish Brigade, in the French colonies – the island of St Domingue, now Haiti, and the mainland colony of New Orleans.[41]

Planting and commerce overlapped; many planters were also general traders. Their agents, often relatives, sold their produce in London, Dublin, Nantes and Bordeaux. The proceeds of cotton grown by John Blake in St Domingue and consigned to Thomas Blake in Bordeaux were passed on to John's brother

Luke in London. There was a triangular relationship between Ireland, the West Indies and France; Irish landowners used profits from their West Indian plantations to set up younger sons in business in Bordeaux and Nantes. John Stapleton, a Tipperary man whose family had a plantation in Antigua, extended his interests first to St Domingue, then to Nantes where Richard Stapleton based his privateer during the Anglo-French wars. John's wife, *née* Helen Skerrett, indentured a Galway blacksmith to work on the Antigua estate. It doubtless helped that Sir William Stapleton was Governor of the Leeward Islands. Difficulties arising from the war caused many Irish planters to move from French and English islands to the neutral Danish island of St Croix. By 1760 there were 250 Catholic Irish on this small island, including twelve plantation owners and a hundred overseers.[42]

In the 1730s Richard Welsh of New Ross, County Wexford, by hiring seasonal labour from his home area insinuated himself into the English cod-fishing operations in Placentia Bay, Newfoundland. Like a cuckoo in the nest, by mid-century he was the biggest operator there. After his death in 1770 Roger Sweetman, of Newbawn, County Wexford, who seems to have been his son-in-law, inherited and expanded his business. By 1788 his company owned dwelling houses, offices and warehouses in Placentia, a dozen ships carrying cod to Irish agents in England, France, Italy, Spain and Portugal, and 140 fishing shallops. Every summer 700 fishermen and shoremen were brought from Wexford to man the shallops and the shore installations. Many wintered in Newfoundland, cutting and hauling timber for building ships, shallops and houses. It was indeed big business, but wilted as the Napoleonic wars reduced trade with the Continent.[43]

By the end of the seventeenth century the supercargo system

was being phased out because Irish exports to France went mainly to St Malo, La Rochelle and Nantes, but exports from France to Ireland came mainly from Bordeaux. Credit and bills of exchange presented no problems so long as Irish merchants in these ports and in London and Dublin trusted one another and shared local knowledge. Thus Dominick and Martin Bodkin were established in La Rochelle in the 1670s, and were joined there by Lynches and Kirwans. In Nantes between 1700 and 1710 Dominick Joyce set up as agent for Dominick Kirwan; Peter French as agent for Martin French; and Peter Browne as agent for Andrew Browne. By 1739 a list of Irish agents in Nantes included the names Walsh, Stitch, Clancey, O'Riordain, Sheil, Kirwan and Kiely. In London, FitzGerald, Kirwans and Trants had been in business since the 1680s. By 1720 there were at least nine Irish firms in London, and by mid-century about twenty, including one headed by two sons of Viscount Barnewall of Kingsland. Between these closely knit groups, a Galway Lynch's bill on a Galway Bodkin in Nantes could settle debts in Dublin and London, and then be used to finance Anglo-French deals, all without cash changing hands. In addition to the more respectable Irish houses in Nantes was an inn of no very high repute kept by Thomas Martin. Its rear premises included a special room frequented by the young of both sexes.[44]

British, French, Austrian and Spanish officers might look down their noses at trade, but not Irish officers. When Nicholas Skerrett sailed to France in 1708 to join his brother in Berwick's, he took with him enough wool, cloth and lead to see him through his early impecunious years as cadet and subaltern. Bryan MacDermot, probably the son of Cathal Roe MacDermot, Prince of Coolavin, who after Limerick had gone first to Spain, left the Irish Brigade after the Treaty of Ryswick for the textile trade in Rouen. James Rutledge from Mayo also exchanged soldiering for a mercantile career, assisted no doubt by his first wife who was a Kirwan and his second who was a Blake.[45]

Patrick D'Arcy of Killtullagh, County Galway, left the Irish Brigade in the 1760s to become a partner of another ex-officer, Thomas Sutton of Clonard, County Wexford, in a vastly lucrative banking and investment business in Paris. They invested mainly in mining and East Indian ventures, advised the government and many private individuals on handling their finances; and Sutton became a director of the French East India Company. They were associated with the firm of Denis McCarthy (of the Earl of Clancarty's family) in Bordeaux, who produced and exported wine to Ireland and the West Indies while his numerous kinsmen in the Brigade were imbibing it in large quantities. Denis McCarthy became a Director of the Chamber of Commerce in 1767, and a count of the French nobility. McCarthys swarmed in France, especially in the Irish Brigade, from Major General Florence McCarthy Reagh, who emigrated to New Orleans, to Jean Baptiste McCarthy, a 'spoilt' priest of Nantes who was executed for brigandage.[46]

The most conspicuous success, still commemorated in the firm's advertisements, was that of Richard Hennessy who joined Dillon's in 1740 from his home at Ballymacoy near Mallow. He was stationed for a while at la Rochelle through which was exported most of the brandy distilled in the Cognac district. Naturally he sent casks of this delicious, nutritious, character-building beverage to his friends in Ireland, without worrying too much about excise duty. He fought at Dettingen and Fontenoy, and in 1752, having been wounded in action, retired from Dillon's and settled down in Cognac where he began distilling the stuff. In the 1760s there was set up the brandy exporting firm of Hennessy, Connelly and Co. His son James followed in his footsteps; and in 1766 the firm of 'Jas Hennessy' (which could stand for James or Jacques) exported 13,000 cases; in 1778, nearly 120,000 cases. The family became completely integrated into the French nobility, to the extent of founding a pack of hounds to hunt wolves, but retained its links with County Cork.[47]

Bordeaux was the base of many Irish families who made and exported wine. The best known were the Protestant Bartons; but Catholic Kirwans, O'Byrnes, D'Arcys, Clarkes and Lynches all owned vineyards and exported the wines of Medoc. Famous, if only as an agile political survivor, was Jean Baptiste Lynch, grandson of Colonel John Lynch who had left Ireland with Sarsfield and set up in Bordeaux as a wool and leather merchant. By 1790 Jean Baptiste, aged fifty-one, had acquired a title, the Chateau Duzac in the Medoc and a vineyard. In revolutionary France he was known as a well-heeled liberal, almost a Girondin republican, what would now be called a 'champagne socialist'. But his title and wealth made him an object of suspicion to the Jacobins, so by a singularly ill-judged change of coat he became an ardent royalist. This resulted in his imprisonment and the loss of his property; but he was saved from the guillotine by the fall of Robespierre, and recovered his estates. He became Mayor of Bordeaux in 1809, and as a reward for his fervent declarations of loyalty was created a Napoleonic *comte*. In January 1812, he pledged his city's devotion to the imperial cause; and in March he greeted the vanguard of the victorious British army, tearing off his tricolour cockade and replacing it with the white cockade of the Bourbons. Napoleon on his return from Elba said he could forgive all who betrayed him but two, one of whom was Jean Baptiste Lynch. However, the *comte* had made his getaway to England, and returned in triumph after Waterloo.[48]

Another Irish Catholic family which made good in France

was that of MacMahon. Many were in the Irish Brigade, but Jean Baptiste MacMahon chose a medical career and studied at Rheims. Having qualified, he put up his plate at Autun in Burgundy. Among his patients were the enormously wealthy owner of the Chateau Sully and his wife. He did not survive MacMahon's ministrations, but his widow did, and married the young doctor. Their grandson was the famous Marshal MacMahon, hero of the Malakoff, Duke of Magenta and in 1873 President of the French Republic.[49]

West Indian plantations were run on slave labour. In a growth industry there was need for a constant flow of newly-captured negroes from West Africa. These were provided by, among others, the talented and versatile Walsh family. After losing his land to a Cromwellian adventurer, James Walsh served in the Restoration navy and captained the ship which carried James II into exile after the Battle of the Boyne. He and his son Philip set up as shipbuilders in St Malo, building several warships for the French navy and augmented their income by privateering under French letter of marque, smuggling and slave-trading. Philip died in 1708 in Madagascar, after a fight with a Dutch ship. He left five sons by his wife, a White of Waterford.

One of these sons, Anthony, born in St Malo in 1703, transferred the family's shipbuilding enterprise to Nantes. He also went privateering in wartime, smuggling and slaving at all times. Slaving was particularly lucrative: in a single round voyage, sailing before the trade winds, a ship took French produce to West Africa, slaves to the West Indies; sugar, coffee, tobacco, cotton and rum back to France.

In 1745 Anthony was recruited by Lord Clare for a Jacobite enterprise, his task being to carry Prince Charles Edward in his frigate *Doutelle* to the west coast of Scotland. *Doutelle* was accompanied by the sixty-four-gun *Elizabeth*, of which the captain was Walter Rutledge of Dunkirk. Of the 'seven men of Moidart' who landed with the prince at Eriskay, four were Irish – George Kelly of Roscommon, Sir Thomas Sheridan of Cavan, John O'Sullivan of Kerry and Colonel John McDonnell of FitzJames's regiment. Scottish Jacobites contended that the '45 would have fared better if all four had stayed at home; but the prince thought well of Anthony Walsh, who 'understands his business perfectly and is an excellent seaman.' After the defeat of his army, the prince was picked up in the Western Isles and carried back to France by another Irishman, Richard Warren, an ex-officer of Lally's and Roche's and a merchant in Marseilles.

In 1753 Anthony went to St Domingue to manage the Walsh plantations there. Meanwhile his younger brother Francis had inherited a large fortune from his uncle, Patrick White of Waterford, and followed the family calling of shipbuilding, privateering and slaving from a new base, Cadiz, which tended to be the preserve of Waterford families. In 1749 Francis bought the Chateau de Serrant in the Loire valley, and was ennobled as the Comte Walsh de Serrant. His son Anthony, the second count, served in the Irish Brigade and became colonel proprietor of the regiment of de Walsh de Serrant. In 1794 he joined General Daniel O'Connell in raising the Irish Brigade in the British army.[50]

In the 1780s, Protestants still controlled most of Irish trade – in Belfast all of it. Nevertheless the largest Dublin sugar merchant was Edward Byrne, closely linked with the Tuites who grew sugar on St Croix island in the West Indies, with Denis McCarthy in Bordeaux, Thomas Sutton in Paris and Patrick Bellew in Cadiz. In 1792 it was calculated that he contributed £80,000 a year to the revenue. The largest silk merchant was Andrew Reynolds; at the head of the Leinster cotton industry was the firm of O'Brien and Comerford; the firm of Duffy,

Byrne and Hamill dominated the calico trade; and Richard McCormick was a worsted and wool tycoon. All these were Catholics and all, at least by their own account, members of gentry families who had lost their all through loyalty to the House of Stuart. Perhaps their social pretensions were taken with a pinch of salt by Plunketts, Prestons and MacDermots; but Charles O'Conor of Belanagare could write of a possible marriage of his nephew Owen (who became O'Conor Don) to a daughter of Edward Byrne. 'It would put the family of Belanagare on a footing of respectability far beyond any other Catholic name in the province.'[51]

Hugh O'Conor, who claimed descent from O'Conor Sligo, established a business in London, Dublin and the Isle of Man (a smuggling centre) to deal in sugar, cotton, rum, wine and spirits. His sons carried on in the business and married a Blake of Tower Hill and a Moore of Mount Browne, a family which supplemented its income from rents by brewing. The Dermots of Usher's Quay, who resumed the Mac in 1784, were shipowners and provision merchants. They came from a branch of the sept in County Louth, distantly related to the MacDermots of Coolavin.[52]

John Keogh served his apprenticeship to an O'Conor on the Isle of Man and was then employed by a haberdasher, Mary Lincoln, in Dublin. (His non-admirers taxed him with being apprenticed to a smuggler, which was not unlikely, and being 'porter and counter-boy to the Widow Lincoln.') From these humble beginnings he became a partner in the firm of Lincoln, Son and Keogh, then set up on his own account in silk and brewing, became extremely rich, and prominent in the affairs of the Catholic Committee.[53]

George Moore and his son, Captain John Moore, had kept their land under the Articles of Limerick. Captain John's eldest son, Robert, inherited the estate; and the younger, George, emigrated to Alicante in Spain where he managed a fleet of ships engaged in the wine trade. In 1780 he returned home to sign the Oath of Allegiance of allegiance to George III; and three years later, on the death of his elder brother without issue, came into the estate. With the money he had made in Spain he bought 800 acres of Blake land and built Moore Hall, in County Mayo, an elegant Georgian mansion. He was worth about £4,000 a year.[54]

Most of these successful merchants bought land as soon as the law enabled them to do so, after the Catholic Relief Act of 1782. Byrne acquired the Mullinahack estate from Lord Allen. Keogh bought land in Roscommon and neighbouring counties, ancient homeland of the MacEochaidhs, and in 1782 claimed to have 2,000 tenants.[55]

There were innumerable complaints, but no proof, that Catholics used their money to buy support in Parliament. Lord Charlemont referred to 'a sort of Papist patronage in both Houses of Parliament.'[56]

The Catholic gentry did not shine in the art world; but Henry Trench, of a Catholic branch of the family established in Mayo, was an accomplished watercolour artist, working mainly in Italy and described in 1712 as 'first of all the young geniuses at Rome for painting'. His work, signed *Enrico Trench, Hibernese*, can be seen in Rome and Lucca. But fame and fortune eluded him: he was 'beggared by a whore and died of the pox' aged only forty.[57]

---

1 Pyers O'Conor-Nash, *History and Heritage of the Royal O'Conors*, 45-6.

2 19 Geo. Ch. 7, II.

3 W. N. Osborough in T. P. Power and Kevin Whelan (eds.), *Endurance and Emergence*, 39; A. Cogan, *Diocese of Meath*, II, 170-3; information from Lord Dunboyne.

4   Mrs M. J. O'Connell, *The Last Colonel of the Irish Brigade*, I, 185; L. M. Cullen in Power and Whelan, *op. cit.*, 74-5; Dalton, *King James's Irish Army List*, I, 217-8; II, 656.

5   J. G. Simms, *Williamite Confiscations*, 75-6; Donogh O'Brien, *History of the O'Briens*, 91; Inchiquin MSS, 1508.

6   R. Hayes, *A Biographical Dictionary of Irishmen in France*, 256, 55-6.

7   *Ibid.*, 316-7; TCD MS, N3, 7, 128.

8   Brian de Breffni, 'Letters from Connaught to a Wild Goose', in *Irish Ancestor*, X, 1978, 92; RIA, BI, l.

9   Mrs M. J. O'Connell, *op. cit.*, I, 101, 217-8.

10 *Ibid.*, I, 101.

11 *Ibid.*, I, 193; J. E. and G. W. Dunleavy (eds.), *O'Conor Papers*, 8.4.SE. 182; L. M. Cullen in Power and Whelan (eds.), *op. cit.*, 78.

12 Mrs M. J. O'Connell, *op. cit.*, I, 221-2.

13 *Ibid.*, 257, 258.

14 John Hayes, 'The Trants: an Enterprising Catholic Family in Eighteeth Century Cork', in *Journal of the Cork Historical and Archaeological Society*, LXXXIV, Vol. I, Jan-June 1981, no. 223, 21-9.

15 R. E. Parkinson, *History of the Grand Lodge of Ireland*, II, 315; Michael Baigent and Richard Lee, *The Temple and the Lodge*, 184.

16 Mrs M. J. O'Connell, *op. cit.*, II, 71-2; I, 172; II, 12.

17 *Ibid.*, I, 41,131.

18 Dalton, *op. cit.*, II, 703.

19 Cogan, *op. cit.*, III, 674; Lucy Sutherland, *The East India Company in Eighteenth Century Politics*, 58-72, 358; Hickey, *Memoirs*, III, 138-9.

20 1 Geo, Ch. 20, II, ; Hickey, *op. cit.*, IV, 259-60; D. J. Macnamara, *The Story of an Irish Sept*, 298-9.

21 L. M. Cullen in Power and Whelan (eds.), *op. cit.*, 76-7.

22 Cogan, *op. cit.*, III, 674.

23 *Ibid.*, II, 285.

24 John Fleetwood, *A History of Medicine in Ireland*, 42, 76, 102, 130, 229; P. Somerville Large, *Dublin*, 160; Hugh MacDermot, *Letters*, no. 16.

25 J. B. Lyons, *Brief Lives of the Irish Doctors*, 36-7, 43-4; Thomas Wyse, *Historical Sketch of the Late Catholic Association*, 34.

26 Lyons, *op cit.*, 47-9.

27 M. R. O'Connell (ed.), *The Correspondence of Daniel O' Connell*, 1230; William Magan, *Umma More: the Story of an Irish Family*, 219; Mrs M. J. O'Connell, *op. cit.*, I, 247.

28 Arthur Young, *A Tour in Ireland*, 207-8.

29 David J. Dickson in Power and Whelan (eds.), *op. cit.*, 86, 94.

30 *Council Book of the Corporation of the City of Cork*, 235, 311, 319, 335.

31 Alexander the Coppersmith, *Remarks upon the Religion, Trade, Government, Policy, Customs, Manners and Maladys of the City of Cork*, 7-8, 98-100.

32 Maureen Wall, *Catholic Ireland in the Eighteenth Century*, 77.

33 'The Trants, an enterprising Catholic Family in Eighteenth Century Cork', in *Journal of the Cork Historical and Archaeological Society*, LXXXIV, Vol. 1, Jan-June 1981, No. 223, 21-5.

34 *Ibid.*, 23-4.

35 Dickson in Power and Whelan (eds.), *op. cit.*, 97.

36 Ida Grehan, *Irish Family Histories*, 231.

37 Wall, *op. cit.*, 78, 87.

38 Karen J. Harvey in Power and Whelan (eds.), *op. cit.*, 178, 183, 185; Wall, *op. cit.*, 79.

39 *Ibid.*, 79.

40 *Ibid.*, 79; Diarmuid Ó Cearbhaill, *Galway Town and Gown*, 74-80.

41 L. M. Cullen and T. G. Smart, *Comparative Aspects of Scottish and Irish Economic and Social History, 1600-1900*, 165ff.

42 Ó Cearbhaill, *op. cit.*, 72-3.

43 John Mannion, in Kevin Whelan (ed.), *Wexford History and Society*, 375-99.

44 Ó Cearbhaill, *op. cit.*, 68, 74.

45 *Ibid.*, 68, 74.

46 Kevin Whelan in Power and Whelan (eds.), *op. cit.*, 135-6; Hayes in Power and Whelan (eds.), *op. cit.*, 165,166.

47 *Ibid.*, 121.

48 *Ibid.*, 160-1.

49 Renagh Holohan, *The Irish Chateaux*, 118-20.

50 Hayes in Power and Whelan (eds.), *op. cit.*, 305, 306-9..

51 Wall, *op. cit.*, 81-3; David J. Dickson in Power and Whelan (eds.), *op. cit.*, 96-8; Dunleavy (eds.), *op. cit.*, 8.4.SE.020.

52 Hugh MacDermot, *Letters*, no. 9; Sir Dermot MacDermot, *The MacDermots of Moylurg and Coolavin*, 249-50.

53 Wall, *op. cit.*, 81-3.

54 Joseph Hone, *The Moores of Moore Hall*, 21-3; Cullen in Power and Whelan (eds.), *op. cit.*, 57.

55 Wall, *op. cit.*, 81.

56 H. M. Charlemont, *Charlemont Correspondence*, I, 45-6.

57 Anne Crookshank and the Knight of Glin, *The Watercolours of Ireland*, 23-4.

9

THE STRUCTURE OF POLITICS
AND THE REPEAL OF SOME PENAL LAWS

Ireland was governed from Westminster. 'Poyning's Law' of
1494 required the Irish Parliament to submit its Bills to the
British government for approval or amendment before they
could be enacted in Dublin. The 'Declaratory Act' of 1720
enabled the British Parliament to legislate for Ireland. The
Lord Lieutenant (or Viceroy) and the Chief Secretary, heads
of the Irish executive, were English political appointees.

This was only the beginning of it. In neither country did
any difference of principle divide government and opposition.
Between 1715 and 1801 *all* British and Irish ministers were
Whigs. The war against the American colonists was provoked,
started, fought, bungled and lost by Whigs. What dominated
the political scene was 'interest' – personal friendships and
enmities, family relationships, favours given and received. The
currency of politics was not generally crude cash, handouts from
the secret service fund or the Civil List: it was in the form of
jobs – peerages at the top of the scale, and lower down
promotions in the army and the church, sinecures about the
Court or on the fringes of government, and innumerable jobs
as judges, civil servants, postmasters, surveyors, revenue officers,
admiralty contractors, tidewaiters. Of these the Crown had at
its disposal far more than any private individual. So the theory
and practice of eighteenth century government was that the

king chose the Prime Minister and then, to enable him to manage Parliament and run the country, put the Crown patronage at his disposal.

The Irish patronage was delegated to the Lord Lieutenant (Viceroy) and the Chief Secretary. The House of Lords presented them with few problems. In the first half of the century it consisted only of about twenty-eight lay peers, four archbishops and eighteen bishops of the Church of Ireland. The prelates were appointed by the government which counted on them as right reverend placemen. Of the lay peers, some were far from affluent, pathetically pleading for £200 pensions as rewards or inducements for being 'ready at all times to attend His Majesty's service in the House of Lords'. After mid-century English ministries made use of Irish peerages for purposes of English political patronage, and the number of Irish peers rose by 1770 to sixty-seven, but many of these were English gentlemen who had no intention of taking part in the proceedings of the Irish House of Lords.

So the Lord Lieutenant's and Chief Secretary's problems were mainly with the House of Commons. Of the 300 members in the 1770s about 104 were 'placemen' – full or part-time government servants including army officers, revenue officials, and functionaries in the lawcourts – or holders of government pensions. These gave the executive its hard core of reliable supporters, but to ensure the majority he needed for governing the country the Lord Lieutenant had to secure the support of another hundred or so. The county members were in theory elected by forty-shilling freeholders, but in fact often nominated by county magnates who instructed the freeholders how to vote. (The system was still going strong in 1841 when a supporter of Daniel O'Connell had trouble persuading his tenants to vote as he desired. The Liberator could not understand his problem: 'He can *command* them.') County members were often the nominees of great men, or great men in their own right, the administration could not rely on them in Parliament: they prided themselves on being 'independent', that is to say, not committed to government support.[1]

For the majorities he required, the Lord Lieutenant must look to the borough members. 'Borough' was a portmanteau term covering ten cities, 110 true boroughs and seven manors, each represented by two members. They varied greatly in size, from Dublin, Cork and Limerick to Bannow in County Wexford which consisted of a mound of sea-sand without a single house, or Harristown in County Kildare, also uninhabited. There were:

> Fifty-three Corporation boroughs in which only the Mayor and Corporation had the vote.
>
> Forty-six Freemen boroughs in which all Freemen had the vote.
>
> Eleven boroughs in which householders, or those in a certain area, had the vote.
>
> Seven manors in which all freeholders voted.

Over half the corporations consisted of less than twenty members, and forty were entirely self-elected. Freemen were generally admitted by the corporations 'by grace especial.'[2]

With franchises like these, it is not surprising that of the ninety-nine Corporation and Freemen boroughs, only six were *not* controlled by patrons, known as borough-owners, who were generally neighbouring landed magnates.

Some borough-owners controlled only a single borough, but Lord Downshire controlled seven, Lord Ely six, and John Ponsonby, Speaker of the House of Commons, directly or indirectly controlled twenty-two. In so far as some peers had political importance, it was as borough-owners, not as members of the Upper House. About 200 members of the House of Commons were nominated by patrons, mainly borough-owners.[3]

Seats were openly bought and sold. In the 1760s one could pick up a borough seat for £600 to £800. To fight a county seat was more prestigious, but more expensive since landowners and freeholders expected to be paid for their trouble, and there was much impersonation and multiple voting. (An elector in Cork complained of being 'tired polling'.)

Gentlemen who had invested such sums expected a return for their money, in cash, power or prestige. The cheapest rewards were a peerage, or a step up in the peerage, perhaps a bishopric or a deanery, or promotion in the army, for the man himself or his close relative; or a seat on the Privy Council. The reward, or inducement, which the authorities least liked bestowing was a pension.

These circumstances facilitated parliamentary management. Provided the placemen, peers, and pensioners remained true to their salt, the bishops did not forget their maker, and enough borough-owners could be kept sweet by 'civility', 'bustle', 'management' or in the last resort 'expense', the Viceroy need fear no evil.[4]

Radicals, and in general those on whom the manna did not fall, frequently demanded the abolition of sinecures and a ban on MPs receiving places and pensions. They got no satisfaction: the administration could not govern the kingdom in any other way; gentlemen in Parliament depended on these handouts to keep them beyond reach of want; and there was always the specious argument that as Members of Parliament were *prima facie* the flower of the nation, it would be foolish to deprive them of the opportunity of serving the nation in public appointments and of being recompensed for their services.[5]

Up to 1767 the Lord Lieutenant and the Chief Secretary

lived in England, rarely if ever visiting the country for which they were responsible. In that year, however, the new Lord Lieutenant, Lord George Townshend, and his Chief Secretary set the precedent of living in Dublin Castle for most of the year. The Castle became the source from which all blessings flowed, direct to the blessed. So long as these satraps were competent managers, the hand of the English government was thereby strengthened; when they were out of their depth in the Irish political bog, English influence waned. When feelings ran really high over some particular issue, and were shared by the great majority of MPs, as was to happen in the Patriot agitation for independence in 1780-82, the power of patronage could even be temporarily defeated. But although concessions sometimes had to be made on non-essentials and constitutional forms, the essentials of power remained in English hands.

Catholics, of course, received no share of the loaves and fishes, which is not to say they would have refused a share had it been offered them.

So anyone who aimed to secure a fair deal for Irish Catholics had to persuade the *British* government that it was time the Penal Laws were repealed.

For the first half of the eighteenth century Catholic affairs had been conducted, if at all, by a few Catholic peers – Gormanston, Kenmare, Trimleston – who generally seemed to be resigned to their boring, frustrating but not uncomfortable lot. Charles O'Conor of Belanagare wasn't; and increasingly from mid-century he took a lead in agitating for the repeal of the Penal Laws. He was well placed to do so. Although untitled, in lineage and Irish antecedents he was at least the equal of any Preston, Browne, Plunkett or Barnewall. By his writings and researches he had done much to restore Catholic pride and self-confidence. He was in cordial agreement with his friend Dr John

Curry, the eminent Dublin physician, who on 3 October 1755 wrote to him in exasperation:

> As for the Papists, they must really be considered
> as living statues if they do not apply for redress.[6]

Both saw that the best way forward was by displaying fervent, ostentatious loyalty to the British Crown and the Hanoverian succession.

As O'Conor wrote to Curry in August 1756:

> The present set of men either in the administration
> or in Parliament imposed no bondage upon us.

The hatred felt for Catholics, in so far as it survived, would not be lessened:

> by a sullen silence, by an unmeaning reservedness
> in time of danger . . .* Will the expression of our
> gratitude for the relaxation of many Penal Laws
> carry no weight at all? Will it offend the monarch
> on his throne to find his Popish subjects at this
> time joining in a testimony to the equity of his
> administration, the lenity of his government?[7]

A year later the Archbishop of Armagh, six bishops and a number of Catholic laymen met at Lord Trimleston's house to draft a joint pastoral letter directing the clergy to pray for George II and his family after Mass on Sundays; and to read out on the first Sunday of every quarter a denial that the Pope

---

* Britain and France were again at war.

had the authority to depose kings and denunciation of other 'odious tenets' falsely imputed to Catholics. They could not carry the other bishops with them, and the Holy See, which recognised 'James III' as King of Great Britain and Ireland, expressed disapproval; but it showed the way the wind was blowing.[8]

For their policy of winning Catholic rights by expressing loyalty to the British Crown, Charles O'Conor and his like have been sneered at by later patriots who won first complete Catholic Emancipation, then the ownership of the land for those who tilled it, and finally independence for twenty-six counties by confrontation, either political and constitutional, or by the 'armed struggle'. The fell epithet 'Castle Catholic' was applied in the nineteenth century to those Catholics who sought Ireland's benefit (and of course in many cases their own) by working with, not against, the government. But in the circumstances of 1750-1800 that policy made sense, and was justified by success, while confrontation was an abysmal failure.

In the third quarter of the eighteenth century the times were propitious. Except in Ulster and from time to time in 'Whiteboy' counties, relations between Catholics and Protestants were improving. Jacobitism was a spent force. While Catholics were no longer suspect as Jacobites, they no longer saw their Anglo-Irish neighbours as anarchists who had murdered one king and thrown out another. The grandsons of Cromwellian planters regarded themselves as Irish, albeit Protestant Irish. Religious prejudices still survived, but were becoming less divisive, at least among the upper and middle classes. Some clergy set an example. For instance the Catholic Archbishop of Cashel, who normally lived at Thurles, had a standing invitation to stay, whenever he visited Cashel, at the Protestant Archbishop's palace; and Protestants attended entertainments offered him on his visitation. Protestants contributed to the building of Catholic churches, and members of the two churches attended one another's funerals and weddings. The parish priest was part of the social scene, hunting, dining and playing at cards with the Protestant squire.

Some rather overdid it. A priest in County Wexford was denounced by Bishop Sweetman for minding 'his dogs and his hunting rather than his flock.' Another got on the wrong side of Sweetman's successor, Dr Caulfield:

> He has been in Ferns about three years and has hunted, sported, visited, etc., but never said Mass or asked leave to say it. He has been idling from one gentleman's house to another in the style of a Buckeen, without observing fast or abstinence.[9]

Nevertheless, improved social relations stopped well short of power-sharing with Catholics, which would endanger every Protestant's right to land acquired since 1641.

In the autumn of 1759 Curry tried to organise a loyal address drafted by O'Conor, to be passed to the king through the Speaker of the Irish House of Commons. A Dublin physician, he naturally canvassed first the Catholic merchants of the capital, among whom Anthony Dermot, the wealthy shipowner and provision merchant of Usher's Quay, was prominent. But in no way would the grander country gentry take a lead from a physician and a merchant. On 15 December Curry reported progress to O'Conor:

> When the clergy and gentry had upbraided the merchants as a presumptuous, low-bred, ignorant multitude whom it was a disgrace to associate with, the Speaker of the House of Commons sent for Mr

> Dermot and ordered him to read the address aloud,
> [which he did]. Mr [Speaker] Ponsonby replied
> that he counted it a favour done him to be put in
> the way of serving so respectable a body as the
> gentlemen who had signed it. He had a better
> opinion of us than the anti-Addressers have, to
> whom we are a riff-raff. But whose fault is it that
> none of the greater gentry's names are on the list?[10]

His Majesty returned a gracious reply. On George III's accession in 1760 two such Addresses from Irish Catholics were actually republished in the *London Gazette*. In that year the Pope decided to omit in future the name 'James III' from his briefs nominating bishops to Irish sees. (Six years later Jacobitism received its quietus when, on the death of Prince James Edward, the 'Old Pretender', the Pope pointedly refused to acknowledge his son, Prince Charles Edward, the 'Young Pretender', as King of Great Britain.)

In February 1760, Curry and his friend Thomas Wyse of the manor of St John's, Waterford, who had lived most of his life in France and had two sons in the Irish Brigade, put to O'Conor a project for forming a Catholic Committee as a pressure-group for the repeal of the Penal Laws. O'Conor approved, so Curry and Wyse set to work. It was with some difficulty that Trimleston was coaxed into joining the Committee, and before long O'Conor, Curry and Wyse were to wish he hadn't.

Wyse was impetuous, easily roused, no intellectual but a compulsive organiser. It grated on him that Lord Trimleston, affable to his equals, humane to the lower orders but haughty to all between, should assume control of the Committee as of aristocratic right and brush off assistance even from gentlemen. Moreover Trimleston kept a grip on the Committee's funds

which were used, *inter alia*, to pay Daniel MacNamara £15,500 as its London agent and a sweetener of £500 to Edmund Burke.*
Wyse's plan of small regular subscriptions from all members, all over the country, had never been implemented because the Catholic hierarchy would not co-operate in the collection; so most of the money was collected from the Dublin merchants – but managed by Trimleston. O'Conor complained again and again of the peer's 'pride and selfishness'; and that he 'usurps the property of the public and refuses to be accountable for it except in his own way, not in ours.' Nicholas Taaffe, of the great Meath and Louth family, a count and field marshal of the Holy Roman Empire, victor over the Turks at Belgrade, resident in Germany but a frequent visitor to the land of the fathers, was one of the few who faced up to Trimleston. Of him Wyse approved: his connections with the Imperial court made him a diplomat 'with the bluntness of a soldier and the honesty of a German.'

In December 1760, Curry again tried to gather in the country gentry:

> We have returned to us upward of four hundred of
> the names of the first Roman Catholics in Cork,
> Waterford and Galway . . . almost all the best
> people have signed, but we have no lords! T—n
> and K——e have sent affronting letters in answer
> to our friendly invitation.[11]

Trimleston was not inactive in the Catholic cause: far from it: but he could not work as a member of a team. He had, however, other useful, indeed endearing, qualities. He was an expert on

---

* Burke, a Westiminster MP, was of course a Protestant but his mother
was a Catholic, a Nagle of Annakissy, and he was always helpful to
Catholics.

the medicinal properties of herbs; and had acquired in Paris a knowledge of 'alternative medicine' which was much in demand in County Meath. He treated the poor free, but expected his more affluent patients to slip something into his fee-box.[12]

With a wrangling crew and rival captains, the Catholic Committee was ineffective, and by 1763 it was moribund. In September of that year O'Conor wrote sadly to Curry:

> You have acted your part honourably, warmly and honestly, and now have nothing to do but give up your political patient.[13]

Ironically, just as the Catholic Committee lapsed into futility, events gave their cause a considerable boost.

The principle feature of the Peace of Paris in 1763 was the cession of French Canada to Britain. The guarantee of religious toleration to French Canadians did not pass unnoticed in Ireland; and the British government's vague suspicion of Ulster Presbyterians was brought into sharp focus. South of the Canadian border the thirteen British colonies had needed, and obtained free of cost to themselves, the protection of British fleets and armies against the French. They no longer needed it and were sure now to cut their links with Britain. Ulster Presbyterians had been subject to many of the same disabilities as Catholics, totally excluded from political life, which they sullenly resented. They had emigrated in large numbers, and of the three million colonists the roughest, toughest and most English-hating were the quarter million 'Scots-Irish' who retained strong links with their kinsmen in Ulster. If, as seemed likely, there was to be trouble with the colonies, it was not the Catholics who were a potential fifth column. O'Conor had warned of this in an anonymous letter, which attracted much attention, to the

London Chronicle, on 30 August 1763: the Presbyterian Scots-Irish in Ulster would be motivated not by their grievances but by 'avowed traitorous intent.'

It would be an exaggeration to say that the government had a deliberate policy of playing the Catholic card against the Presbyterians, but at Westminster it seemed prudent to conciliate the Catholics, whether the Irish Parliament liked it or not.[14]

That Parliament was noted for baroque oratory rather than for political talent. Able Irish politicians like Edmund Burke gravitated to Westminster, the real centre of power. In College Green Henry Grattan was witty and popular, an inspired orator with vaguely liberal views, but not much more. His rival, Henry Flood, was a more forceful man, strongly anti-Papist. So although the Penal Laws were hardly enforced, prejudice and inertia kept them on the statute books.

Protestant bigotry could be rationalised by the refusal of Catholics to take oaths of supremacy and abjuration which contained words offensive to their religion. They could thus easily be charged with disaffection to the House of Hanover, despite all their loyal addresses. In 1772 some Catholics, headed by Curry, petitioned the Lord Lieutenant to be allowed to take an oath of loyalty the wording of which would not offend their consciences. Probably under pressure from Westminster, an act to that effect was passed by the Irish Parliament in 1774. A Catholic was by this act allowed to swear allegiance to the House of Hanover and abjuration to the House of Stuart; to denounce any presumed duty of Catholics to murder heretics or break faith with them; to deny that the Pope could depose kings; 'and I do declare that I do not believe the Pope of Rome . . . hath or ought to have any temporal or civil jurisdiction within this realm.'

The Catholic Committee tried to obtain a less objectionable wording, since it was no part of their religion that they should murder or break faith with heretics. But some Catholics believed that although the wording was indeed odious, there was nothing in the oath to which a Catholic could not swear. The bishops and laity were divided on this for a year, until the deadlock was broken by Lord Trimleston leading a march of sixty Catholic 'gentlemen of property and eminent merchants' to the King's Bench to take the oath. About 1,500 Catholics followed their example.[15]

This could not have come at a better time for the government, for in 1775 war broke out against the American colonists with whom many Irish (and not a few English) Protestants were in sympathy. Not so Irish Catholics. A body representing Catholic gentry humbly presumed:

> to lay at His Majesty's feet two million of loyal, faithful and affectionate hearts and hands, unarmed indeed but zealous, ready and desirous of exerting themselves strenuously in defence of His Majesty's most sacred person and government.

Lord Shelburne, a large Irish landowner albeit often absentee, wrote to a friend in England:

> In every Protestant or Dissenter's house the established toast is 'Success to the Americans!' Among the Roman Catholics they not only talk but act very freely on the other side.[16]

As early as 1776 able-bodied Catholic convicts were being released from prison to join the navy; and although by law Catholics could not bear arms, Catholic landowners encouraged recruiting by their tenants and offered bounties to any who joined up.

In 1778, when the regular British army was in America and a considerable part of it had surrendered at Saratoga, when France and Spain were obviously about to join Britain's enemies, the British government (strenuously lobbied by Daniel MacNamara) passed an act removing many restrictions from English Catholics. This was a signal to Dublin and Luke Gardiner, MP for Dublin city, seconded by Barry Barry of the Cork convert family (who had many Catholic relatives), proposed a Catholic Relief Bill. Under pressure from the Castle, the Irish Commons passed this on 20 June and sent it to Westminster for approval. Again MacNamara got to work, and in August the Bill was returned to Dublin. It was passed by the Commons to wild applause from 'a shoal of Papists in the gallery', and the Lords responded favourably to the usual inducements. On 14 August it received royal assent.

It did nothing much for other Catholics, but was of enormous benefit to Catholic landowners, repealing the sections of the 1704 anti-Popery Act most obnoxious to them. Thereafter a Catholic, although not yet able to acquire land in fee simple, could lease it for 999 years or five lives. He need not gavel his estate; and his eldest son could not, by conforming, acquire the entire estate, relegating his father to the position of tenant-for-life. The benefits of the act were restricted to Catholics who took the 1774 Oath of Allegiance, which most proceeded to do.[17]

Insofar as the object of the act was to secure Catholic support against the rebel colonists, it worked.

But the 'Patriots' or 'Protestant nation' aspired under Lord Charlemont, Henry Flood and Henry Grattan to follow in a moderate and constitutional way the American example. To this end they built up a force of Volunteers ostensibly for internal security and to defend the country, in the absence of the regular army, from French invasion. The Volunteers were a middle-class army: every man bought his own, often very expensive, uniform; they were a private army, unpaid, independent of the government; they swore no Oath of Allegiance; their officers, elected by the men, did not hold the king's commission. They revelled in parades, musketry practices, and field-days in clement weather. Officers and men dined together with animated political discussions and many toasts drunk. They were highly politicised, providing the Patriot leaders with a nationwide framework and ginger-group in the campaign for independence, and Presbyterians with a political platform they had hitherto lacked. Although hardly formidable against the French, they would, wrote Lord Charlemont, 'certainly have been an object of terror to the wisest and strongest administration, and the present one was neither wise nor strong.'[18]

Political motivation was strongest in and around Belfast where most Volunteers were ardent supporters of their American cousins. From the early 1780s there was grouping round William Drennan, a Presbyterian physician educated in Glasgow (a hotbed of republicanism) and a keen Volunteer, an 'interior circle' of Belfast Volunteers who drew inspiration from the 'Good Old Cause' of Commonwealth against the Crown, and Dissent against the Church. In their eagerness to sever all links with England, they were even prepared to enter into partnership with like-minded Catholics. William Drennan was the first United Irishman, long before the term was ever invented. In this unexpected, and to the government most unwelcome, development, it is likely that Freemasonry played a part. In some companies almost every Volunteer was a Mason, in some Lodges almost every Mason of military age was a Volunteer. Drennan was probably a Mason: certainly most of his 'interior circle' were. And there were Catholic Masons, with links back to Jacobite

Freemasonry, such as the Bellews of Barmeath.[19]

Some Volunteer corps included Catholics and in a few, Catholics formed a majority. Charles O'Conor questioned the propriety of them joining up when they were not allowed to bear arms. But to his son Denis, he described not without pride a parade in Dublin:

> The Catholics (mixed with a few Protestants) have formed themselves into an Irish Brigade and last Sunday presented a splendid appearance in scarlet uniform.[20]

In the west and south the Volunteers were keener on internal security than on politics. Robert FitzGerald, Knight of Kerry, wrote in February 1780 to his friend Maurice O'Connell ('Hunting Cap'):

> I have been thinking of a scheme to prevent the barony of Iveragh from being made the asylum of rogues and vagabonds . . . Why should not a [Volunteer] corps be raised in that barony? The gentlemen of property of your religion, uniting with the Protestants, might soon raise a body of men . . . that might be relied upon for executing the above purpose . . . I will furnish them with firelocks.

But Hunting Cap, up to his eyes in farming, smuggling and supporting his younger relatives in another Irish Brigade, was in no mood to waste time playing, unpaid, at soldiers, and replied:

It is much to be wished that the land be purged
of outlaws and vagabonds. Not only that, but that
it should possess some little force for repelling and
pillaging of scampering privateers . . . I am fully
convinced that the Roman Catholic gentry of
Iveragh would readily unite with Protestant neighbours to form a corps, did they think that such a
measure would meet with the approbation of the
legislature . . . But what can they do when the laws
of their country forbid them the use of arms?[21]

Essentially the Volunteers were a political force. Grattan and his
'Patriot' colleagues made adroit political use of them – with the
implied threat of something more – to obtain notional independence for Ireland in 1782. But it was not real independence:
although Poyning's Law and the Declaratory Act were repealed,
the Viceroy and Chief Secretary were still appointed from
Westminster and still wielded the Crown patronage.

Some Patriots, including Grattan but not Flood, would enlist
Catholics' support by promising them more concessions, but
stopping well short of power-sharing. Under their influence a
Volunteer convention at Dungannon had passed a resolution to
that effect. But events were to show that for most Protestants
this was a tactical play: their hearts were not in it.[22]

Early in 1782, with the war going from bad to worse, the
British government made another move to conciliate Catholics.
On 4 May, again under strong pressure from the Castle, the Irish
Parliament passed another Catholic Relief Bill proposed by
Luke Gardiner and seconded by John Dillon of a convert family.
By it Catholics were allowed to purchase, inherit and bequeath
land just like Protestants. They were even allowed to own horses

worth more that £5. Catholic bishops were allowed to function as they had been functioning for fifty years, and the remaining restrictions on the work of diocesan priests were lifted. Shortly afterwards another Act allowed Catholics to run Catholic schools as they had been doing for two generations, and to be guardians of Catholic children. Mixed marriages remained illegal, though the law was widely disregarded. (A Protestant, it was remarked, could marry a negro or a Turk but not the Catholic girl next door.) The Catholic hierarchy's dislike of mixed marriages was as strong as that of the Protestant Ascendancy: Bishop Sweetman of Ferns denounced one of his priests as 'an infamous and incorrigible couple-beggar' for uniting in Holy Matrimony many mixed couples.[23]

The government was highly gratified by the number of Catholic recruits for the army and navy. A somewhat atypical recruit was Eoghan Ruadh Ó Súilleabháin, an *aisling* poet from Kerry who had had a grounding in English, Latin and Greek, and had been tutor to the Nagle family of Annakissy, County Cork; but owing to misbehaviour (perhaps with the Nagle girls?) had been obliged to flee the house, his employer expediting his departure with a shotgun. He joined in the Battle of the Saints which finished a disastrous war against the colonies with an overwhelming victory over the French and Spanish fleets, and wrote in English an appropriate poem:

> Now may prosperity attend
> Brave Rodney and his Irishmen,
> And may he never want a friend
> While he shall reign commander.
> Success to our Irish officers,
> Seamen bold and jolly tars
> Who like the darling sons of Mars

> Take delight in the fight
> And vindicate bold England's right,
> And die for Erin's glory.

Someone sent the poem to the admiral who, much gratified, sent for the poet and offered him promotion; but all the poet wanted was release from the navy. A Lieutenant McCarthy, also from Kerry, was present and said, 'Anything but that.' The poet muttered in Irish, 'I will play some other trick on you.' Said McCarthy, 'I'll take good care, Sullivan, you will not.' Trick or no, O'Sullivan was invalided out and returned to schoolmastering in Munster.[24]

Lord Trimleston died in 1779 and Curry in 1780. As O'Conor, born in 1710 and Wyse, some ten years older, began to slow down, Sir Patrick Bellew of Barmeath Castle in County Louth took an increasing part in the affairs of a revived Catholic Committee. The Viceroy, the Duke of Rutland, considered that he 'carried his ideas of mischief as far as any Catholic in Ireland'; but actually Bellew was a moderate, a born fence-sitter. Some of the more radical Volunteer leaders, bent on parliamentary reform, sought to enlist the Committee as allies, offering Catholics the vote in return for their support. Bellew wrote:

> The Roman Catholics are the objects of the wishes
> of both parties [the government and the radicals]
> and if they go on in the decent and manly manner
> they have of late, my opinion is that they may make
> their own terms.[25]

In other words, sit on the fence.

All through 1784 the Catholic Committee was divided. The conservatives, mainly landed gentry, were confident that 'the government will take us up.' Bellew believed that Catholics would soon be called to the Bar, and hold commissions in the army, 'but they must not think of having a right to vote.' Kenmare, Archbishop Butler and others believed that their best hope was to be pro-government, anti-reform and anti-Volunteer. But the radicals, mainly Dublin merchants led by John Keogh and Thomas Braughall who had joined the Volunteers after the Dungannon convention, were all for horse-trading with the reformers. When a new Lord Lieutenant, the Duke of Rutland, arrived in March 1784, they even boycotted the Committee meeting drawing up an Address of Welcome. Privately, Rutland urged the Committee to support the government and distance themselves from the Volunteers, but the Committee could no more agree on that than on dealing with them. In vain did the Belfast Volunteers parade in front of Papist chapels, and even venture through the portals of the Scarlet Woman to suffer a sermon by a Popish priest: the Catholic Committee would not, or could not, descend from its perch on the fence but remained there as though impaled, one leg on each side. Anyway, there were not many Volunteers who would contemplate *political* concessions to Catholics: these included Henry Grattan, described by Archbishop Butler as being 'all in all with the Catholics', but they did not include his parliamentary rival Henry Flood, or Lord Charlemont, the Volunteer Supremo.

So the Catholic Committee, divided between conservative landed gentry and radical Dublin merchants, unable to agree on anything, again became marginalised, ignored by the Volunteers and by the government which, with the war over, no longer needed its support. And with the war over, there was no ostensible purpose for the Volunteers. So what was the point of all their drilling and marching, pipe-playing and starching, in gawdy uniforms which were losing their novelty and becoming a little tawdry? Rutland would have liked to disband these 'armed legislators' but had not dared to do so. Now he needn't: they quietly faded away, leaving only a few dormant political volcanoes such as the Dublin Protestant colonel, Napper Tandy, slightly absurd and generally inebriated. Parliamentary reform and Catholic Emancipation would both have to wait.[26]

At least the Catholic Committee did not make itself ridiculous as did the Dublin Parliament during the royal malady in 1789. Counting on the king never recovering, they sent a delegation to pledge their undying devotion to the Prince of Wales who did not trouble to conceal his impatience to assume his father's powers. It arrived in London only to find that the king had recovered. The Protestant Parliament having so spectacularly wrong-footed itself, the Catholic Committee hastened to congratulate His Majesty on his 'happy restoration to health' and the 'personal exercise of his authority.' The Catholic Archbishop of Dublin, Dr Troy, conducted a solemn service of thanksgiving with a congregation of some 3,000 including many Protestant peers and Members of Parliament, and an elaborate musical performance concluding with *God Save the King*.[27]

Four months later the storming of the Bastille gave a shake to the political kaleidoscope, and the pieces settled in a different pattern.

---

1   E. and A. Porritt, *The Unreformed House of Commons*, II, 450-3, 418; M. R. O'Connell, *Irish Politics and Social Conflict in the Age of American Revolution*, 364; M. R. O'Connell (ed.),*The Correspondence of Daniel O'Connell*, 2903.

2   Porritt, *op. cit.*, II, 187; O'Connell, *Irish Politics*, 366, 298; Angus MacIntyre, *The Liberator: Daniel O'Connell and the Irish Party*, (London, 1965), 232.

3   O'Connell, *Irish Politics*, 298, 303, 306, 359-60; MacIntyre, *op. cit.*, 233; James Kelly, *Prelude to Union*, 69.

4   O'Connell, *Irish Politics*, 357-8, 359; Porritt, *op. cit.*, II, 207, 215, 362, 418.

5   Porritt, *op. cit.*, 417; Kelly, *op. cit.*, 19.

6 RIA MSS B I 1.

7 R. E. and C. C. Ward (eds.), *Letters of Charles O'Conor of Belanagare*, 15.

8 Maureen Wall, *Catholic Ireland in the Eighteenth Century*, 99; Patrick J. Corish, *The Catholic Community in the Seventeenth and Eighteenth Centuries*, 119.

9 Corish, *op. cit.*, 119-20; A. Cogan, *The Diocese of Meath*, III, 83; Kevin Whelan (ed.), *Wexford History and Society*, 306.

10 RIA MSS B I 1.

11 Thomas Wyse, *A Historical Sketch of the Late Catholic Association*, I, 63-76; Ward (eds.), *op. cit.*, 84, 111, 115, 123; Burke, *Peerage, Baronetage and Knightage*, 1750; Wall, *op. cit.*, 110.

12 *McVeagh (ed.), Richard Pocock's Irish Tours*, 140.

13 Wall, *op. cit.*, 119; Ward (eds.), *op. cit.*, 115, 124, 130.

14 Ward (eds.), *op. cit.*, 131 fn. 1, 134; Charles O'Conor, *Memoirs of Charles O'Conor of Belanagare, 167;* Wall, *op. cit., 127-8.*

15 Wall, *op. cit.*, 122-3.

16 *Ibid.*, 124; W. E. H. Lecky, *History of Ireland in the Eighteenth Century*, II, 165; M. R. O'Connell, *Irish Politics*, 124.

17 17 and 18 George Ch. 42, III; Wall, *op. cit.*, 125-33, 197 fn 29.

18 A. T. Q. Stewart, *A Deeper Silence*, 6, 19-22.

19 The Republican 'interior circle' of Belfast Volunteers is traced by Stewart, *op. cit.*, 62, 71, 85, 87, 91-3, 130-1, 136, 138, 164-78.

20 Ward (eds.), *op. cit.*, 324, 351, 355.

21 Mrs M. J. O'Connell, *The Last Colonel of the Irish Brigade*, I, 265-6.

22 Stewart, *op. cit.,* 37.

23 21 and 22 Geo Ch. 62, III; Wall, *op. cit.*, 142; Patrick J. Corish, *Wexford*, 242.

24 Daniel Corkery, *The Hidden Ireland*, 194-9.

25 Wall, *op. cit.*, 150.

26 Thomas Wyse, *op. cit.*, I, 123; Wall, *op. cit.*, 151-3.

27 Wall, *op. cit.*, 150.

10

Fin de Siècle

The French Revolution came as no surprise to Charles O'Conor who had often predicted that French troops serving alongside the Americans would pick up from them republican ideas which they would carry back to France. In Ireland it produced, most notably in Belfast but also in Dublin – where Trinity College pulsated with advanced radical politics – a middle-class republican intelligentsia, steeped in the writings of Rousseau and Paine, almost wholly Protestant. Some were no more revolutionary than their idol, Charles Fox; others addressed one another as 'Citizen', cropped their hair in the Jacobin fashion, rejoiced in the revolution which had brought their class to power in France and even in Louis XVI's execution and the excesses of the Terror: and looked forward to a repeat performance in Ireland. They were strongly Francophile, especially in Belfast where the crypto-republicanism of the 'interior circle' of Volunteers became trendy.[1]

There, where the Volunteers enjoyed a revival, a Society of United Irishmen was formed, essentially the republican 'interior circle' of Volunteers. Prominent at its formation in Belfast was a young Protestant lawyer, Theobald Wolfe Tone, who went on to form a second branch in Dublin. Its general idea was to unite Catholic, Anglicans and Presbyterians 'under the single denomination of Irishmen'. To this end it intended to reduce the power of the Crown; to loosen the links with England; to introduce universal male franchise; to abolish pensions, sinecures and rotten boroughs. This was a perfectly respectable radical programme in the eighteenth century tradition of Wilkes and Daniel O'Connell, with no social or economic policies, aiming neither at making the poor richer or even the rich poorer. An analysis of the Dublin Society of United Irishmen in 1792–3 shows that it included 130 Protestants and 140 Catholics, including Dr Hugh MacDermot, who was not prominent. All but one of the most active leaders were Protestants. Although in its early years it was no more than a radical debating society, Wolfe Tone and other leaders had a hidden agenda.[2]

Meanwhile the Catholic Committee, almost moribund under Lords Kenmare and Fingall and Sir Patrick Bellew, was taken over and injected with new vigour by the Dublin merchant gang of four – John Keogh, Thomas Broughall, Edward Byrne and Anthony Dermot. In September 1791, Wolfe Tone published a pamphlet, *An Argument on Behalf of the Catholics of Ireland*, which brought him into contact with Keogh, the first Catholic he had ever met socially. As a result of this, although a Protestant, he was appointed the Catholic Committee's stipendiary secretary. The Committee was certainly not republican, but its secretary was, and Keogh was inclined that way. Nor was it formally connected with the United Irishmen, though they had about thirty members in common, including Dr Hugh MacDermot, a terrific admirer of Wolfe Tone's pamphlet, 'in merit beyond my feeble commendations'. The Catholic Committee might make common cause with the United Irishmen, but only if they could thereby obtain emancipation. That was what mattered to them – not the more radical items on the United Irish programme.[3]

Since the mid-1780s there had been rumbles of a low-key guerrilla war in the north-eastern counties, the most populous part of Ireland where there was fierce competition for farms and rents were accordingly high. The protagonists were the Protestant Peep o' Day Boys, so called for their dawn raids on Papists' houses, and the Catholic Defenders. Both made their points by secret oaths, beatings, intimidation and raiding gentry houses for arms, just like the Whiteboys only more so. Like the Whiteboys, their grievances were economic, too high rents and tithes; their enemies were the landlords, and of course one another. The Peep o' Day Boys specialised in a form of ethnic cleansing known as 'papering' – affixing to a Catholic's house a written notice warning the occupants to be gone. It was effective. Many Defenders moved to more Catholic areas in Leinster and Connaught, bringing with them their grievances and their violence. They also in the early 1790s began to be politicised, republican and anti-government, as well as anti-Protestant and anti-landlord.

Landowners, of course, abhorred the Defenders, and it must have shocked his family when Francis Bellew, son of Sir Patrick of Barmeath, was arraigned in 1792 for 'appearing in arms with a mob of Defenders'. The principal prosecution witness was asked, 'Did you see a person of the name Bellew there?' He replied:

> I saw a person riding very fast coming towards the people there assembled. Some of the people said he was the son of Sir Patrick Bellew. He told the people that there was a troop of Light Horse coming to attack them, and they would be cut to pieces if they remained. . . . His horse was in a great sweat, and both he and his horse appeared as if they had rode a long way in a great hurry.

A succession of gentlemen who had dined at Barmeath that night gave evidence for the defence. The accused had left the dinner-table only for a few minutes, and had not been dressed for riding; nor did he return hot and disordered as though from a hard gallop. His father had formed a Volunteer corps from his tenants and was 'one of the first in the list of Roman Catholics. To suppose that such a man, either in his own person or through the medium of his son, would encourage the Defenders was out of all line of probability.'

Francis Bellew was acquitted and left the court without a stain on his character. Nevertheless family legend holds that, having heard some dinner guests discussing an operation to surprise a rally of Defenders, he did gallop off to warn them – – not out of any sympathy for Defenders, but because he did not want Barmeath tenants and labourers to get into trouble.

It would be interesting to know if any of the defence witnesses, like the Bellews, were Freemasons. The Defenders had shadowy links with Freemasonry.[4]

The Revolution had a shattering effect on the Irish Brigade in the French service. At first, while Louis XVI was still nominally king, most Irish officers went along with the constitutional changes, and fought in defence of France against the kings of Europe. To Generals Arthur Dillon and Kilmaine[*] was due much of the credit for the repulse of the Prussians at Valmy in 1792. General O'Moran, who had served twenty-one years in Dillon's, conducted an expert defence of French Flanders. But in 1792 Dillon's, its polyglot rank-and-file infected with revolutionary zeal, mutinied and murdered any of their officers they could catch, including Lieutenant Colonel Theobald Dillon.

---

[*] His real name was Jennings. Kilmaine was his family estate in County Mayo.

Captain O'Conor was murdered by a mob in the same year. The moderate Girondin reformers were ousted and executed by the Jacobins; Generals Arthur Dillon, Ward and O'Moran went to the guillotine, other Irish officers to prison. In the savage civil war in the Vendée, Irish officers fought on both sides: William Bulkeley, from Clonmel, who had married a Vendéean lady, was captured by the republicans and executed; Charles O'Sullivan, on the royalist side, who had sought refuge with his brother John on the republican side, was handed over by that brother to be guillotined. Wrote the Mayor of Angers to the Mayor of Calais,

> Our Holy Mother the Guillotine is busy at work. Within the last three days she has shaved eleven priests, one *ci-devant* nobleman, a general and a man [Bulkeley] of splendid physique of six foot, whose head was too large for the guillotine; it is now in the sack.[5]

John O'Sullivan was considered peculiarly savage in his republican zeal. He assisted at the infamous *noyades* of Nantes, in which counterrevolutionaries were crammed into barges which were then sunk, because to guillotine them all would take too long. At least two of his victims, Anne Sheil and Anne Stapleton, were Irish. There is a legend that one day the officer in command of the troops round the scaffold in Paris called out in Irish, as the victims queued up for death, 'Are there any Irish here?' There were seven, and he managed to fiddle the procedure, so that they were returned to prison, and survived. It is more certain that the officer commanding the troops at Louis XVI's execution was half-Irish, his mother being Louise Murphy, one of the more celebrated of Louis XV's mistresses, who had married a Frenchman.[6]

Most Irish officers, however, were fervently royalist, the more so after the humiliations to which the king and queen were subjected after being caught trying to flee the country. General Daniel Charles O'Connell proposed to surround their majesties with Irish, Swiss and Swedish regiments and disperse the *canaille* with a whiff of grapeshot; but the placid, phlegmatic king would not authorise anything so drastic. The Chevalier Trant and Captain James Rice planned to rescue at least the queen, and laid on relays of horses to carry her to the coast whence an Irish ship would take her to the Rice house at Dingle. But that too came to nothing, so both king and queen went to the guillotine.[7]

The foreign corps, distrusted by the Jacobins, were disbanded. A few Irish officers remained in the French service: *'le brave'* Kilmaine was let out of prison and became one of the best cavalry commanders in Napoleon's Italian campaigns of 1796 and 1797. He died a year later, bitterly disappointed at not commanding an invasion of Ireland. An O'Meara was one of Napoleon's generals.[8]

Some Irish officers joined the ranks of the *émigré* corps (O'Connell as a trooper of hussars) which fought, rather badly, in the 'Grand Old' Duke of York's ineffective Flanders campaign of 1794. Others went to London, where they found an old friend, the long retired Chevalier de Fagan, busy pulling strings to obtain for his sons and nephews commissions in the service of the East India Company.

The law which denied commissions to Catholics having been repealed, General O'Connell took a leading part in persuading the British government to form from Irish officers in the French service and other ranks enlisted in Ireland a new Irish Brigade of five one-battalion regiments bearing the old and honoured names. Because they were considered less reliable and more expendable than English and Scottish regiments, it was stipulated that they serve only outside Europe, which meant in the West Indies where they suffered appalling losses (including the Liberator's brother) from disease.

However, many survived and some had distinguished careers in the British army. Lieutenant Maurice O'Connell became Lieutenant General and Governor of New South Wales. Eugene McCarthy also became a general. Stack, who had boarded the *Serapis* with him, as a colonel applied for promotion. 'What is your religion?' he was asked. 'The religion of major-generals,' he firmly replied. Henry MacDermot of Coolavin survived the West Indies and transferred to the Connaught Rangers in which he served in all the great Peninsular battles – Fuentes d'Onoro, Busaco, Badajoz, Salamanca, Vittoria – only to be killed in the last battle of the war, at Orthez in southern France.[9]

Nicholas Trant, of the Catholic, Cork branch of the family, who had been in Walsh's, also survived the West Indies. At the start of the Peninsular War he was seconded to the Portuguese army, in which he had a career of extraordinary distinction. He led Portuguese regulars, organised the Portuguese guerrillas who harried the French supply lines (and rescued several French prisoners from death by torture at their hands). He formed a band of high-spirited Irish theological students at Salamanca University into a sort of intelligence corps which gave Wellington a very good idea of what was going on 'the other side of the hill'. At his death many years later, the Duke pronounced his nostalgic obituary, 'Trant, poor fellow, a very good officer, but as drunken a dog as ever lived.'[10]

The radical clique which from 1790 dominated the Catholic Committee was led by Keogh, 'roughly hewn', in the words of Sir Thomas Wyse, 'in both mind and body.' The conservative element clustered round Kenmare whom Wyse dismissed as:

cold, unconciliating, timid yet fond of petty power,
influenced by puny ambition, hovering between
Catholic and Protestant and sacrificing alternately,
and generally unprofitably, to the evil genius around
the Castle on one side and chained spirit of his
country on the other . . . a mere second-rate
negotiator.

But with Keogh in the ascendant, and very thick with the United
Irishmen though he had not yet joined them, the government
ceased to regard the Catholic Committee as a useful counterweight
to Protestant republicanism. The Presbyterians were becoming
every month more militant in Belfast. They seemed bent on
moulding the Volunteers into the shape of the French National
Guard and dressing them in French-style uniforms. Freemason
Lodges in Belfast and the north-eastern counties called for
parliamentary reform and full Catholic Emancipation. On 14
July 1792, the Belfast Volunteers staged a grand parade and
march past, drums thudding and banners waving, to celebrate
the anniversary of the storming of the Bastille. War with France
broke out in February 1793; and a month later, not before time,
the Volunteers, 'those armed legislators', were disbanded.[11]

With the United Irishmen demanding Catholic Emancipation
and Keogh calling the tune for the Catholic Committee, the
Castle and its masters at Westminster were disinclined to give
the Catholics an inch. Kenmare was content merely to put up
with this and await better times. Keogh wasn't, and in the winter
of 1791-2 went to London to put the Catholic case to Edmund
Burke. He and Burke argued that if Catholics' loyalty was not
rewarded, they would join the United Irishmen. The implication
was that if their loyalty was rewarded, they wouldn't.

Ministers in London were impressed by Keogh's arguments

but the Viceroy, Lord Westmorland, and his advisers were not. Keogh, they said, was an upstart of no account, repudiated by Catholics of quality. Indeed while Keogh was in London, Lord Kenmare, Archbishop Troy and several of the landed gentry and merchants resigned from the Committee. However in 1792, as a reward to Kenmare for his forbearance, a Relief Act was passed which admitted Catholics to the Inns of Court and allowed them to practise as barristers and solicitors. Furthermore, restrictions were lifted on mixed marriages, Catholic schools in Ireland and foreign education.[12]

As FitzGibbon, Flood and other Protestant zealots had predicted, these concessions whetted the Catholics' appetite for more. Keogh's Catholic Committee promoted in Dublin an elected Catholic Convention (the very word reeked of the French revolution) to agitate for their cause. Keogh bustled around organising the elections in the provinces, energetically seconded by Tone who in private derided him as 'Gog': 'Gog is jealous of everybody'; 'Gog insufferably vain'; 'Gog must do or seem to do all himself'. A year after his first visit to London Keogh made a second, to present to the king the Convention's petition for the redress of their grievances. Under strong pressure from Westminster another Relief Act was passed in April of 1793. Keogh preened himself that this was the result of his masterly diplomacy, but it wasn't. Since February Britain had been again at war with France. The ministry wanted Catholic Ireland to stay quiet, Catholic Irishmen to join the army and navy in large numbers, which they did; and its Catholic allies, the Empire and Spain, to see England as the defender of the faith against atheist France.

By the Relief Act of 1793 a Catholic could enter Trinity College; carry arms provided he owned landed property worth £10 a year or chattels worth £300; vote in parliamentary elections on the same basis as Protestants, viz. as a forty-shilling freeholder. He was debarred from Parliament and from the highest offices of state such as Governor General, Privy Councillor, judge, sheriff, general in the army, by the requirement under the Test Act of 1678 and the Bill of Rights of 1689 that these persons take an oath the wording of which was incompatible with the Catholic faith. But he could become a colonel in the army,* Justice of the Peace, Grand Juryman, Deputy Governor of a county. Most Catholic gentry thought this handsome, including Maurice O'Connell (Hunting Cap) who became a JP and Deputy Governor of Kerry. His nephew, Daniel, began to read for the Bar.13

A freeholder was a man holding his land by a lease of indefinite length, commonly for two or more lives, not by a lease of fixed length such as thirty-one years. To qualify for the franchise a man had either to own land worth more than forty shillings a year in rent, or to lease freehold land worth forty shillings a year after payment of rent. In 1430 when these criteria had been laid down forty shillings was a tidy sum, conferring on its owner a degree of independence and respectability. By 1793 a 'forty-shillinger' could be a very poor man, vulnerable to landlord pressure. So long as he paid his rent he could not be evicted; but if he failed to 'pay his landlord the compliment of his freehold', that is to vote as his landlord directed, he would smart for it when his lease expired and came up for renegotiation, for sale by 'cant' (auction) or for allocation to a more dutiful tenant. So the grant of the franchise to Irish Catholics – which was more than English Catholics had – did not mean a great deal so long as they could only send to Parliament a Protestant of their landlord's choice. Wolfe Tone, shrewd when not biased

---

* Soon, without further legislation, Catholics in the army were rising to any rank.

by wishful thinking, pointed to the illogic of allowing poor, uneducated Catholics to vote while preventing Catholic gentlemen from sitting in Parliament:

> If the Catholics deserve what has been granted, they deserve what has been withheld; if they do not deserve what has been withheld, what has been granted should have been refused.[14]

After 1793 'Catholic Emancipation' meant essentially altering an MP's oath so that a Catholic could take it.

Keogh before going to London had sworn that he would accept nothing short of full emancipation; but he returned to Dublin (like others who have negotiated with British governments) arguing that three-quarters of a loaf was better than no bread. Wolfe Tone was scathing: 'and so Gog's puffing has come to this. I always thought that when the crisis arrived he would be shy.' But the Catholic Committee, after some argument, accepted Keogh's view and dissolved itself, its job (nearly) done.[15]

By now Keogh had joined the United Irishmen, but the firebrand of the Catholic Committee was a cooling ember in this milieu. By 1797 he had made his peace with the Castle, and he played no part in the events of the following year.

The Catholic Relief Act of 1793, passed reluctantly by the Irish Parliament was the *ne plus ultra* for most Irish Protestants. Allowing a Catholic forty-shillinger to vote a Protestant gentleman into Parliament did no great harm; but to allow Catholics to be elected to Parliament would very soon result in their having an overwhelming majority in the Commons, as they had had in 1688; and what price then a Protestant landlord's hundred-year old title to his estate? As Lord Westmorland wrote to Pitt, 'Every man holds his estate and his political consequence by dispossession of Catholics.'

Westmorland's successor at the Castle was Earl Fitzwilliam, more high-minded than politically sagacious. He arrived in Dublin in December 1794, and, believing in Catholic Emancipation, could hardly wait to dismiss a number of officials who were known to oppose it. Without even softening up the opposition by the customary methods, he openly presented a plan for emancipation, and Grattan introduced a bill in the Commons to that effect. This was too much! There was a terrific uproar from FitzGibbon and the anti-Papist stalwarts, and in April Fitzwilliam was peremptorily dismissed. In May Grattan's bill was overwhelmingly defeated, and Fitzwilliam's successor, Lord Camden, proscribed the United Irishmen as an unlawful organisation.

These events made it clear that parliamentary reform and Catholic Emancipation could not be achieved, in the present climate, by constitutional methods.

Early in 1793, to replace the Volunteers for home defence, the government raised 16,000 men in county regiments of militia. Conscripts, drawn by lot, were in most counties almost entirely Catholic and of exactly the same class as the Defenders. Their loyalty was suspect, and they had very little military value, but they were to be guilty in 1798 of most of the atrocities committed against Catholic rebels.

Moderate United Irishmen like Dr Hugh MacDermot accepted the proscription of their society. (In 1793, marriage to his first cousin Bessie O'Conor and the death of his father, which burdened him with the management of Coolavin, somewhat distanced MacDermot from active politics.) The thoughts of more militant United Irishmen turned to armed rebellion. As a debating club they were strong in intellect, but as rebels they were weak in muscle; so they sought allies among the Presbyterian republicans in the north-east and the Catholic Defenders in the rest of the country. Tone's bibulous colleague, Napper Tandy, took the Defender oath and, betrayed by informers, decamped to Paris where, on the strength of his experience as a colonel in the Volunteers, he set up as a military expert among the finest soldiers in the world; and was an inexhaustible mine of inaccurate information, to the French about the situation in Ireland, and to the Irish about the French intentions.

In 1795 the government raised, for internal security, a force of Yeomanry. They were volunteers, organised in local units, composed mainly of the sort of farmers who would own good horses, and officered by local gentry. They were mainly Protestant, but contained some units raised by Catholic gentry.

In 1795, after a battle between Defenders and Protestant Peep o' Day Boys, the latter reorganised as the Orange Order. It was a bizarre situation: the proscribed United Irishmen were linked on one hand to the Defenders and on the other to Presbyterian ex-Volunteers who were linked to the Orange Order who were fighting the Defenders. And all drew some support from Freemason Lodges.

Contacts with the United Irishmen politicised the Defenders who became more consciously republican. Under pressure from the Orangemen, Defender outrages – raiding gentry houses for arms, cutting down ash trees to make pike-shafts, intimidating juries, cutting out the tongues of people who spoke out of turn – spread south and west from Ulster. Again and again Catholic bishops denounced them to very little effect; and the victims of some of their worst atrocities were Catholic magistrates.[16]

It was fundamental to United Irish thinking that no rebellion could succeed without a prior French landing; and it was fundamental to French military thinking that a rebellion must precede a landing. The United Irishmen were assured that the French *would* come by an authority more impressive than Napper Tandy. Lord Edward FitzGerald, a younger brother of the Duke of Leinster, had embraced extreme republicanism in Paris and had been cashiered from the British army for recommending that *The British Grenadiers* be replaced as a regimental march by *La Marseillaise*. With his beautiful wife, his great wealth, his aristocratic connections, his trendy opinions and his hair cropped short in Jacobin style, he was (as Roy Foster remarked) the epitome of radical chic; but his charisma was not matched by his competence. He was said to be 'not fit to command a sergeant's guard'.[17]

Soon after Lord Edward left Paris, Wolfe Tone went there and set about persuading the French that the best way to defeat England was by landing first in Ireland. It says much for his power of persuasion and fast talk that he brought the Directory round, more or less, to his strategy. But with all his ability and good qualities, Tone led the French badly astray. He reported the situation in Ireland not as it was but as he thought it should be. Religious differences, he insisted, were of the past. Catholic, Anglican and Presbyterian were alike awaiting the dawn of liberty. If only one good general and 20,000 French veterans landed, preferably in the north, with 20,000 spare muskets and plenty of cannon, hundreds of thousands of Irishmen would hasten to fight alongside them. But the French must first provide this *point d'appui*; otherwise a premature rising would fail.[18]

In December 1797, the French did land, or came within yards of doing so. Forty-six ships crammed with troops, spare muskets, green cockades and green uniforms sailed from Brest. Unfortunately the frigate carrying the general and admiral in command got lost in a fog and were not seen again for three weeks. On 21 December sixteen ships, led by the third-in-command who had no orders and very little idea of what he was supposed to do, sailed into Bantry Bay. It was the wrong place, at the wrong time, and their Irish allies had not been given the smallest inkling of what to expect, nor of when and where to expect it. They arrived in the evening; it was snowing, and next morning the bleak snow-streaked hills looked most uninviting. And where were the welcoming Irish? Among the few peasants who watched them they could discern no trace of fraternity or *camaraderie.* For the next two days, while Wolfe Tone bit his nails in frustration, an offshore gale made landing impossible. On the third day the captains cut their cables and headed back to Brest. If they had landed, only the raw Bantry Yeomanry would have stood between them and Cork. It was, wrote Tone, the luckiest escape England had had since the Armada.[19]

The United Irishmen were disappointed, but at least the French had come, and could come again. The affair was followed by a spectacular upsurge of Defender outrages; and in March General Lake, commanding in Ulster, was ordered to disarm the province. His operation was attended with some success, but was carried out so ferociously that it went far to make a reality of the worst possible case, the nightmare of the Castle, an effective alliance between the United Irishmen and the Defenders. Promoting this sinister development, yet in some degree insuring against it, was the increasing takeover of the newly raised Yeomanry, with its roots in the old Volunteers, by the Orange Order. A friend of Lord Charlemont wrote to him:

> Your old Louth Volunteers, who six months ago were all United Irishmen, are now complete Orangemen, which is more congenial to their feelings.

The term Yeomanry became almost synonymous with 'Orange-men', except in a few corps raised by Catholic magnates such as Lord Fingall, Sir Thomas Esmonde and Sir Patrick Bellew.[20]

In early summer Lord Edward's Supreme Directorate of the United Irishmen appointed colonels and lieutenant colonels to their battalions, ordered company officers and NCOs to be democratically elected, called for returns of strengths, pikes and muskets. But it was all in Lord Edward's mind: nothing much happened on the ground except near Dublin and Belfast and in County Wexford.[21]

The Supreme Directorate was composed almost entirely of Protestants, and Lord Edward himself was one, if somewhat lapsed. Watching their every move were some very efficient secret agents for the government, notably Leonard McNally and Francis Magan, Catholic barristers, and Thomas Reynolds, also a Catholic but Wolfe Tone's brother-in-law, related to Lord Edward and a member of the Directorate. Through these, all those members of the Directorate who were present at an important meeting were put in the bag, with all their documents. Lord Edward, characteristically late for the meeting, was afterwards mortally wounded while resisting arrest.[22]

The rank-and-file of the rebels were Presbyterians in the north-east and elsewhere Catholic Defenders. The government was greatly worried about the attitudes of the Catholic Church and the Catholic gentry. It need not have been. The hierarchy again and again denounced the Defenders, and only about 4 per cent of the priests contracted 'the French disease'.[23] Most gentry, detesting both Orangemen and 'croppies*, kept their heads down. Some joined Catholic Yeomanry corps in which they would be welcome. Dan O'Connell, a promising young lawyer in Dublin, wrote to his uncle, 'Hunting Cap', who would have

---

* So called because they had their hair cropped in Jacobin fashion.

to pay for his uniform:

> I am the only man so far as I can learn in the body
> of lawyers or students of the law who has not
> entered into some corps.

Actually he had, and was already doing his gunnery training with
the Lawyers' Artillery Corps.[24]

What the rebels lacked was leadership at battalion and
company level: it would not be provided by fashionable young
Protestants with their cropped hair and well-thumbed copies of
Tom Paine's *Rights of Man*, calling one another 'Citizen' and
debating in Trinity College the most extreme republican dogma.
Where the Defenders had as their officers their own natural
leaders – Catholic gentry and middlemen, strong Catholic
farmers and a handful of militant priests – they fought well. In
County Kildare their leader was Michael Reynolds, a hunting
farmer, a great horseman and a Catholic. In simultaneous night
attacks they stormed Prosperous and Clane and butchered the
garrisons. The attack on Prosperous was actually led by Dr John
Esmonde, a younger brother of Sir Thomas Esmonde Bart.* He
was later arrested, and as he held a commission in the Yeomanry,
he was hanged wearing his uniform jacket inside out to show
he was a turncoat.[25]

---

* Dr John was probably made a rebel by the murder by troops of his
brother, a priest who was hearing croppies' confessions. Of Dr John's
sons, one inherited the title and the estate in County Wexford; one was
a priest and first Rector of Clongowes College; one was a colonel in
the French Grenadiers; and one commanded *HMS Lion* at Trafalgar.
The son of the Trafalgar captain won the VC in the Crimea; and his
great-grand-nephew, Lieutenant Commander Eugene Esmonde, won
the DSO and a posthumous VC in World War II. An Esmonde girl
served in the Cumann na mBan in the War of Independence; and the
fourteenth baronet was a Nationalist MP and a Free State Senator. A
remarkable family.

For a time it looked as though Counties Kildare and Meath might be lost to the rebels, who could then link up with the Presbyterian rebels in the north. From this position of humiliation and impotence the government was rescued by a remarkable charge by Lord Fingall's Catholic Yeomanry, led by His Lordship himself, which dispersed a rebel force on the hill of Tara. Next day the local butcher offered to show Fingall where many exhausted rebels were asleep in a barn, and could be killed as they slept. 'Butcher,' replied Fingall, 'it may be your trade but it is not the trade of a Plunkett to kill sleeping men.'[26]

Ambitious plans were made and complicated orders issued for a rising by dockers and coalheavers in Dublin itself. But it all petered out with the young gentlemen elected to lead them wandering round asking each other where they were supposed to go and what they were supposed to do.[27]

County Wexford was where the authorities least expected trouble. They had not managed to secure a copy of the United Irishmen's order of battle there because Robert Graham, carrying with him the reports for the Directorate, arrived too late for the meeting at which they were all arrested.[28] The county was generally prosperous with numerous farms of twenty to forty acres growing grain and providing employment. There had been no Whiteboyism here, so troops did not seem to be needed. It was one of the most anglicised of counties and Irish was understood only along its western borders.

Nevertheless there were factors in Wexford, not immediately apparent, which were conducive to rebellion. Except for the Esmondes, the Catholic landowners were on a modest scale, not like the great lords of the Pale or the Butlers and Mathews of County Tipperary strongly interested in maintaining the *status quo*. Middlemen, being phased out elsewhere, were here many and influential. Catholic middlemen were mainly of gentry families, obsessed with their ancestry and gentry status maintained in more than one case by a 'very steady hand and a good aim'. Many were leasing land which their ancestors had owned, and they hoped one day to own it themselves. They saw themselves as a sort of underground aristocracy, and were seen as such by their neighbours who looked to them rather than to Protestant magistrates to adjudicate in disputes. Most Catholic gentry had strong links with Europe which, together with proximity to Dublin, exposed them to republican infection. Many became, and remained, United Irishmen. Sympathy for French republicanism fused with ancient resentment.[29] The Byrnes of Monaseed, surrounded by lands which O'Byrnes had once owned, could neither forgive nor forget. Miles Byrne fumed:

> How often has he my father shown me the lands
> which belonged to our ancestors now in the hands
> of the descendants of the sanguinary followers of
> Cromwell who preserved their plunder and robberies
> after the restoration of that scoundrel Charles II.[30]

Sectarian tensions were strong in Wexford. Basically this was because middlemen and farmers, competing economically, were less tolerant than more or less satisfied landowners elsewhere. Over most of Ireland converts to the established church, nearly all remaining Catholic in sympathy, linked the two communities. But in Wexford there were very few converts – fifty-nine for the whole of the eighteenth century compared with 395 in Galway, and 239 in Tipperary. Wexford was the only county in which Catholics were banned from the Volunteers in 1782. (However in Sir Thomas Esmonde's Castletown Yeomanry there were many Catholics.)[31]

There were economic causes for discontent. The county's

prosperity depended largely on the malting trade. The malt-houses and the ships carrying malt to Dublin, Britain and the Continent were almost entirely Catholic-owned. But the course of the war had closed the continental outlet and the price dropped catastrophically in 1797, ruining many maltsters and shipowners and causing much unemployment, of which United Irish propagandists took full advantage.[32]

There is doubt about the strength of the United Irishmen in Wexford and their responsibility for the rising. It used to be accepted that this was a mere peasants' revolt into which upper and middle-class figures were pressed, more or less unwillingly, by the threat of death if they refused. This is the picture painted by Thomas Cloney of Moneyhore, one of the rebel leaders, in his *Personal narrative of those transactions ... in Wexford ... in 1798*, published in 1832. It was also the story of several other rebel leaders brought to trial or seeking pardon after the revolt was defeated. But another leader, Miles Byrne, in his memoirs written in the 1830s, supported by much circumstantial evidence, insists that there was a strong and active United Irishmen organisation in the county well before the rebellion started:

> It was well understood that the ensuing spring was finally fixed for the rising; therefore the winter of 1797 and 1798 only remained to complete the preparation. Nothing could exceed the readiness of the United Irishmen to comply with the instructions that they procure arms, ammunition etc., notwith-standing the difficulties and perils they underwent procuring these articles. Every man had firearms of some sort, or a pike ... Since almost every blacksmith was a United Irishman, the pike-blades were soon to be had, but it was difficult to procure

handles for them, and the cutting down of young trees awoke attention.[33]

The conflicting accounts can be easily explained. Cloney in his narrative published many years later simply repeated what he had said immediately after the rebellion, while in prison and hoping for a pardon (which he obtained), insisting that the rising was not the work of a subversive organisation but the spontaneous reaction to Orange murders, flogging and pitchcapping;* and that he joined it reluctantly, under compulsion. But Miles Byrne escaped to France immediately after the rebellion and lived the rest of his life there, safe from prosecution. He is the better witness.

The circumstantial evidence in favour of Miles Byrne's account may thus be summarised. Several priests were disciplined by Dr Caulfield, Bishop of Ferns, for United Irish activities before the rising. Someone must have organised the collection and distribution of arms. Within two days of the outbreak of the rebellion, which was certainly spontaneous, gentlemen with the rank of United Irish colonels were taking over battalions already existing in cadre. Within ten days two of these headed the attack on New Ross. After the rebellion there was found a list of colonels and captains.[34]

Professor L. M. Cullen convincingly postulates six battalions organised at least as cadres before the revolt started. These, each commanded by a colonel with eight captains, formed the hard core of the rebel host, round which gathered less organised masses.[35]

---

* 'Pitchcapping' was a torture frequently applied to croppies. A paper bowl was filled with pitch and gunpowder, crammed on to the victim's head and set alight.

The rebellion in Wexford was unique in having as its leaders a large number of Catholic gentry, both landowners and middlemen. In Miles Byrne's words:

> Young men, sons of gentlemen farmers and the farmers' sons were the men to whom the people looked up with confidence in this perilous struggle, and in no instance were they deceived. These brave, modest young men, who would have thought it a dishonour to be engaged in a fight at a fair, were now everywhere seen, first in the danger, leading their men to victory.[36]

Of the United colonels, one of the best was Thomas Cloney, a big, twenty-six-year-old hunting squire, educated in England, of a family described by himself as 'respectable middlemen', farming themselves some 300 acres. He denied that he was ever a United Irishman, but it is clear from Miles Byrne that he was. He commanded one of the two Bantry battalions in the west of the county. The other was commanded by John Kelly of Killane, whom Cloney describes as 'son of a man of respectability' and Miles Byrne as 'the best battle commander; the Hoche of Ireland'. The northern battalion was commanded by Anthony Perry, a Protestant married to a Catholic, related to the Catholic Hays and the FitzGeralds of New Park. The three eastern battalions were commanded by Edward FitzGerald of New Park and Edward Roche of Garrylough, who had been wealthy maltsters before the slump and who had some military experience from the Yeomanry; and by Edmund Kyan who in the course of an eventful life had lost an arm and gained a good knowledge of artillery. All these were United Irishmen, and all were Catholics except for Perry.[37]

Among the United captains named by Miles Byrne were his kinsman, Garrett Byrne, a stylish landowner. He and his younger brother Billy, six and a half feet of muscled male beauty, were ardent United Irishmen. Two former 'French' officers, John Hay and William Barker, late of Walsh's, contributed much needed military experience. Dr John Colclough, grandson of the great Caesar Colclough's Catholic brother, and Edward Hay served the cause as civilians. Miles Byrne mentions many more captains of the same class as himself – several Byrnes, two Devereaux, two Furlongs, Fornen, Fennell, Murphy, Doyle, Kennedy, Carty, Sheehan, Mallow, Neill. All were Catholics. It was they who made the rebellion in Wexford so much more formidable than elsewhere.[38]

Of eighty-five priests in the diocese, eleven took part in the rebellion. According to their bishop, they were by no means the flower of the priesthood. Seven had a drink problem, described by Kevin Whelan as an occupational hazard of priests who participated too enthusiastically in the activities of the countryside. Five, however, displayed notable courage and leadership as United captains. Father Philip Roche was a boisterous six-footer who might have been invented by Boccaccio and had been reprimanded by his bishop for debauchery. But he had a way with him, and was an inspiring leader though not always in the right direction. The bishop had nothing much against Father Michael Murphy but his drinking, and nothing at all against Father John Murphy except that he was 'giddy but not noted for immorality'. Both Fathers Murphy made first class United captains.[39]

Trouble came to Wexford from the north, provoked by tales of flogging and pitchcapping in Carlow and Kildare. Anthony Perry himself was pitchcapped by men of the brutal North Cork Militia, and in his agony revealed something of the United

Irishmen's plans. The incident which started the rebellion was the slaughter, with pikes and pitchforks, of a party of Yeomanry searching for arms. It was planned by Father John Murphy. There followed tit-for-tat burnings of Catholic and Protestant churches and houses; and the total and unexpected rout, fourteen miles form Wexford town, of a company of North Cork Militia.

Next, against very feeble opposition, the rebels stormed Enniscorthy. Leading them across the deep and rapid river Slaney was a gentleman of sixty, Thomas Synnott, and his two nephews. The croppies set up a standing camp on Vinegar Hill just outside the town, and celebrated their victory with Irish jigs, French *carmagnoles*, whiskey and the slaughter of fifteen suspected Orangemen. Cloney arrived, according to his own account alone and still undecided on whether or not to join the rebels; but Miles Byrne describes him as 'joining camp at the head of a splendid corps of fine, determined fellows.'[40]

At this point William Barker, the old soldier of Walsh's, urged them to go straight for New Ross, the key to counties Waterford and Tipperary, by far the most worthwhile objective and virtually undefended.[41] But these new soldiers elected instead to move on Wexford, the garrison of which promptly moved out. They elected, or appointed, as their commander-in-chief Beauchamp Bagenal Harvey, small, mild and Protestant, a philosophical United Irishman qualified as a rebel leader only by his wealth and social eminence. Ignoring Barker's advice, he and his colleagues made the usual mistake of amateur strategists, dispersing instead of concentrating their efforts. Concentrated, the rebels might have taken New Ross and spread the rebellion into Munster; or moved north to blow on the embers in Carlow and Kildare; or even marched up the coast and galvanised into rising the Defenders in Dublin. They could not do all three.

The largest force moved in a leisurely manner on New Ross,

giving ample time for the garrison to be strengthened. The hard core of the rebel army consisted of two battalions from the west of the county, commanded by Cloney and his friend John Kelly of Killane. If the weakness of the United Irishmen was in the high command, their strength was in the fighting quality of the rank-and-file, pikemen and musketeers, commanded by men such as Cloney and Kelly. Colonel Crawfurd, the future hero of the Peninsular War, said of their men in New Ross that he 'never saw any troops attacking with more enthusiasm and bravery'. But the high command failed to concentrate the storming parties or to provide them with reserves to exploit their early success. After a desperate day's fighting they withdrew, leaving Kelly badly wounded.[42]

Meanwhile an appalling massacre had taken place at Scullabogue House of over a hundred loyalist prisoners, men, women and children, shot on the lawn or roasted alive in a locked barn. Harvey, shocked by this horror, left the army and returned despondently to Wexford. He was succeeded as commander-in-chief by Father Philip Roche who was equally devoid of military experience but whose 'boisterous spirit pleased the multitude'.[43]

The detachment directed against Carlow and Kildare captured Newtownbarry; but then celebrated their victory so lavishly that they fell victims to a counterattack and were dispersed far and wide, most of them dropping their weapons and going off home. Miles Byrne made his way to Edward FitzGerald's army (his own regiment, Kyan's and Perry's) which was moving up the coast towards Dublin. It was probably Father Michael Murphy who wrote to a friend in Dublin:

> Great events are ripening. We shall have an army
> of brave republicans one hundred thousand strong
> with fourteen pieces of cannon, on Tuesday before

Dublin. You will rise with proportionate force.

But at Arklow the croppies met for the first time well trained British Fencibles,* armed with sufficient artillery. Kyan sited his guns skilfully and scored a hit with his first shot. Three battalions of pikemen then charged behind Miles Byrne, Father John and Father Michael Murphy. Father Michael was killed thirty yards from the guns, and a shell blew off Kyan's cork arm and half the stump. But courage and pikes could not prevail against grapeshot at a few yards' range.[44]

The battles of New Ross and Arklow cost the rebels the initiative, and there is nothing so helpless as a rebellion on the defensive. Overwhelming numbers of regular British troops moved in for the kill.

In the last few days of the rebellion the croppies in Wexford paraded a hundred prisoners on the bridge over the Slaney. One by one each was made to kneel and four executioners drove pikes into his stomach and back and tossed him writhing over the parapet into the river. After ninety-seven had thus been despatched, up galloped Colonel Edward Roche and ordered every man to march to the relief of Vinegar Hill, about to be attacked by the enemy. The last three prisoners were left kneeling in the blood on the bridge.

The rebels on Vinegar Hill, many thousands in number but no longer an army, were bombarded with artillery until they took to their heels, and the troops could proceed at leisure with the customary shooting of prisoners and wounded. William Barker, the former 'French' officer, lost his arm in the battle but was smuggled down to Wexford and into a ship bound for Hamburg.

---

* Full-time soldiers but enlisted only for home defence.

If only he had been in command instead of Bagenal Harvey and Father Roche . . . [45]

Among the rebel leaders Father Roche, Harvey, Dr Colclough, John Kelly and Billy Byrne were hanged. Miles Byrne escaped to France. Most of the others, including Cloney, were saved by an amnesty proclaimed by the new Viceroy and Commander-in Chief, the Earl of Cornwallis.

The rising in Ulster, birthplace of Irish republicanism of which the United Irishmen hoped and government feared most, proved a fiasco. The Presbyterians had little stomach for the fight and their plans were leaked to the authorities by Nicholas Magin, a Catholic farmer, who was a United colonel. Afterwards the Presbyterians claimed that the Papists had let them down and would have to be dealt with next.[46]

By mid-August of 1789 the rebellion seemed to be over and scores of thousands of croppies submitted and handed in their weapons. But on the twenty-third of the month, by a masterpiece of mistiming, the French landed at Killala in County Mayo. It was not only the wrong time but the wrong place. Connaught was the only province in which there was no United Irishmen organisation and precious few Defenders, and it was far from any worthwhile objective. However, there were the French, 1,099 veterans under General Humbert with 6,000 spare muskets, three cannon and a job lot of gaudy uniforms for the Irish who would join them. Humbert's task was to form a bridgehead for 7,000 more French who, as he believed, were already embarked and ready to sail. They were not embarked and did not sail.

The French occupied Killala without difficulty and established their headquarters in the house of Dr Stock, the Protestant bishop, behaving most correctly. Within three days some 5,000 peasants had rallied to the tricolour, but the French were amazed by their uncouthness and amused by their naivety as they congratulated these atheists on coming to Ireland to fight for the Blessed Virgin. As many as possible were put in uniforms and handed muskets, but that did not make them soldiers: indeed it seemed as though nothing would. Few could speak English, none French, so instruction was difficult. An old French officer said to Stock, 'I would pick one third and by the Lord I would shoot the rest.'[47]

What Humbert needed was the sort of Catholics who had led the rebellion in Wexford, but speaking Irish and if possible French. He had been assured by such as Wolfe Tone and Napper Tandy that any number of them would ride to his standard, but very few turned up. The best was George Blake of Garacloone, one of the Ballyglunin Blakes, known as 'Pistol' Blake after being cashiered from the British army for killing a brother officer in a somewhat dubious duel. James McDonnell had been a member of the Supreme Directorate of the United Irishmen but had missed that fatal meeting because his coach broke down. Two other local gentlemen joined: Austen O'Malley, a fine young buck who knew all about duelling but nothing about soldiering; and James O'Dowd, who had served in the Austrian army and in the Yeomanry. On Humbert's staff were two County Antrim Catholics, Matthew and Bartolemew Teeling; Wolfe Tone's brother Matthew and the enigmatic Henry O'Kane who was improbably both a priest and a French army captain. He was first ashore at Killala, kissing the ground and greeting the natives in fluent Irish. He was indeed a useful man, but what were these among so many recruits to be trained? Fifty good officers would have been too few.[48]

As a propaganda move Humbert formed a Provisional Government of Connaught and more or less conscripted as its President John Moore of Moore Hall. He had never been a United Irishman and insisted that he had accepted office only because he would otherwise have been shot, and did no more than sign assignats (IOUs) for commandeered horses, cattle and sheep. It was later alleged by a rebel priest that Dr Dominick Bellew, the Catholic Bishop of Killala, had acted as President of the Committee of Public Safety set up by Humbert. It seems most unlikely. It was the sort of thing that could easily be proved but it was not even tested in court, though there must have been plenty of Protestants glad to see a Catholic bishop in the dock. Dr Bellew was no democrat. But he was quarrelsome, and no doubt there were disgruntled priests in his diocese. Perhaps this was one of them. He could hardly have been pleased by the arrival of his slovenly, ne'er-do-well brother Matthew at Killala. Because he had served in the Russian and Austrian armies, Humbert made him generalissimo of all the Irish levies, but soon had to cashier him for incapacity and drunkenness.[49]

On 26 August Humbert attacked General Lake's force at Castlebar. His veterans of the German and Italian campaigns were of far higher quality than Lake's Militia and Yeomanry; and at the first cannon shot Humber's Irish levies fled in one direction and the militia with equal celerity in another. 5,000 more Irish joined Humbert after the 'Castlebar Races', but they only added to his problems.

If Humbert had marched on Galway, he would have found the West Bridge guarded by a sandalled and robed friar carrying a musket 'to prevent entry of disaffected persons'.[50] Instead he marched towards Sligo, and then turned south with Lake at his heels and Cornwallis with 20,000 men between him and Dublin. Cornwallis was using a sledgehammer, but there are worse ways of cracking a nut if a sledgehammer is available. On 8 September the three armies met at Ballinamuck in County Longford. The French were old enough soldiers to know when to surrender, and were repatriated to France. Their Irish allies were slaughtered during the battle and hanged in droves after it, the militia making up for deficiencies in action by their zeal as executioners.

George Blake, on the refusal of his request to be shot rather than hanged, called for soap which he rubbed into the rope so that the noose would run more freely, and assisted the in-experienced executioner to adjust the knot properly. As James O'Dowd was about to be strung up, a Yeomanry officer called out, 'See where this has brought you! I believe your father is a gentleman and keeps a pack of hounds.' 'He keeps three,' replied the O'Dowd's son, 'and his whippers-in are better gentlemen than you.' It was a good exit-line. The Teelings and Matthew Tone were also hanged, despite their French commissions; as was Matthew Bellew who had been left behind, permanently sozzled, at Killala. John Moore, condemned to transportation, died on the way to the ship at Cork. Austen O'Malley and McDonnell escaped to France.[51]

Nine days after Humbert's surrender Napper Tandy stepped ashore at Rathlin Island off the Donegal coast. He was part of an expedition consisting of 270 French troops and a large quantity of weapons and saddlery for the Irish army which they expected to find awaiting them. When the postmaster broke it to them that Humbert and his whole army were prisoners, there was nothing for it but to re-embark. Napper Tandy had celebrated his return to the Old Sod to such effect that he had to be carried aboard, urinating copiously over the shoulders of his bearers. On 12 October a British squadron intercepted a small French fleet off the Donegal coast and captured eight out of ten ships. Among the prisoners, jaunty and defiant, his French uniform blackened with gunpowder from fighting his battery, was Wolfe Tone. He was taken to Dublin and condemned to death for high treason, but escaped the hangman by committing suicide. His reputation is, perhaps, higher than he deserved. His courage in adversity was flawless. His ideal of Catholic, Protestant and Dissenter uniting under the common denomination of Irishmen still inspires all Irish patriots, although further than ever from reality in six counties of Ireland. But his judgement was distorted by wishful thinking; and by grievously misleading the French, he was largely responsible both for Humbert's landing and for its failure.[52]

Tone's one-time disciple, Dr Hugh MacDermot, wrote of these events to his brother Henry, a lieutenant in Dillon's Regiment in the British service:

> You will be happy to hear that none of our friends are in any degree implicated in the late rebellion. Indeed no Catholic of sense, character or property, none but the lowest rabble and a few gentlemen of desperate fortune and unprincipled character, joined the French. In many places there has been a destruction of property, partly by the excesses of the rebels, partly by the marches of the army, by plundering, pilfering, pressing horses etc. As for my part, by living in the retired place which is a mile off the high road, I escaped the slightest loss of any kind.[53]

During the rebellion Pitt and Cornwallis gave much thought to preventing another. The safeguard they favoured was union between Great Britain and Ireland, under one Crown and one Parliament. It was thought highly unsatisfactory that the British government, which was *de facto* responsible for the government of a country seen as vital for Britain's defence, should have to work through the creaking, corrupt Castle bureaucracy. In a union there would be no such conflict of interests and differences of opinion which had happened and delayed action in 1798. If ever it were thought desirable to admit Catholics to Parliament, they would form a small and harmless minority at Westminster, but would dominate an Irish Parliament as they had in 1689.

Irish opinion was divided. Most politically conscious Catholics tended to favour the Union. They had no reason to trust 'Grattan's Parliament', which had never done anyting for them except under pressure from Westminster. But there was an anti-Union minority, including Dr Hugh MacDermot.[54] On the whole Protestants were against Union. Gentlemen whose grandfathers had called themselves English, now thought of themselves as emphatically Irish, more Irish (as Daniel O'Connell said) than the Irish themselves. They regarded Grattan's Parliament with a devotion that it did not deserve, greatly exaggerating its independence. It was obvious that with only a hundred MPs at Westminster instead of 300 in College Green, and an equivalent reduction of Irish representation in the Upper House, the loaves and fishes would be in short supply. The English were unsound about Papists, and only a Protestant Parliament in Dublin could really protect Irish Protestant interests. Dubliners were generally anti-Union, resenting their Dublin being relegated from capital city to provincial town; they feared that, without 300 or 400 peers and MPs spending six months there every other year, business would slump and property prices fall. Lawyers stood to lose much litigation and fees for drafting parliamentary bills. Cork on the whole was for the Union, believing that with Dublin being downgraded, their city would prosper. But the mass of the people, Cornwallis believed, did not care 'one farthing': anyone could get up a petition anywhere on either side.

In January 1799, the Commons refused, by 111 votes to 106 even to discuss the matter. 'We are yet a nation,' exulted Charlemont, 'the abominable project is defeated.'[55]

But he exulted too soon, for the Castle machine swung promptly into action. There was less plain bribery than is generally believed. Anyway, how can one distinguish, in the political climate of the time, between a bribe for a vote, a reward for steady support and compensation for losses? Cornwallis, never given to understatement, was appalled to find himself:

> negotiating and jobbing with the most corrupt people under heaven . . . I despise and hate myself every hour for being engaged in such dirty work.

Yet he was convinced that a union was best for both countries; and if it could be achieved only by wholesale trade in borough stock, so be it; but:

> how I long to kick those whom my public duty obliges me to court.

On expert advice, he gave priority to compensating for their losses to the following:

1   Borough proprietors: eighty-four boroughs were to be disenfranchised, and of the remainder all but Dublin reduced to one-member constituencies. Since borough ownership had brought them the highest offices, the largest fortunes, this was the class that would suffer most from the Union. £1,260,000 was distributed among them to soften the blow – £13,800 per disenfranchised borough, which they certainly regarded as compensation for their losses, not as bribes. Lord Downshire, the biggest borough-owner of all, pocketed his com-

pensation – but still voted against the Union.

2 Interest in counties: since counties would continue to send two members each to Parliament, albeit to Westminster instead of College Green, those who managed county elections would suffer little loss. But they were a respected and influential class, who must be kept sweet.

3 Barristers, of whom there were about fifty in the Lower House, each regarded a seat as the road to preferment. In future there would be less than twenty.

4 Purchasers of seats, to whom would be refunded their purchase money.

5 Residents and property owners in Dublin.

During the past twenty years the number of placemen and pensioners in the Commons had been allowed to fall to seventy-three. Now twenty-six new places were distributed. Opponents of the Union were persuaded to vacate their seats and were replaced by supporters. Sixteen borough proprietors were given United Kingdom peerages, carrying seats in the House of Lords; twenty-six new Irish peers were created; twenty Irish peers were raised in rank.[56]

From this unseemly scramble the Catholic gentry withdrew the skirts of their garments. It was not that they were unbribable, but they were not worth bribing. In any case most of them favoured the Union, fearing after '98 a triumphant Orangeism entrenched in the Irish Parliament. They thought they were more likely to be completely emancipated by English than by Irish MPs, and the history of the past twenty-two years seemed to support that view. Nevertheless Cornwallis had seen that the case for Union would be strengthened by strong Catholic support, and after the fiasco in January 1799, he wrote, 'If ever a second trial of the Union is to be made, the Catholics must be included.' Pitt, too, believed that Catholic Emancipation must follow the Union. He could not, of course, say so publicly, or make any promise to that effect without enraging Irish Protestants; but by many a nudge and a wink Catholics were given that impression. Among Catholic supporters of the Union was Maurice O'Connell, 'Hunting Cap', who pointed out to his nephew Daniel that everything Catholics had gained in the past twenty-two years had been granted by the government, not in response to any agitation.

Prominent in noisy denunciations of the Union was Daniel O'Connell, aged twenty-five. He resented the diminution of his country's status. He believed that Irish MPs, albeit Protestants, disliked meeting every hour neighbours who 'looked shame on them', and that there was more to be hoped from them than from Englishmen. In January 1800, he made his first public political speech. It had, he said, been industriously circulated, that Catholics' support for the Union had been brought by promises of Emancipation.

> Can they remain silent under so horrible a calumny? Let every man who feels with me proclaim that if the alternatives were offered him of Union or the re-enactment of the penal code with all its pristine horrors, he would prefer without hesitation the latter . . . that he would rather confide in the justice of his brethren, the Protestants of Ireland, than lay his country at the feet of foreigners . . . I know that the Catholics of Ireland still remember that they have a country, and that they will never accept any advantages as a *sect* which would debase and destroy them as a *people*.

He sat down to tumultuous applause such as he would hear many times in the next forty years. 'Popular applause is always shortlived but the inconveniences may be serious and lasting,' Hunting Cap reprimanded him. Dan promised to mend his ways but had no intention to doing so. Four days after Dan's great speech, Dr Hugh MacDermot joined a procession of Freemen and Freeholders of Dublin to address Grattan and the Speaker. 'The concourse of people was innumerable, and the hopes of defeating the Union are this day sanguine in the extreme.'[57]

But the gravy-train towards Union could not be halted, least of all by Catholics with no place in it. The Irish House of Commons, by 158 votes to 115, voted for Union with Great Britain, to come into effect on 1 January 1801.

Catholics did not get any *quid pro quo* for their support. Pitt, having half-promised Emancipation, could not deliver. George III was no bigot; he had nothing much against Catholics, except that his eldest son was unlawfully married to one. He had been glad to grant religious freedom to French Canadians, and had given a secret service pension to the Cardinal Duke of York, pretender to his throne. But at his coronation he had sworn an oath, devised in 1689, the express purpose of which was to deny to Papists places of authority under the Crown. Clearly this was incompatible with admitting them to Parliament. 'Where is that power on earth,' he asked, 'to absolve me from the due observance of every sentence of that oath?. . . I had rather beg my bread from door to door.' If Pitt's supporters had been behind him on this issue he might have put it to the king that the oath had been devised in very different circumstances, when all Catholics were Jacobites, and Jacobites were subversive in peace and enemies in war. Even then it would have been hard to convince His Majesty that an oath could be broken for reasons of political expediency. But Pitt's followers, both English and the newly-arrived Irish

MPs, were opposed to Catholic Emancipation. It hardly needed the king to make it known that he would regard as his enemy anyone who voted for it. Moreover, pushing the king too hard on what he saw as a matter of honour might well bring on another onset of the royal malady, of which there had recently been disturbing symptoms, with the prospect of a regency, and a government headed by the Regent's friend, Charles Fox.[58]

So Catholics had to wait for full emancipation. Sir Arthur Wellesley, Chief Secretary in 1807, left Lord Fingall under no illusions; the Popery laws would be implemented with 'mildness and good temper', but they would not be repealed in the foreseeable future.[59]

It was not until 1829 that Daniel O'Connell, scion of an old landed family in Kerry, by an extraordinary campaign of populist mass agitation, won:

> a great and glorious triumph . . . Catholics can be judges, mayors, sheriffs, common counselmen, aldermen, peers of parliament, members of parliament, in short everything.[60]

He led to victory the rising Catholic middle class – merchants, journalists, strong farmers and above all lawyers. The Catholic gentry were solidly on his side, so long as he agitated only for emancipation. The Irish Party which he led in Parliament, 'O'Connell's Tail', consisted in 1832 of thirty-two members, of whom twenty-three were Catholic gentry; of the nine Protestants, eight were of Irish convert families (Butler, Callaghan, O'Brien, two Macnamaras, Mullins, O'Connor, Roche).[61]

Many a Catholic family which had survived the Penal Laws went under after the Famine, ruined by the cost of keeping its dependents alive. Successive Reform Acts and the increasing pressures of democracy transferred their political power first to the Catholic middle classes, then to the Catholic masses. During the century after Emancipation, Catholic, like Protestant, landlords almost disappeared. But through the whole of the eighteenth century this endangered species, simply by surviving, had kept alive the possibility that Irishmen might one day run their own country.

1 A. T. Q. Stewart, *A Deeper Silence*, 146-7.

2 Marianne Elliott, *Partners in Revolution: The United Irishmen and France*, 23-5; Maureen Wall, *Catholic Ireland in the Eighteenth Century*, 164-6; R. B. McDowell, *Irish Historical Studies*, 2, 1940, 14-15, 39.

3 Wall, *op. cit.*, 164-6; Hugh MacDermot, *Letters*, no. 38.

4 *Trial of Francis Bellew Esquire . . . for appearing in arms with a mob of Defenders*, NLI, Jolly Collection, 1058.

5 Miles Byrne, *Memoirs of Miles Byrne*, I, 261; R. Hayes, *A Biographical Dictionary of Irishmen in France* 17, 61, 62, 69, 129, 247-8, 310-11.

6 *Ibid.*, 72, 207, 243-8, 254-5.

7 Mrs M. J O'Connell, *The Last Colonel of the Irish Brigade*, II, 91-2, 134.

8 Hayes, *op. cit.*, 129-31.

9 Mrs M. J. O'Connell, *op. cit.*, II, 141; MacDermot, *op. cit.*, 265.

10 John Hayes, 'The Trants: an Enterprising Family in Eighteenth Century Cork', in *Journal of the Cork Historical and Archaeological Society*, LXXXXVI, no. 243, Jan–June 1981, 21-9; Elizabeth Longford, *Wellington: The Years of the Sword*, 146.

11 Thomas Wyse, *Historical Sketch of the Late Catholic Association*, 102, 123; Stewart, *op. cit.*, 147-8, 185; Elliott, *op. cit.*, 35-48.

12 32 George, Ch. 21, III, .

13 33 George, Ch. 21, III, ; Wall, *op. cit.*, 167-8.

14 Quoted by Robert Kee, *The Green Flag*, 57 fn.

15 Maureen Wall, *op. cit.*, 168.

16 Elliott, *op. cit.*, 40-4, 49, 96; T. Bartlett, 'Defenders and Defenderism', in *Irish Historical Studies*, XXIV, no. 95, May 1985, 374-9, 464, 476.

17 Elliott, *op. cit.*, 25, 60-1; Thomas Pakenham, *The Year of Liberty*, 48; R. F. Foster, *Modern Ireland*, 268.

18 Elliott, *op. cit.*, 71, 79, 81-5, 109.

19 *Ibid.*, 101-3; Kee, *op. cit.* 81-4.

20 Elliott, *op. cit.*, 127-9; Kee, *op. cit.*, 86-90.

21 Elliott, *op. cit.*, 123-4, 189; Kee, *op. cit.*, 93-4.

22 Elliott, *op. cit.*, 193-5, Packenham, *op. cit.*, 37, 43, 77-8. 91. 115-7.

23 Daire Keogh, *The French Disease: the Catholic Church and Nationalism in Ireland, 1790-1800*, 199.

24 M. R. O'Connell, *The Correspondence of Daniel O'Connell*, 24A.

25 Pakenham, *op. cit.*, 111-24.

26 Countess of Fingall, *Seventy Years Young*, 108–9; Kee, *op. cit.*, 105-6; 108-9; Pakenham, *op. cit.*, 159-60.

27 Pakenham, *op. cit.*, 90-100, 103.

28 Byrne, *op. cit.*, I, 8, 40.

29 Daniel Gahan in Kevin Whelan (ed.), *Wexford History and Society*, 213-4; Edward Hay, *The History of the Irish Insurrection of 1798*, 38; Kevin Whelan in T. P. Power and Kevin Whelan (eds.), *Endurance and Emergence*, 135-9, 142-3.

30 Byrne, *op. cit.*, I, 3.

31 T. P. Power in T. P. Power and Kevin Whelan (eds.), *op. cit.*, 104-5, 124.

32 Nicholas Furlong in Whelan (ed.), *op. cit.*, 170-1.

33 Thomas Cloney, *A Personal Narrative of . . . 1798*, 18; Byrne, *op. cit.*, I, 7, 8, 21; L. M. Cullen in Whelan (ed.), *op. cit.*, 269.

34 *Ibid.*, 269-70.

35 *Ibid.*, 260-1, 269-70.

36 Byrne, *op. cit.*, I, 169.

37 Cloney in Whelan (ed.), *op. cit.*, 320-2; Byrne, *op. cit.*, I, 76, 55-6; L. M. Cullen in Whelan (ed.), *op. cit.*, 269-70

38 Byrne, I, *op. cit.*, 48, 53, 56, 78.

39 L. M. Cullen in Whelan (ed.), *op. cit.*, 285-6; Kevin Whelan in Whelan (ed.), *op. cit.*, 305-7.

40 Cloney, *op. cit.*, 13; Byrne, *op. cit.*, I, 46-8; Hay, *op. cit.*, 84-5.

41 Byrne, *op. cit.*, I, 48-9.

42 Cloney, *op. cit.*, 34-42; Pakenham, *op. cit.*, 200-7.

43 Pakenham, *op. cit.*, 100; Hay, *op. cit.*, 153; Byrne, *op. cit.*, I, 192-3.

44 Byrne, *op. cit.*, I, 76-9; Pakenham, *op. cit.*, 211.

45 *Ibid.*, 170-3.

46 *Ibid.*, 216-31.

47 Bishop Stock, *Diary*, 3, 4, 12.

48 Hayes, *op. cit.*, 131-2; Hayes, *Last Invasion*, 17; Byrne, *op. cit.*, II, 7, 197, 206; Elliott, *op. cit.*, 224-5; Kee, *op. cit.*, 134-7.

49 Hayes, *op. cit.*, 261; Bishop Stock, *op. cit.*, 24; J. Hone, *The Moores of Moore Hall*, 39-40; Keogh, *op. cit.*, 185.

50 J. Hardiman, *A History of Galway*, II, 183.

51 Pakenham, *op. cit.*, 326-7; Hayes, *op. cit.*, 202, 205, 284; Martin J. Blake, *Blake Family Records*, 199; Kee, *op. cit.*, 140-1; Hone, *op. cit.*, 40-1; Bishop Stock, *op. cit.*, 24, 35.

52 Elliott, *op. cit.*, 233; Kee, *op. cit.*, 141-2.

53 Hugh MacDermot, *Letters*, no. 66.

54 *Ibid.*, nos. 71, 73.

55 Foster, *op. cit.*, 283-4; C. Ross (ed.), *Cornwallis Correspondence*, III, 111; Charlemont MSS II, 34.

56 Ross (ed.), *op. cit.*, III, 81, 102; Foster, *op. cit.*, 284; Kee, *op. cit.*, 157-8; E. and A. Porritt, *The Unreformed House of Commons*, II, 406.

57 *The Dublin Evening Post*, 14 Jan 1800; M. R. O'Connell, *op. cit.*, 3378; Hugh MacDermot, *Letters*, no. 73.

58 John Brooke, *King George III*, (London, 1972), 366-8.

59 Elizabeth Longford, *Wellington, The Years of the Sword*, (London, 1969), 131.

60 M. R. O'Connell, *op. cit.*, 1529.

61 Angus MacIntyre, *The Liberator: Daniel O'Connell and the Irish Party*, Appendix B, 301-7.

SELECT BIBLIOGRAPHY

TCD: Trinity College Dublin
NLI: National Library of Ireland
RIA: Royal Irish Academy
PRONI: Public Records Office of Northern Ireland

Baigent, Michael and Richard Lee. *The Temple and The Lodge*. (London, 1989).

Bartlett, T. 'Defenders and Defenderism', *Irish Historical Studies*, XXIV, 95, May 1985.

Begemann, Wilhelm. *Freemasonry in Ireland*. (MS in Freemasons' Library, Dublin).

The Trial of Francis Bellew Esquire. Pamphlet in NLI, Jolly Collection 1058.

Blake, Martin J. *Blake Family Records 1600-1700*. (London, 1905).

Brooke, John. *King George III*. (London, 1972).

Byrne, Miles. *Memoirs of Miles Byrne*. (Dublin, 1907).

Campbell, T. *A Philosophical Survey of the South of Ireland*. (London, 1777).

Carty, Mary Rose. *The History of Killeen Castle, County Meath*. (Dunsany, County Meath, Carty/Lynch, 1991).

Caulfield, J. (ed.). *Correspondence of lst Earl of Charlemont*. 2 vols. (London, 1891–2).

Cloney, Thomas. *A personal narrative of. . . 1798*. (Dublin, 1832).

Cogan, A. *Diocese of Meath*. 3 vols. (London, 1872).

Corish, Patrick J. *The Catholic Community in the 17th and 18th Centuries*. (Dublin, 1981).

Corkery, Daniel. *The Hidden Ireland*. (Dublin, 1924).

Cullen, L. M. *The Emergence of Modern Ireland*. (London, 1981).

——————. *Life in Ireland*. (London, 1968).

Dalton, J. *King James's Irish Army List, 1689*. (Dublin, 1860).

Dern, Laurence. *Ahimon Rezon or Help to a Brother*. (Belfast, 1782).

Dunboyne, Lord. *Butler Family History*. (Kilkenny, 1991).

Dunleavy, G. W. and J. E. (eds.). *O'Conor Papers* (Unpublished MSS in TCD).

Elliott, Marianne. *Partners in Revolution: The United Irishmen and France*. (Yale, 1982).

Foster, R. F. *Modern Ireland 1600-1972*. (London, 1988).

Fingall, Countess Elizabeth. *Seventy Years Young*. (London, 1937).

Fahey, J. *History and Antiquities of the Diocese of Kilmacduagh*. (Dublin, 1883).

Grace, Sheffield. *Memoirs of the Family of Grace*. (London, 1823).

Gaughan, J. Anthony. *The Knights of Glin*. (Dublin, 1978).

Hardiman, J. *A History of Galway*. 2 vols. (Dublin, 1820).

Hay, Edward. *History of the Irish Insurrection of 1798*. (Dublin, 1847).

Hayes, R. *A Biographical Dictionary of Irishmen in France*. (Dublin, 1949).

——————————. *The Last Invasion of Ireland*. (Dublin, 1939).

Hickson, Mary Ann. *Old Kerry Records*. 2 vols. (London, 1872–4).

Holohan, Renagh. *The Irish Chateaux*. (Dublin 1989)

Hone, J. *The Moores of Moore Hall*. (London, 1939).

Howard, G. E. *Several Special Cases in the Laws Against the Further Growth of Popery*. (Dublin, 1775).

Kee, Robert. *The Green Flag*. (London, 1972).

Keogh, Daire. *The French Disease: the Catholic Church and Nationalism in Ireland, 1790–1800*. (Dublin, 1993).

Kelly, James. *Prelude to Union*. (Cork, 1990).

MacLysaght, Edward (ed.). *The Kenmare Papers*. (Dublin, 1941).

Lecky, W. E. H. *History of Ireland in the 18th Century*. (London, 1892).

Lodge, John. *The Peerage of Ireland*. 6 vols. (London, 1789).

Lynam, Shevawn. *Humanity Dick Martin*. (London, 1975).

McCarthy, S. T. *The McCarthys of Munster*. (Dundalk, 1922).

MacDermot, B. C. (ed.). *Letters of Hugh MacDermot*. (Unpublished.)

MacDermot, Sir Dermot. *The MacDermots of Moylurg and Coolavin*. (Unpublished, 1981).

MacEwan, Michael. *The Ryan Family and the Scarteen Hounds*. (Wilton, 1989).

MacIntyre, Angus. *The Liberator: Daniel O'Connell and the Irish Party 1830–1847*. (Hamilton, 1965).

MacNamara, N. G. *The Story of an Irish Sept*. (Dublin, 1896).

Magan, William. *Umma More: the Story of an Irish Family*. (Shaftesbury, 1983).

Marnane, D. G. *Land and Violence in West Tipperary*. (PhD Thesis, 1985).

Melvin, Patrick. 'The Composition of the Galway Gentry', *Irish Genealogist*, 1936.

Nolan, W. (ed.). *Tipperary History and Society*. (Dublin, 1985).

O'Brien, Donough. *History of the O'Briens*. (London, 1949).

O'Byrne, Eileen (ed.). *The Convert Rolls*. (Dublin, 1981).

Ó Cearbhaill, D. *Galway, Town and Gown*. (Dublin, 1984).

O'Connell, Mrs M. J. *The Last Colonel of the Irish Brigade*. 2 vols. (London, 1892).

O'Connell, M. R. *Irish Politics and Social Conflict in the Age of the American Revolution*. (Philadelphia, 1965).

O'Connell, M. R. (ed.). *The Correspondence of Daniel O'Connell*. 8 vols. (Dublin, 1972–1980).

O'Conor, Charles. *Memoirs of Charles O'Conor of Belanagare.* (Dublin, 1796).

O'Conor Don, S. J., C. O. *The Early Life of Charles O'Conor.* (Dublin, 1991).

O'Conor Nash, Pyers. *The history of . . . the Royal O'Conors.* (Castlerea, 1990).

Pakenham, Thomas. *The Year of Liberty.* (London, 1968).

Parkinson, R. E. *The History of the Grand Lodge of Ireland.* (Lodge of Research, 1957).

Porritt, E. and A. *The Unreformed House of Commons.* 2 vols. (London, 1909).

Power, T. P. and Kevin Whelan (eds.). *Endurance and Emergence: Catholics in Ireland in the 18th Century.* (Dublin, 1990).

Ross, C. (ed.) *Cornwallis Correspondence.* 3 vols. (London, 1859).

Shepherd, Robert. *Ireland's Fate.* (London, 1990).

Simms, J. G. 'Irish Jacobites', *Analectica Hibernia,* 22, 1960.

——————————. *The Treaty of Limerick.* Irish Historical Series No. 3. (Dublin, 1965).

——————————. *Williamite Confiscations in Ireland.* (London, 1956).

Staples, H. P. (ed.). *The Ireland of Jonah Barrington.* (London, 1968).

Stewart, A. T. Q. *A Deeper Silence: the Hidden Origins of the United Irishmen.* (London, 1993).

Stock, Bishop. *Killala Diary of Bishop Stock.* (MS in TCD).

Wall, Maureen. *Catholic Ireland in the 18th century.* (*Collected Essays,* ed. G. O'Brien.) (Dublin, 1989).

Ward, C. C. and R. E. (eds.). *Letters of Charles O'Conor of Belanagare.* (Ann Arbor, 1980).

Whelan, Kevin (ed.). *Wexford History and Society.* (Dublin 1992).

——————————. *Tintern Abbey, County Wexford.* (Saltmills, 1992).

Wyse, Thomas. *A Historical Sketch of the Late Catholic Association.* 2 vols. (London, 1829).

Young, Arthur. *A Tour in Ireland.* Ed. C. Maxwell. (Cambridge, 1925).

INDEX

abduction of women, 103, 183–4
Albemarle, Duke of (Monck), 138–9
  Earl of (Keppel), 48, 85
Alexander the Coppersmith, 232–4
American colonies, 259–60, 261–2, 263
Anne, Queen, 54
Antrim (McDonnell), Alastair, 4th Earl, 40
  5th Earl, 57
Arklow, battle of, 295–6
Arthur, Patrick, 236
'Articlemen', 35, 38–9, 40–5
Asgill, John, 117
Athlone, 16, 26, 31
Attainder, Irish Act of, 21
Aughrim, battle of, 31

Baggot, Mark, 47–8
Baldwin, James, 193–4
Ballinamuck, battle of, 299–300
Bantry Bay, French landing, 195, 284–5
Barker, William, 293, 294, 296–7
Barnewall, Nicholas, 3rd Viscount
  Barnewall of Kingsland, 41, 133
  Sir Patrick, Bart, 41
  Father John, 53–4
  Father Patrick, 134
base tenure, base fee, 72–3, 74fn
Bellew of Barmeath, 1st Bart, Sir
  Patrick, 126
  2nd Bart, Sir John, 31, 46, 126
  5th Bart, Sir Patrick, 126, 267–8
  Bishop Dominick, 127, 299
  Francis, 273–4
  Matthew, 299–300
Bellew of Mount Bellew, family, 109–10
  Christopher, 65
  Michael, 65
  Christopher, 65, 237
  Michael, 65
  Luke, 237
  Patrick, 237
  Francis, 238
  Sir Patrick (also of Barmeath), 100
Barrington, Jonah, 83–4, 106–7
Berwick (Stuart), Duke of, 23, 30
Blake of Ballyglunin, Martin, 18, 89
  others, 89, 238
Blake of Menlo, Colonel Walter, 32, 69
  others, 89, 238
Blake of Moyne, 88
Blake of Ardfry, 89
Blake of Muckiness, 90
Blake of Tower Hill, Isidore, 237–8
  John, 238

  of Garraclune, George, 298, 300
Bophin, Lord, see Clanrickard
Bowes, John, 59
Boyne, battle of the, 23
Braughall, Thomas, 272
Browne of the Neale, Sir John, 86–7
  Peter, 87
Brownrigge, Henry, 140
Bulkeley, William, 275
Burke, Edmund, 207, 258fn, 260, 278
Bushe, Amyas, 153–4
Butler of Kilcash, Thomas, 147
  Lady Iva, 147
  John, 147
  John, of Garryricken, 148
  Walter, 148
  Lady Eleanor, 148
  Archbishop Christopher, 149
Butler, Sir Theobald (Toby), 1, 33, 58,
  61–2, 140
  Archbishop James, 149
  Archbishop James, 149
  Bishop John, 149
  Robert, of Ballyragget, 167
  Captain Whitwell, 197–9
Byrne, Edward, 244–5
  Miles, 289–91, 295–6
  Garrett, 293
  'Billy', 293, 297

Cahir (Butler), Theobald, 1st Lord, 22,
  146
  James, 9th Lord, 146, 166
Camden (Pratt), John Jeffreys, 1st
  Marquess, 282
Carlingford (Taaffe), Nicholas, 1st
  Viscount, 25
Carolan, Turlough, 115–6
'Castlebar Races', 299
Catholic Church, under pressure, 78–9
  pressure relaxed, 79
  career option for younger sons, 223–4
  general, 255–6, 266
Catholic Committee, 119, 257–9, 267–9,
  272, 277–8
Catholic Emancipation, 281, 304, 306–7
Catholic Relief Acts, 1778, 262
  1782, 265–6
  1792, 279
  1793, 279–80
Catholic schools, 79, 266
Charlemont (Caulfield), James, 1st Earl
  of, 262–3, 268
Charles Edward Stuart, Prince ('The
  Young Pretender'), 162, 243–4, 257

INDEX

Scully, Jeremiah, 161
James, 161
Denis, 161
Settlement, Act of, 17, 21
sexual relations (see also abduction of
women), 103
Sheehy, Father Nicholas, 163–5
Edward ('Buck'), 166
Sheldon, Lord Dominick, 23
slave trade, 243
smuggling, 'free trade', 92, 196–200
Spanish Navy, 221
Stack, Lieutenant, 214
Lieutenant Colonel, 277
Stapleton, Lieutenant Colonel, 215
John, 239
Starkie, family, 76
Stock, Bishop J., 297–8
Sullivan, Laurence, 222
Sutton, Thomas, 241, 244

Taaffe (see also Carlingford), Count and
Field Marshal Nicholas, 258
Tandy, James Napper, 269, 283, 300
Teeling, Matthew, 298–300
Bartholomew, 298–300
Test Act, 51, 280
Thomond (O'Brien), Henry, 8th Earl of,
213
Tone, Theobald Wolfe, 93, 271–2, 279,
280, 284, 285, 300–1
Matthew, 298, 300
Trant, Sir Patrick, 18, 234
Ignatius, 234–5
Dominick, 235
Thomas, 222–3
Chevalier Thomas, 219, 276
Colonel Nicholas, 277
treason, indictments for, 21, 24, 25–6
penalties for, 21
Trench, Rev John, 31fn
'Billy', 100
Henry, 246
Trimleston (Barnewall), Mathias, 10th
Lord, 25
John, 11th Lord, 26
Robert, 12th Lord, 133–4, 253, 254,
257–9, 261, 267
Trinity College, Dublin, 189–90, 226,
271, 279, 287

Troy, Archbishop John Thomas, 269, 279
Tyrconnell (Talbot), Richard, 1st Duke
of, 18–19, 20–1, 26, 28, 32–3,
Duchess of, 47
Trustees for Forfeited Estates, 41, 42,
133, 177
Tyrone (Power), Richard, 1st Earl of,
167

Ulster, 16–17, 122–4, 259–60, 263, 271,
278, 285, 297
Union of Britain and Ireland, 301–6
United Irishmen, 271–2, 278, 281, 282–
4, 285, 286, 288, 289, 290, 292, 297,
298

Vinegar Hill, 294, 296
Volunteers, 262–5, 268, 271, 278, 282

Walsh, James, 243
Philip, 243
Anthony, 243
Francis, 1st Comte Walsh de Serrant,
244
Anthony, 2nd Comte Walsh de Serrant,
244
Walsh's Regiment, 34, 210, 216–7, 217–
9, 244
War of 1689–91 (Williamite War), 15–36
Welsh, Richard, 239
Wellesley, Sir Arthur, later Lord
Wellington and Duke of Wellington,
148fn, 173–4, 277, 307
West Indian plantations, 97, 238–9, 243
Westmorland, Earl of, 279, 281, 282
Wexford, County, 141–4
elections, 141–3
rebellion of 1798, 268–97
Wild Geese, 34–5, 196, 214, 215
William III, of Orange, King, 20–8, 46–7
Wogan, Charles, 214
Whiteboys, 162–7
Whyte of Loughbrickland, 47, 122
John, 122–3
Charles, 123
Wyse, Sir Thomas, 119, 237, 257, 267

Yeomanry, 283, 288, 289
younger sons of Catholic landowners,
100–1, 210–46

[319]